D0098123

SEASONS OF REAL FLORIDA

The Florida History and Culture Series

UNIVERSITY PRESS OF FLORIDA
STATE UNIVERSITY SYSTEM

Florida A&M University, Tallahassee
Florida Atlantic University, Boca Raton
Florida Gulf Coast University, Ft. Myers
Florida International University, Miami
Florida State University, Tallahassee
University of Central Florida, Orlando
University of Florida, Gainesville
University of North Florida, Jacksonville
University of South Florida, Tampa
University of West Florida, Pensacola

SEASONS OF

Foreword by Randy Wayne White

Series Foreword by Raymond Arsenault and Gary R. Mormino

UNIVERSITY PRESS OF FLORIDA

Gainesville · Tallahassee · Tampa · Boca Raton

Pensacola · Orlando · Miami · Jacksonville · Ft. Myers

Jeff Klinkenberg

REAL FLORIDA

Copyright 2004 by the *St. Petersburg Times*, the Times Publishing Company
Printed in the United States of America on acid-free paper

09 08 07 06 05 04   6 5 4 3 2 1

LIBRARY OF CONGRESS CATALOGING-IN-PUBLICATION DATA
Klinkenberg, Jeff.
Seasons of real Florida / Jeff Klinkenberg; foreword by Randy Wayne White.
p. cm.—(The Florida history and culture series)
ISBN 0-8130-2713-6 (acid-free paper)
1. Florida—Description and travel—Anecdotes. 2. Florida—Biography—
Anecdotes. 3. Florida—Social life and customs—Anecdotes. I. Title. II. Series.
F316.2.K575 2004
917.5'904—dc22   2003066598

The University Press of Florida is the scholarly publishing agency for
the State University System of Florida, comprising Florida A&M University,
Florida Atlantic University, Florida Gulf Coast University, Florida International
University, Florida State University, University of Central Florida, University
of Florida, University of North Florida, University of South Florida, and
University of West Florida

University Press of Florida
15 Northwest 15th Street
Gainesville, FL 32611-2079
http://www.upf.com

For Susan
with love

Contents

Series Foreword   ix
Foreword by Randy Wayne White   xi
Preface   xiii

FALL

1. The Subtle Season   3
2. Peebles   6
3. Flamingo Tourists   11
4. Inmate No. 793362   16
5. Clyde Butcher   23
6. The Smallwood Store   28
7. Pictures of History   32
8. Travels with a Bear Man   38
9. Torreya State Park   43
10. The Herlong Mansion   47
11. Old Woman River   56

WINTER

12. Last Fish Monger   67
13. Fruit Hog   73
14. Mister Citrifacts   76
15. Miss Ruby   80
16. In the Footsteps of the Masters   86
17. Smoked Fish   94
18. Winter Perfume   98
19. Minding the Manatees   103
20. What Lies Beneath   107
21. The Yearling Restaurant   114
22. Black Seminoles   119
23. His Father's Voice   124

SPRING

24. Coconuts and Alligators — 135
25. Bartram's Travels Through Our Dreams — 139
26. Idella — 146
27. Mastry's Bait and Tackle — 154
28. Barren Beauty — 158
29. Tom Gaskins — 162
30. The Guru of Fly-Fishing — 165
31. Marjory Stoneman Douglas — 168
32. Builder of Boats, Keeper of History — 171
33. No Such Thing as a Dead Gator — 176
34. When Trees Talk — 183

SUMMER

35. A Florida Boy Keeps His Cool — 193
36. Loincloth Man — 196
37. Kiss of the Swamp Angels — 200
38. Cracker Cattle — 205
39. Florida's Deepest Roots — 210
40. Shell Woman — 217
41. Wakulla Springs — 222
42. A Fisherman Named Hemingway — 225
43. Man out of Time — 230
44. For a Song — 235
45. Soul Food — 239
46. Dark Night of the Soul — 244
47. Firefly Doc — 253

Credits — 261

Series Foreword

During the past half-century, the burgeoning population and increased national and international visibility of Florida have sparked a great deal of popular interest in the state's past, present, and future. As the favorite destination of countless tourists and as the new home for millions of retirees and other migrants, modern Florida has become a demographic, political, and cultural bellwether. In an effort to explore the Sunshine State in all its complexity, past and present, the University Press of Florida has established the Florida History and Culture series.

As coeditors of the series, we are committed to the creation of an eclectic but carefully crafted set of books that will provide the field of Florida studies with a new focus and that will encourage Florida researchers and writers to consider the broader implications and context of their work. The series includes standard academic monographs, works of synthesis, memoirs, and anthologies. And, while the series features books of historical interest, we encourage authors researching Florida's environment, politics, literature, and popular or material culture to submit their manuscripts as well. We want each book to retain a distinct personality and voice, but at the same time we hope to foster a sense of community and collaboration among Florida scholars.

For many decades, writers have searched Florida's coastal eddies and hinterlands for authentic Florida personalities. During the Great Depression, the New Deal's Federal Writers Project helped capture a vanishing Florida culture. Stetson Kennedy and Zora Neale Hurston rescued the voices of muleskinners, turpentiners, and spongers. Jeff Klinkenberg's *Seasons of Real Florida* fits squarely in that venerable tradition.

Klinkenberg, a *St. Petersburg Times* reporter, stands on the shoulders of some giants in Florida journalism. When Klinkenberg was growing up in 1950s Miami, the *Herald*'s Stephen Trumbull and Nixon Smiley earned well-deserved reputations for their statewide dispatches. Al Burt succeeded Trumbull and Nixon, writing about Floridians and Floridiana with grace and tenderness.

Seasons of Real Florida introduces an extraordinary cast of characters: Professor Lloyd, the "Firefly Doc" at the University of Florida; Carol Sellars, the 85-year-old "shell woman" of Cayo Costa Key; Jack Kepler, the salvager of rare Upper Keys trees; Columbus White, the Lochloosa gator trapper; Glen Simmons, the last of the Everglade skiff builders; Tom Gaskins and his cypress knee attraction; Buster Agliano, Ybor City's last fishmonger; and Frank Wilson, Bradenton fruit hog. Klinkenberg brings sensitivity to Florida's places and subcultures: the Yearling restaurant at Cross Creek; Ted Peters's smoked fish establishment in South Pasadena; Miss Ruby Williams's fruit and vegetable stand at Bealsville, bear country in the Weeki Wachee preserve; the Ted Smallwood store at Chokoloskee.

Readers will delight in reading and rereading these portraits of pure Floridiana. Enjoy them with a glass of fresh-squeezed Frostproof orange juice and smoked mackerel with crackers.

Raymond Arsenault and Gary R. Mormino
Series Editors

Foreword

Tourists tell me they've visited Florida, by which they mean the city-sized experiential computer arcades, Disney and Epcot, or spring break territory where 7-Elevens sell brain-freezes by the cup for good reason.

I tell them that's not Florida. What is raw, alive, and essential about Florida is becoming more difficult to find, true, but it's still possible to experience it. A good place to start is any story or book by Jeff Klinkenberg.

Jeff is a man with clear vision and an excellent eye. The stories collected here make a valuable primer for the newcomer who cares enough to seek direction. *Seasons of Real Florida*, and the field work invested in its creation, remind us that to interact with Florida we must get off our dead butts, leave the air-conditioning and the automotive cocoon, and get outside. To people like Jeff who adore this region, it is a small price. They delight in mucking through swamp, bushwhacking through cypress, and tracking down unusual characters.

Florida has a visual brilliance that can be accessed only one small section at a time. Last night, for instance, I rigged my kayak at my old house on the Indian mound and paddled a quarter mile onto Pine Island Sound before pausing: Deserted islands all around. The moon was smoky with Earth-shadow, only a white crescent showing. Water was black, islands blue.

As I paddled, I spooked fish—big fish. Maybe snook, at least one slow shark. I could feel the expanding surface pressure as they passed beneath the boat, and I gauged their size by luminous wakes. Estuaries here are a soup of plankton that glows when agitated. I was afloat on a waterspace of green meteorites and comets. Each stroke created sparks. Overhead, diminished by light-years, distant suns seemed a less interesting starscape.

It became more pleasurable to drift than to paddle. If I turned the kayak slightly, I could see the village that is my home: a curvature of island fringed by coconut palms, fronds interlaced like macaw feathers. Houses appeared buoyant but somehow adrift on the raft of land, as if a fresh wind could blow the village out to sea. Beyond darkness was the Everglades. More than a hundred miles beyond that, Miami sprawled beneath a mushroom dome of neon.

Florida will not come to you. You must seek it out in small and private ways. Jeff does this as well as or better than any Florida writer working today, and he does it passionately. Jeff loves Florida. It shows.

Randy Wayne White
Pineland, Florida

Preface

I will try to make this quick.

First, a few things about me. I was born in Chicago in 1949, a fact I blame on my parents. They moved to Florida in 1951. My dad was a musician, a piano player, and we lived wherever he could find work, in Key West and Madeira Beach, near St. Petersburg, before finally settling in Miami.

When I tell my wife I'm a barefoot boy from Miami, she laughs. She only knows today's Miami. But when I was growing up, it was a different place. For most of my boyhood I wore shoes only to church and to school or in the coldest weather. Looking back, I think my life could have been a chapter straight out of *Huckleberry Finn*.

My dad adored the outdoors, especially fishing and camping in the Keys and in the Everglades. I inherited my own love of wild places from him. My mother was entirely a city person who was blessed with the gift of gab and boundless curiosity. She knew everybody in our neighborhood and what they were up to. Like her, I am a busybody. I like to talk but even more I like to listen. I think everybody has a story to tell.

I attended St. Rose of Lima Elementary in Miami Shores, graduated from Miami Edison High School, and got a journalism degree from the University of Florida in Gainesville. I worked as a sports writer for the *Miami News* and the *Ft. Lauderdale News*, afternoon papers that are no more. I started writing for the *St. Petersburg Times* in 1977.

I have written about Real Florida for more than two decades. When I say Real Florida I generally mean a culture shaped by the history, folkways, landscape, animals, and weather of our state. For example, a tourist who visits us during summer may be tempted to order stone crab claws at a restaurant. If he gets them, which is doubtful, they will be frozen. Real Floridians know that stone crab season starts October 15. We associate stone crabs with fall.

That's another thing. In Real Florida, we have real seasons, even if we don't have colorful leaves and hot apple cider sold at roadside stands. We have wildlife migrations and our own seasonal foods. We have dormant alligators or active alligators, mosquitoes or no mosquitoes. We have art unique to Florida and our own ways of doing things. We have our own way of coping with what modern Florida throws at us, from development to crime. I could go on, but I'll let you read my essays for yourself.

I have arranged them by seasons, beginning with fall. Fall in Real Florida is like spring in the North. Having survived our harshest season, we feel renewed. Real Florida is both a real place and a state of mind. It is most obvious in the country, but you can also find it around the corner from the nearest big-city mall. I live on Florida's Gulf Coast, in Pinellas, one of the most crowded counties in all of Florida. I hate the traffic and all those shopping malls that sprout like crabgrass along our roads. They represent generic Florida to me, generic U.S.A.

But the other day a bald eagle flew over my truck as I barreled down Park Street toward my office in St. Petersburg. Eagles are Real Florida. A few hours later, I was pedaling my bicycle past all those fancy houses on Coffee Pot Bayou when I spotted the nose of a timid manatee gulping down air. Another Real Florida moment. For dinner I drove up Martin Luther King to Atwater's Cafeteria, where I ate collards and fried chicken, washed down by some Real Florida lemonade. If you're looking for Real Florida, pay attention not only to your eyes and your ears and your nostrils but also to your stomach.

In a way, I consider myself a travel writer in the tradition of other people who have documented Real Florida, mainly William Bartram in the eighteenth century, Harriet Beecher Stowe in the nineteenth century, and a bunch of other heroes in the twentieth century. When I was growing up, I read Marjorie Kinnan Rawlings books by flashlight under sweaty sheets at night. She was Real Florida. As a young boy, I read Nixon Smiley's Florida columns in the *Miami Herald*. Still older, I became enamored by Al Burt's essays about Florida in the *Herald*. Al retired in the 1980s, and I have tried to pick up where he left off.

What the other writers did, and what I do, is travel the state from one end to the other, visit beautiful places, and chat with fascinating people who have something worth saying. My job is telling their stories of Real Florida to readers who may be unaware of what is happening beyond the city limits or what they see on the TV news or read elsewhere in the newspaper. When they know, they're interested. When they're interested, they have a stake in taking care of Real Florida.

With this book you can travel with me and never leave the seat of your chair. But even better, I hope you will use these essays as the inspiration to get out and discover Real Florida on your own.

Acknowledgments

I want to thank the following people for their encouragement and inspiration over the years: Ray Arsenault, Susan Aschoff, John Barry, Jerry Bledsoe, Richard Bockman, Kristin Klinkenberg Bowman, Missy Brewer, Al Burt, Clyde Butcher, Sue Carlton, Susan Cerulean, Roy Peter Clark, John Crittenden, Buddy Davis, Eric Deggans, Cherie Diez, Marjory Stoneman Douglas, Mary Evertz, Jim Fitch, Mike Foley, Jaime Francis, Tom French, Neville Green, Jeanne Grinstead, Carl Hiaasen, Ray Hinst, John Hires, Charles Hirsch, Gabriel Horn, William Howarth, Anne Hull, Sheryl James, Scott Keeler, Frank King, Lindsay King, Loretta King, Susan King, Stephen Klemawesch, Beatrice Mary Grace O'Donnell Klinkenberg, Ernest J. Klinkenberg, Katie Klinkenberg, Marty Klinkenberg, Peter Klinkenberg, Bill Landry, Lucinda Lane, Suzanne Lash, Jeanne Malmgren, Peter Matthiessen, Bill Maxwell, Rue Morgan, Gary Mormino, Meredith Morris-Babb, Eugene Patterson, Peggy Peterman, Howell Raines, Jack Sanders, Chip Scanlan, Bob Shacochis, Dorothy Shea, Paul Shea, Patricia Shiflett, Florence Snyder, John Stewart, Sheila Stewart, Jack Stevenson, Christopher Still, Sandra Thompson, Jean Tyson, Jim Ward, Randy Wayne White, and Mike Wilson.

Special thanks to everyone at the *St. Petersburg Times*, especially Andrew Barnes, Paul Tash, and Neil Brown.

FALL

1 The Subtle Season

We have no autumn in Florida. The word "autumn" suggests golden leaves, frost on the pumpkins, the cutting of firewood by graying men wearing flannel shirts, maybe a cold glass of apple cider at home. What we have in Florida is something different. We call it "fall."

Many who move here from north of the Mason-Dixon line never get over the disappointment of losing their beloved autumn. But others, the kind who immerse themselves in the culture and nature of their adopted state, learn to love the fall that's here.

Fall in Florida is not going to blind you with electric leaves. As subtle as a dandelion tuft, the season floats along on warm breezes for weeks before finally taking root. Our fall has little to do with outside temperatures, though of course it's always a bonus if the air turns dry any time before November. To enjoy our season, pay attention to the comings and goings of wildlife. Fall rides into Florida on wing and scale.

In the fall, our state is a birder's Eden. Snowbirds—the kind with feathers—descend on Florida like hungry tourists. I live in West Central Florida, where we look for our birds in the trees and in the ponds at Fort DeSoto, Sawgrass Lake, Honeymoon Island, Shell Key, and on any Tampa Bay tidal flat. But we can do the same at St. Joseph's Peninsula State Park in the Panhandle, at Wekiva Springs State Park near Orlando, or at Flamingo in the Everglades.

My favorite spur-of-the-moment place is Boyd Hill Nature Park in St. Petersburg, a five-minute drive from where I work downtown. I can eat my bag lunch there, go for a walk, chat with ranger Donna Heinrich, hear about the arrival of the summer tanagers, see my fall's first ruby-throated hummingbird, and be back at my desk by 1 P.M.

Ranger Donna keeps me informed. When she tells me eagles have returned to the park, I know summer indeed is over. Nobody knows where our eagles vacation during the hottest months—Chesapeake Bay probably. Then I guess they get bored or hungry or notice sunset is earlier every day and feel the need to take wing. On a warm September morning, somebody sees one roosting on a snag next to a golf course fairway in Lakewood Estates. In the afternoon, its mate is resting in a tall pine next to the soccer field adjacent to the park. It's fall.

As weeks pass, we watch our pair add branches to their rickety old nest. A few months later, when they begin sitting on their nest, we hold our collective breath. Some years our eagles produce no young. Some years they give Florida a pair. I love my eagles. Hawks, too. During summer we are happy to see just about any hawk. But when fall arrives, our red-shouldered hawks are joined almost daily by migrating red-tails and broadwings and who knows what. We see them perched on telephone poles and the tops of cabbage palms. They watch the ground for dinner: feckless lizards, snakes, and doves. I like birds of prey because I can usually identify them. The warblers, those tiny colorful birds that dart nervously among the leaves, are the challenge of fall.

The birds pour into the state during fall, pour into Florida by the thousands, stopping for rest before continuing journeys that will take many into South America. As we drive past the mall, as we wash our supper dishes, as we complain to our spouses about Florida's disappointing autumn, fall is happening overhead.

It is hard to notice fall unless you participate in Florida. Participation requires leaving the house and car and maybe taking a stroll in the woods or on a seawall that abuts the bay or the beach. I watch mullet during fall. At first, I see them milling about in small pods in Tampa Bay. As fall thickens, so do the mullet. They put on weight and swim together in massive schools because their safety depends on numbers. Fattening with roe, they wait for the right moment—perhaps an honest-to-goodness cold front or a full-moon tide—and then leave the bayous, canals, and creeks and enter the bay, where they become prey to dolphins and pelicans and fishers with nets. Mullet that reach the gulf have a chance of reproducing.

Over the years I have become a lazy angler. In the worst heat of summer, if I want a chance at a fish supper, it means an appearance on the water before dawn or after dusk. No thank you. In the fall, banker's hours are a possibility. Spotted sea trout, which hide in cooler deep water all summer, show up hungry in the shallows in the fall, waiting to ambush whatever comes along. I like to throw their way a plastic minnow imitation known as a MirrOlure and retrieve it in an erratic manner.

"Look at me!" the drunken MirrOlure almost bellows. "Easy pickings."

Bang! Trout on.

Trout are beautiful fish, silver and green with golden spots, but a trout at the end of your line won't wear you out. Nor will trout ever replace snapper as a favorite table fish. Still, a well-prepared, just-from-the-water trout will fry up good in cracker crumbs, accompanied by stone-ground grits drowned in butter. Fall food.

Fall would be incomplete without a plate or two of stone crab claws. The pugnacious crabs are on the move in the fall, skulking about the gulf near shore, waiting for a genuine cold front or at least a solid blow to provoke travel. Sadly for them, but good for us, they often seek shelter in heavy wooden boxes scattered across the gulf bottom from here to the Everglades: commercial crab traps.

When stone crab season opens officially in mid-October, fall is a full-blown reality no matter the temperature or plain-green leaves. Dip the white meat into hot drawn butter if you must—it's the Yankee way—but around here in the fall, we prefer to eat them cold with a mayonnaise-mustard sauce. Of course, we will wash down our claws with fall's liquid treat, fresh-squeezed—has to be fresh-squeezed—orange juice.

Many Floridians, at least new ones, take awhile to catch on to what our fall is all about. I tell new folks or folks who have paid scant attention in the past that our fall is like a northern spring. It's a time of celebration. In our case, we have survived summer, our most trying season. Now months of fair weather, good food, and a chance to enjoy nature lie ahead.

It all starts now.

❷ Peebles

Fall is definitely here. I know because the "Open" sign finally is hanging from the front door at Peebles Bar-B-Q in Auburndale. I have to tell you that hungry folks throughout Central Florida look forward to the great day as a child waits for Christmas.

At 11 A.M. on the Thursday after Labor Day, fall officially commences. After a long summer without real barbecue, customers virtually burst through the door, stomachs growling and mouths watering for ribs, pork, and beef, with maybe some baked beans, cole slaw, and potato salad on the side. Forget about the Big Mouse up Orlando way. Auburndale, the little community outside Lakeland, has its own institution.

Ellie and Gladys Peebles began selling their barbecue from a little stand in their front yard in 1947. Decades later, the Peebles clan has its own restaurant, which is actually more like a big patio, air-conditioned by nature, windows covered by screens to frustrate the flies.

Ronnie Peebles, Ellie's and Gladys's son, owns the place now with his brother-in-law, Dale Strickland. But they pretty much do everything the way Old Man Peebles did back when Truman was president and Florida was still mostly wilderness. "We don't go in for too many changes around here," Ronnie Peebles once told me. "I think that's what people like about us."

Barbecue lovers suffer in Florida. Oh, we have no trouble finding delicious stone crab claws, smoked mullet, Cuban sandwiches, a bowl of Spanish bean soup, a great Duncan grapefruit. But we have a definite barbecue deficit. Connoisseurs often have to settle for second best, especially if we live in the big coastal cities, where choices often are limited to franchised barbecue restaurants. When we do stumble upon a good place, we're likely to keep it secret.

For great barbecue, usually we are compelled to travel north into the Deep South—into Alabama, Georgia, or North Carolina. In the summer, I tell friends I am going to the mountains for the scenery, but really I go to eat barbecue. We exit the interstate in Georgia, near Macon, and take the back road north. Every little town seems to have a neat barbecue spot. So much barbecue, so little time!

In North Carolina, even the bad barbecue places are pretty good, and the good ones are out of this world. My favorite, a little roadside stand that was open only on Saturdays for lunch, disappeared a few years ago. We have been told that Mr. Barbecue found himself a better patch of road, but nobody seemed to know, or was willing to tell us, where that patch of road might be. We mourned until we found another restaurant, one that had tables, thank you, and we're feeling better now. In Florida, I mostly feel frustrated. In my job, I travel from the Keys to the Panhandle, usually in my pickup truck, usually in disappointment because of mediocre barbecue. But I never stop hoping.

Five years ago, an old friend from Miami moved to Plant City, his hometown. He said he'd take me to a great barbecue joint if I ever drove his way. I never did. I now am sure he was going to take me to Peebles, but when he died the name of the restaurant died with him.

Then I started hanging out with Jim Fitch, the curator of the Museum of Florida Art and Culture in Avon Park, who was helping me on a story. Fitch is a Florida native who seems to know everything important about our state. He is an amateur anthropologist, archaeologist, folklorist, naturalist, and, most important, a gourmet. His wife, Anne, makes the best cole slaw I have ever tasted. I begged for the recipe, but months passed before Fitch knew me well enough to hand it over.

Fitch did not tell me about Peebles right away either. As a wily Cracker, he first had to take my measure. Yes, I appreciated a good cole slaw, but was I the kind of man who would drop everything for good barbecue? Eventually he spilled the beans during a four-hour motor trip through Central Florida. I would like to believe I passed the Cracker test, but I think he just ran out of things to talk about.

It was a desperate fall morning. Circumstances beyond my control had kept me away from the mountains and their colorful leaves and delicious barbecue. Suffering, I remembered what Jim Fitch had told me about Peebles. Hands shaking, I telephoned the restaurant. When I asked Ronnie Peebles whether I could drive over to discuss barbecue, and maybe eat some, I got the impression he was less than overjoyed. Nothing is more awkward than dead air on the telephone, but that's what I was hearing for a moment so long I was ready to beg forgiveness. "Well, I guess you can come on by," he finally said. I shouldn't have been surprised by his reluctance. Although most restaurants will do anything for good publicity, the great ones don't need it. They already have all the customers they want.

Once, in the Keys, I ran into the same antipublicity problem when I stopped at the last restaurant in Florida that served what I considered a genuine Key lime pie. When I hauled out my notebook to record for posterity the owner's achievement, she almost tossed me out through her screen door. "I been makin' pies for thirty-one years," she stormed. "I want to retire. I don't need people from Tampa coming down here and making more business."

I wore her down, I am almost sorry to say, and she talked. But she perversely refused to give me her name or let me take her photograph. She has since passed away, and her restaurant is gone. At Peebles—I smelled the barbecue two blocks before I saw the restaurant on 503 Dixie Highway—Ronnie Peebles met me in the kitchen with nary a smile. "You don't have to take a picture, do you?" he growled. A photo might mean even more positive publicity, more hordes of customers from Tampa Bay.

It was a little after 11 A.M. on a Thursday, I should tell you, and the gravel parking lot was nearly filled with pickup trucks, semi-trailers, sports utility vehicles, luxury cars, and jalopies. Inside it was even more crowded. All sixty-five tables were filled with barbecue lovers white, black, rich, and poor. An obese man who had forgotten to wear a shirt, and a belt, waited at the counter for takeout. The crowded parking lot, the diverse customers, even the slob patron constituted a sign of good barbecue.

"My daddy came from Georgia," Peebles told me when I asked for history. We were standing in the kitchen near his three hard-working barbecue pits. "When he moved to Auburndale he drove a school bus and had a produce stand. But he cooked barbecue like he had in Georgia. Barbecue was just a Saturday and Sunday thing for him at first. Then our family went to Friday and Saturday. Business got better. Now we're open Thursday through Saturday. We go through about five thousand pounds of meat, and 125 gallons of barbecue sauce, on a good weekend.

"We still do everything the way Mom and Dad did, using their recipes. People ask for the recipes," he said, looking me hard in the eyes, "but we don't give it out. It's a family secret."

At Peebles, they start working on their oak-hickory fires, and their meat, a full day before the restaurant opens. And they don't stop cooking until Saturday night. I wish I could describe the aroma coming out of the chimney. I sidled up to Dale Strickland, Peebles's brother-in-law, the main cook.

"I never get tired of eating barbecue," he said, turning ribs. "I am one of those guys who eats too much barbecue. Sometimes I'll cook some up at home, and when I'm traveling, I'll even stop to try somebody else's barbecue. I like barbecue so much I even eat it at a place like Bennigan's."

I asked how he likes chain-restaurant barbecue. He was raised to be polite, so he only smiled. Eventually, I got a table, always at a premium. I ordered a regular chopped pork plate. My companion ordered sliced beef. We both wanted potato salad, cole slaw, and baked beans. Our orders arrived in throwaway dishes with plastic forks—a good sign. The Peebles family believes in keeping overhead low. Tables and chairs don't match either. As for the heat that builds in the dining room most afternoons, thank goodness for floor fans and the breeze that seeps through the window screens.

The slaw was perfection itself: sweet-sour and freshly prepared. I am picky about baked beans—you can ask anyone—but Peebles served an excellent brew, moist without being watery, strongly flavored by pork and brown sugar. My companion's beef was pretty good, but the chopped pork on my plate was heavenly, the melt-in-your mouth variety, subtly flavored by wood coals and, I thought, apple-cider vinegar. The barbecue sauce was a mystery dark-brown potion with more kick than the bland stuff you'd get in a franchise restaurant. I soaked up every extra drop with the two slices of white bread that come with the meal.

I felt like a tick ready to burst, as we say in Real Florida. Standing, patting my belly, resisting the urge to belch, I prepared to pay my bill. I had hardly taken a step toward the cash register when some eager beaver customer slunk behind me to take my table. They don't waste time at Peebles. Eat and get out is the prevailing credo.

In the parking lot, I bumped into Bill Richardson, who teaches college in Lakeland. He had just finished a big lunch, but he was going home with takeout too. "The best way to keep my marriage together," he joked, "is bringing home some barbecue." He had been a customer for twenty-five years. I asked what he does when Peebles closes for the summer at the end of June.

"Mourn," he said.

❸ Flamingo Tourists

If flamingos were not real birds, we would have to invent them. Ugly and beautiful, clumsy and graceful, they represent everything nerdy and cool about our state.

So speaketh a man who knows that flamingos may not even be native Floridians. As a Chicago-born guy who has been known to decorate his lawn with plastic flamingos, I can live with the contradiction.

Whether the flamingos I see so rarely in the Florida wild are actually escaped zoo birds hardly matters to me. As a lifelong member of what I call the cult of the flamingo, I'll take my flamingos however I can get them. I saw my first live one in the early 1950s at a Miccosukee Indian village near Miami. The tame flamingos pranced, stretched their wings, and honked. Mainly they looked like weird, pink, upside-down croquet mallets from *Alice in Wonderland*.

Nobody knows for sure when flamingos came to symbolize the Florida tropics. We do know that John James Audubon, the famous painter and naturalist, saw a flock in the Florida Keys in 1832. Back in London, he must have dreamed of pink feathers. Audubon implored friends in America to kindly shoot him a flamingo and send it his way. Six years passed before he received a model from Cuba. It was dead, of course, but Audubon gave it a kind of immortality. His painting is the most famous rendition of the bird ever captured on canvas.

The flamingo has always vexed Florida birders. Are they or are they not Florida residents? A prominent ornithologist described seeing an immense flock—more than two thousand birds—near Cape Sable, in the western Everglades, in 1884. In 1901, an expert birder reported seeing a number of flamingos at Sugarloaf Key, near Key West, sitting on what appeared to be nests. Many experts today scoff. It's the only account of a flamingo nursery in the Florida wild. But nobody wants to say it's impossible.

These days the best place to see a flamingo in the wild is at, appropriately, the tiny community of Flamingo, perched on Florida Bay at the southernmost point of the mainland. From canoe, I've seen a few stragglers near the visitor center, and a decade ago I saw a good-sized flock from—well, you won't believe me.

When I tell people I saw a flock of flamingos from the seat of my bike, they usually think I'm telling a fish story. But no, it's a flamingo tale, and true. From a Florida Bay boardwalk, I spotted a flock of twenty-three. I enjoyed them until mosquitoes almost as big as flamingos sent me pedaling like Lance Armstrong.

It's easier to see a plastic flamingo on a lawn than a feathered one on a Florida bay. I used to have two plastic specimens in my yard. A guy I talked to recently has fifty-seven in his yard in Fitchburg, Massachusetts. Donald Featherstone has the perfect name for a flamingo fancier. Featherstone is the inventor of the plastic flamingo as we know it.

An art school graduate, he dreamed of creating a masterpiece. In 1957 he did, at Union Products, a New England company that makes plastic animals. His first creation, a duck, sold respectably. "But everybody loved flamingos," he told me by telephone. "I got myself a *National Geographic* magazine and found a photograph to use as a model. And I made myself a plastic one."

The company has sold twenty million. Since 1987, each flamingo has carried Featherstone's signature. "I never made a penny from it except for my salary," he said. He retired in 2001 at age sixty-five. "I know some people think plastic flamingos are tasteless and tacky, but I love them." In fact, when Harvard University honored him with one of its humorous Ig Nobel Awards, he attended. "The award is for an endeavor that should never have been undertaken," he said, and laughed.

I hate plastic flamingo snobs. It is hard to imagine a Florida without flamingos, plastic or otherwise. They are part of a culture that includes coconut-head dolls and seashell lamps.

A few years ago, in St. Petersburg, a city that appreciates its flamingos—flamingo kitsch was once celebrated at its history museum—a guy named Ron Mason walked outside early one morning to pick up his paper. The Sunday newspaper was roosting on the lawn, and so was a big flock of plastic flamingos. Mason, who used to be a city councilman, didn't have to laugh, but he did.

For years, he was known for his affection for anything having to do with flamingos. He had plastic flamingos, flamingo dolls, flamingo candleholders, and flamingo salt shakers. He once shook up his neighborhood at Christmas by displaying a nativity scene in which plastic flamingos were substitutes for traditional camels. Under the suit he wore to city council meetings—and I am only taking his word for this—he sometimes wore flamingo-decorated underpants.

So who and why had somebody put sixty plastic flamingos on his lawn?

He had been flocked. "Flocked" is a relatively new term in Americana. It means somebody who likes you, or maybe doesn't like you, sneaks into your yard at night and decorates the lawn with a flock of tacky plastic flamingos.

Ron Mason and his wife, Pat, go to First United Methodist Church of St. Petersburg. The church's youth club wanted to raise money for its programs. Some genius suggested the idea of selling flocking insurance to members of the congregation. For a small donation, church members could buy insurance against flocking. For some reason, nobody approached the Masons. And so they got flocked one Saturday night. Pat Mason packed her car with the flamingos and asked her church for the names of other people who had neglected to buy flocking insurance. She got a name.

"A banker's wife and I did the flocking after Bible study," she said. "It was a nice yard in Allendale. We were very scared that somebody would come out of the house with a shotgun. But we got away with our little crime."

Warning: R-rated—maybe even X-rated—flamingo talk ahead.

Laura Wittish sleeps with flamingos. She is an animal curator at Busch Gardens in Tampa. Busch Gardens has the largest collection of real flamingos in our part of the state. She oversees a flock of three hundred Caribbean flamingos, kept semiwild, at the attraction. Their wings are clipped regularly, but otherwise they have little interaction with people.

A smaller flock of birds, raised from eggs, is tame. When a television talk show host wants a live flamingo or two for a program, Laura brings them. When Busch Gardens attends trade shows, Laura goes and does flamingo public relations.

"Flamingos stay in the room with me," she said. Startled by her confession, I forgot to ask if she ordered room service, and if she did, if the waiter asked what a single woman was doing in a hotel room with a flock of flamingos, at least one of them a male. "The first thing you do is flamingo-proof the room as best you can. You put the toilet seat down, otherwise the flamingos will play in the water. The shower curtain goes up out of reach. You hide the toilet paper.

"Flamingos are like curious children. They want to play with everything in the room. They go around and peck at everything. It's important to keep them amused, so we do bring lots of mirrors. Flamingos like to look at themselves. I put up blankets or something as barriers during the night so I can sleep. The flamingos sometimes take a while to settle down. I always remember to turn on a night light. Flamingos are a little scared of the dark."

In the spring, things get even spicier. It's mating season.

Here we get to the X-rated stuff. Male flamingos march in unison among the rest of the flock. They bob their heads in unison and look quickly to left and right, also in unison. Imagine a large company of performers dancing like Egyptians and you get the idea. Every once in a while, a male flamingo displays his wings and struts around like some lothario in a Zoot suit. And near the end of the mating ritual, Casanova will suddenly hide his head behind his posterior. Of course, this hard-to-get behavior drives the object of his affection wild. Now she wants him; she wants him bad. She leaves the flock and enters the water, the boudoir. It's the signal for amore.

Afterward, the new couple builds a small nest out of mud. A nest looks like a volcano, with an excavation in the middle. That's where she deposits the single egg. Both parents take turns sitting on it. A day or so before hatching, the chick starts chirping from inside the egg. The parents now and forever know the sound of their offspring. After it hatches, after it starts stretching its legs, they can always find it by its chirp.

Flamingos eat little things, bugs and tiny shrimp, but they especially are fond of blue-green algae. It's what gives them their pink color. Parents that are feeding their young often lose their pinkness. All their energy is going to baby.

I don't live near Busch Gardens, but I pass Sunken Gardens in St. Petersburg all the time. Sunken Gardens has a modest flock of flamingos from Chile. They're smaller than Caribbean flamingos and maybe a little stinkier. But, hey, my personal hygiene is not always perfect either.

The last time I visited Sunken Gardens, I looked up my old friend Candace Arnold, a park ranger who has an in with the flamingos. "You want to go in the flamingo pit?" she asked. I did.

"Squat down. Don't move around. Stay quiet."

Out of the corner of my eye I watched a flamingo approach from the side. I felt something exploring my shoelaces and my pants leg and the back of my shirt. It was the flamingo's bill, grooming me.

"You're being loved by a flamingo," Candace said.

Fall. Morning. Tampa Bay. Near the mouth of the Alafia River.
Rich Paul, of National Audubon, who monitors the bay's bird-infested islands, was steering the boat.

I was hoping to see a flamingo in the wild, the longest of long shots, especially in Tampa Bay. Yet I had hope. From time to time, people do report seeing a flamingo at the mouth of the bay, near Anna Maria Island, at Egmont Key, even Fort DeSoto. Most of us dismiss such reports. Lots of people mistake those pink roseate spoonbills for flamingos.

"What's that?" my guide suddenly asked, whipping out binoculars. A half mile away was something tall and pink.

We had our flamingo. Behind it, rising in the mist, were stacks of gypsum—a phosphate plant. Just like in the rest of Florida, where shopping centers tickle cypress swamps, we had beauty and the beast: a flamingo and a phosphate plant. Welcome to *Alice in Wonderland* country.

I watched in fascination. Flamingos have the longest necks in the bird kingdom. They must have the strangest way of eating, too. They move their feet to knock stuff off the bottom, then stick their heads, upside down, into the soup. They filter the goop through their bills. Then they start all over again. "They're shy birds," Rich said. "If we get too close, they fly away."

The tide was high, and we got closer. "What we're seeing is probably an escaped bird," Rich Paul said. A few years ago, one flew away from Lowry Park in Tampa. A few others escaped from a park in Sarasota. "But there is no way of knowing if this is one of those birds."

Now we drifted, closer and closer. The flamingo tried to stare us down from thirty yards away. As the tide fell, as we drifted past our flamingo, I felt more and more like someone named Alice.

4   Inmate No. 793362

If Al Black had a favorite place on earth, it was Florida's east coast. At dawn on a fall morning, the south fork of the Indian River seemed dark and mysterious. A bit like him.

During summer, at high noon, he always enjoyed visiting the Fort Pierce waterfront for the poinciana trees. Their blood-orange blossoms made him feel alive. At dusk, on overcast winter evenings when the cold-front clouds scud above the cypress, he always favored a majestic swamp in the east Everglades. Curlews glided into their roosts.

When I visited him at his new home, he lacked a view of nature's beauty. When he gazed out his barred window, he saw an interstate and, peeking over the interstate, the top of a dying pine tree. Dominating the bleak landscape was a ten-foot fence wrapped with razor wire.

"I never thought I'd end up here," he said.

Al Black, Inmate No. 793362, was assigned to Room 201-A of the Central Florida Reception Center near Orlando. Prison is a hellish place for a landscape artist to find himself, but Black, a charter member of an obscure African American art tradition known as the "Highwaymen," always managed to go down the wrong road.

Blessed with the talent to paint striking scenes of natural Florida, he possessed the charm of a born salesman who could knock on a mahogany office door in Palm Beach, lower his brown eyes in humility, and persuade a bow-tied white architect to buy a trunkload of landscapes. He had an unfortunate darker side as well. He was a thief and a cocaine addict. Now he was fifty-four, a career criminal doing twelve years for stealing from an old woman who had tried to help him stay sober and concentrate on art.

The man who once lived to paint scenes of natural Florida hadn't seen a real river in years. As for the Everglades, pine forests, and poinciana trees, he thanked the Lord for his good memory.

"It's all in my head now," he said. "I carry nature in my head. It can be hard sometimes when you don't have nothing to feed off of."

When Black entered prison in late 1996, painting a pretty picture was far from his mind. His tasks were adjusting to life without freedom and understanding why his world had fallen apart. He had never been a religious man, but like the saying goes, "There are no atheists in foxholes," and so it was that Al Black got down on his knees and prayed for help. And it came to pass that help found him.

On his regular visit to the medical clinic one afternoon, Dr. Dianne Rechtine studied his face. "You the Al Black I read about?" she asked. The doctor had seen a magazine article I had written about the Highwaymen that told how Black had thrown away his talent for a cocaine high. At the end of that story, Black no longer was painting; he lived in a crack house and hustled for every dime. By the look in his eyes—the doctor saw the pride—she knew the man on her exam table was her guy.

"There's something I'd like you to do for me," the doctor said.

Black was a year into his sentence when Rechtine bought him paints and brushes. She gave him a job painting a landscape on the wall of her prison clinic. He painted her a river scene. It was a classic Highwayman landscape, with bent palm trees, a crooked river, flapping birds, and a surreal sky. Black did not labor months on it. Nor did he spend a week, or even a day. He did the painting in minutes.

"So fast," Rechtine said.

"I'm like lightning," Black said.

In the years that followed, he painted more than one hundred murals throughout the prison, in the mess hall, on the walls of the exercise yard, in the staff break room, in the warden's office. Some were a foot or two long. A few stretched thirty feet. Some were as colorful as a gaudy quilt. More often they were as brooding as one of those Robert Johnson blues songs about the devil. The surf in Black's seascapes looked ferocious. The fog in the riverscapes was thick enough to swallow a canoe.

Black had been telling guards and inmates about his painting career. "You painted houses?" they would ask. Now he pushed a cart filled with paints and brushes donated to him by Rechtine, by art historian Gary Monroe of Daytona Beach Community College, and by other Highwaymen fans who had found out he was working again. Black stopped to touch up a painting.

"That's my favorite, man," said an inmate, looking over his shoulder. Ron McAndrew, the warden, told me how much he enjoyed watching Black transform a lime-green hall into Florida wilderness. "They take the

Al Black, one of Florida's highwaymen. Photo by Gary Monroe.

breath away," he said. "When you look at this kind of talent, you wonder what went wrong."

Black wondered the same. But for him and the Highwaymen, life always seemed to turn out more trial than triumph. Their tradition began in 1954 in Fort Pierce, a sleepy community an hour north of Palm Beach. A black teenager, Alfred Hair, took painting lessons from a prominent white landscape artist, A. E. "Bean" Backus. Hair, painting in his own backyard, created landscapes in the style of his mentor, but with a twist.

Backus could devote months to a painting because his art commanded a high price tag. Hair painted fast and sold cheap. His customers, mostly middle-class white people, were seldom willing to pay more than thirty dollars for a painting. Of course, thirty bucks represented more than Hair could earn picking oranges in a day.

Hair talked other talented black friends into painting Florida scenes. He hired a silver-tongued teenaged relative, Al Black, to sell everybody's work. Black loaded paintings into his car and hit the road, selling them at mom-and-pop motels, doctor's offices, and intersections up and down U.S. 1. "If you give me fifty paintings to sell, I'll sell fifty paintings," he liked to brag. "Just give me 30 percent of your profits."

Eventually Hair handed Black a paintbrush. He turned out to be as good an artist as he was a salesman. And the fastest painter his friends had ever seen. "They didn't think of themselves, at least back then, as real artists," said Jim Fitch, who documented the Highwaymen tradition for the Museum of Florida Art and Culture in Avon Park. "Their idea was to make money as quickly as possible and not have to do farm work."

Nobody liked turning a quick buck more than Al Black. Fitch once wrote about Black in an anthropological journal: "Not willing to invest any more of his time, talent or material in a painting than is absolutely necessary, he has developed a style that is free of laborious toil. He puts it down and lets it be."

Many of the Highwaymen died obscure and poor; by the turn of the century, their work sometimes fetched thousands of dollars. The survivors experienced modest fame. James Gibson, Roy McClendon, and the only woman of the group, Mary Carroll, were frequent guest speakers at art and history museums. Still dripping wet, their new paintings often sold for hundreds of dollars or more.

If Black had been a free man, he could have enjoyed the same money and celebrity. Instead he shared a small cell with two other convicts, read his Bible, and prayed that God would grant him a few healthy years if he lived long enough to enjoy freedom outside prison.

With his self-destructive tendencies apparently under control, Al Black began transforming a prison for 2,500 convicts into an art gallery. "I think prison saved my life," he told me as he painted a woodsy landscape in the pavilion where prisoners visit their families.

I watched him work. He first painted a section of the wall white. Then he started with the sky, adding grays and oranges and blues as he moved along. He stepped back, rocked on his heels and wiped his hands on his white uniform. "The colors, they're the hard part."

I asked what he thinks about as he paints. If a room is dark, he said, he might take advantage of the low light and do a sunset or a sunrise. If there's a window, or if the fluorescent light is bright, he'll bring out the sun. Then come the trees and the water. He often finishes with three birds, which represent the Father, the Son, and the Holy Ghost.

Raised on the Bible, he had a hard time following it. He fled Mississippi when he was fourteen, tired of picking cotton. He ended up picking potatoes, string beans, and cucumbers up and down the Atlantic Coast until somebody asked if he could drive. Because it meant more money, he said yes, and drove a produce truck from the fields to the packing houses. He settled in Fort Pierce and became a Highwayman. He was all of nineteen years old. He married and divorced and had other women friends. He fathered eight children—including a son now serving thirty years in another prison for home invasion—and has twenty grandchildren. He told me he hopes his grandbabies never take cocaine.

His rap sheet, which dated to 1971, was nearly eleven feet long when I saw it. He had been arrested for assault, contempt of court, writing worthless checks, and probation violations. He was arrested for sexual assault, though charges were dropped. He was arrested for pretending he was a more successful artist and overcharging the customer for a painting.

His first cocaine arrest came on Halloween in 1988. He told me he still remembered the first satisfying snort and who introduced him to white powder. He didn't blame Eugene; Eugene didn't make him put those rocks in the pipe, didn't make him inhale the smoke. Like that Blind Willie Johnson blues song says, he did it to himself.

"When you're on cocaine, there's nothing you can do," he said in a buttermilk drawl. His brown hair was flecked with gray, and the chin that anchors his baby face was graced by a sinkhole of a dimple. "I used to do ten paintings a day and go out and sell them for nice money. I had nice clothes, a nice place to live. I even had a limousine. I think I was the onliest black man who wasn't an undertaker to have his own limousine.

"Then cocaine. At first, I'd take it to limber me up when I'd start to paint. But I ended up hurting myself and lots of people. I thank the Lord I was able to stop. Jesus Christ is my savior now."

At the recreation hall, inmates played dominoes. A guard said no inmate had ever vandalized an Al Black painting. They lean up against them or touch a scene still wet but never deliberately ruin one.

"I've come into my own since I come here," Black said. He wondered what his old painter friends might say if they could see him. None of the other Highwaymen had visited, of course; they liked him, but they shook their heads about his dishonest ways. Among other things, some suspected he took more than his share when he sold their paintings.

In the prison recreation hall, as I listened, Black talked about his paintings to other inmates like a museum docent. He pointed out his favorite swamp scenes, tortured cabbage palms shrouded by fog, oak hammocks, and pine forests.

"I did this one in about ten minutes." In another he invested a half an hour. "This here poinciana tree took me thirty-five minutes."

Once a week he made his regular visit to the medical clinic where Dr. Rechtine treats his autoimmune disease. Every wall boasts a mural. When the doctor delivers bad news about TB or AIDS, the inmate can gaze over her head at a beach full of coconut trees.

"You'll never see two paintings of mine quite alike," Black boasted. "I always try to change at least one little thing. Sometimes it's the season, sometimes it's the time of the day, where the sun or the moon is."

A guard opened a gate, allowing Black and me entry to another section of the prison. Michelangelo had the Sistine Chapel; Al Black has the prison mess hall. It features more poinciana trees, and pine forests and foggy mornings on the Indian River. He clearly had spent more time on these paintings, his best work at the prison.

His favorite was an Everglades scene stretching about thirty feet. It was painted on a metal door that rolled down over the cafeteria line. "I did that in about an hour, an hour and a half," he said. "I'm a wild man with a paint brush."

Black offered me a tour of his cell, which was more like a small dormitory room. His was the bottom bunk. He had been working on sketches, kept in a drawer under his bed. They were 8-by-11-inch depictions of the best of Florida—flowering trees along lonely river roads and moss-draped pines that line heron-filled marshes.

"I've come a long way since I got to prison. Strange, ain't it?" Strange all right. Black brought up the day in 1995 that art historian Jim Fitch and I had found him living in a crack house in the worst neighborhood in Fort Pierce. His eyes that day were watery and he looked like a skeleton.

"I wouldn't look you in the eye, hardly talked and didn't want to sit next to you in your truck, so I rode in the back. Know why? I knew you'd smell the crack on my breath."

That day he had begged Fitch for three hundred dollars. Knowing the money would end up in a crack pipe, Fitch instead handed Black ten bucks for dinner and still wondered if he'd been conned. That was Black's reputation. "He's 100 percent artist, and 100 percent con man," Fitch always told people. "You do the math."

Black acknowledged his old problems. "Now I look you in the eye and talk to you plain," he said. "I get up, wash my face, brush my teeth, take care of myself. That don't seem like much, but used to be I didn't do even that."

Crack addicts are notoriously careless with their bodies. Shortly before my prison visit, Black had been diagnosed with the virus that leads to AIDS. He said he didn't know how he got it and feels fine.

His release date was scheduled for 2008, but with time off for good behavior, he hoped he might get out earlier. If he makes it, if he ever lives outside of prison again, he vowed with God's help he will take a higher road. He will paint and teach and stay out of trouble.

He is a Baptist but kept a Catholic rosary on his bedpost because of the cross. He reached under his pillow for his big red Bible. He told me he favored the New Testament. He liked the part when Jesus raises Lazarus from the dead because it reminded him of his own redemption. He said he also liked the Acts of the Apostles, especially when Saul is knocked off his horse and is reborn as God's fiery messenger, Paul.

"God took the scales from his eyes," Black said. "Same as me."

He said he was looking forward to a new life on the outside, where he might once again cast new eyes on real rivers and swamps and beaches and paint heavenly pictures. But that would have to wait. As a prisoner, his dreams had to be less ambitious. I asked what he was thinking about?

"Supper."

Maybe they'd be serving his favorite, spaghetti and meatballs. As he dipped garlic bread into the sauce, he could admire his own handiwork and look for bare patches of wall that could use a landscape, perhaps a palm tree and sunlight cutting through the morning fog.

He would add his trademark birds, curlews, three of them, representing God's Holy Trinity. As Al Black tried to survive life in prison, they remained his most reliable friends.

5   Clyde Butcher

Clyde Butcher, at home in snake and alligator country, slithered out of the airboat. "Bottom seems solid," he said with false optimism. A solid bottom is important to a bearish three-hundred-pound man who otherwise would sink into the mud like an anvil. I handed him the seventy-pound pack containing his camera equipment. Using his tripod as a staff, he lumbered through the saw grass into a wet, dense tropical forest in the middle of Everglades National Park.

Puffing from exertion, Clyde disappeared into the green shadows. "There should be moccasins here," he called over his shoulder. At sixty, Clyde had endured several close calls with the heavy-bodied, venomous snakes before. Once, stuck in the mud and unable to move, he watched a big one slither past him, inches away.

The day he let me tag along, we crept deeper into the aquatic forest, snapping dead branches and ducking tree limbs. Vines wrapped around our legs as we stepped over fallen logs. As the bottom grew softer, we began to sink.

As the unofficial photographer laureate of natural Florida, Clyde had ventured where few photographers go, carrying a giant camera that made spectacular black-and-white prints. He long had been famous for his pictures of Everglades wetlands, especially the Big Cypress, where he lived on an orchid-covered island. "My idea is to take photos of places people won't ever visit," he told me.

The foreboding tree island, something out of *King Kong*, seemed to me such a place, miles by airboat from the Tamiami Trail, the road that connects Miami and Naples. Clyde ducked a spider web, mosquitoes hovered, and water beetles jetted out of his way. Clyde held up his hands.

"This looks like a good spot to make a photo," he said. "I like this fern."

Although my job was to hand him stuff from his pack, I neglected to hand over his stun gun. A stun gun is an electrified self-defense weapon normally used to thwart human predators. There were no muggers here, but there were those pesky moccasins. Clyde had read about Amazon rain forest travelers, days away from medical help, who used stun guns to treat snakebite.

"I don't know if it really even works," he said. "You're supposed to hit yourself where the snake bit you. The idea is supposedly that the electricity destroys the protein that causes the pain and makes you sick." I wondered whether the cure was worse than the bite. "Your chances of being bitten are pretty slim," he said. "The odds are against it."

The mosquitoes were kind the day I visited, hardly a bother. In summer, Clyde sometimes submerges himself neck-deep to escape. Summer, of course, produces more than mosquitoes. He has never been struck by lightning, but a few times storms passed so close the hair on his body stood up. "Also, I've seen—what do you call it?—St. Elmo's fire. It's like a blue spark and it shoots out of my hands when there's a lot of electricity in the air."

With no storm in sight, he set up the tripod and crouched low enough for me to open the pack suspended from his massive shoulders. I removed the heavy, collapsed camera box and handed it over. Clyde opened the box to full size. It was his Deardorff camera, built in 1945 but looking something like what Civil War photographer Matthew Brady must have used. The size of a small television, it fit the tripod.

"I've never fallen and wet my camera, but once I set it up on a tripod, covered it with a plastic bag and came back later. The tripod had sunk into the mud and the camera was half under. But it was only fresh water, and it was fine." I felt like I was assisting a surgeon. "Lens," Clyde went on, and I placed the 90mm Super Angulon Excel into his meaty hand. I passed him his light meter, his cable release, his film. The film was an 8-by-10-inch plate, and he slid it into his camera.

He pointed the camera toward green. "What I like here is the contrast between the leather fern and the arrowhead leaf and the dappled-light effect coming through the trees." He asked that I stand still; otherwise my wake might disturb the plants and throw his picture out of focus. "I'm going to shoot this at one-eighth of a second."

One-eighth of a second was quick for him. Once, on a foggy morning in Central Florida, he sauntered into the woods in the dark and set up his

Through his eyes. Photo by Scott Keeler.

camera. Exposing his film forty-five minutes, he captured the dawn. It remains among his most atmospheric photos.

He takes sixty photographs a year. If he is lucky, he ends up with four or five he likes. "I have no idea how this one will turn out," he said, preparing to shoot. "I depend on intuition. I think it's going to be okay. Does that make sense?" He touched the cable release that opens and closes the shutter. That was it—a Clyde Butcher photo. He disassembled his camera, and I stuffed everything into the pack. We were ready to go.

"I can't move," Clyde said. He had sunk into the mud to midcalf. "I'm going to lose my boots. Trying to get my boots, I've had the mud suck the wedding ring off my finger. Twice."

He is married to Niki. They met when they were college students in California. After graduation, Clyde and Niki lived on a hill next door to LSD guru Timothy Leary. With his scruffy gray beard and glasses, Clyde looked to me like Jerry Garcia, the late, dope-smoking guitar player for the Grateful Dead. That's where the resemblance ended. Clyde avoids alcohol and drugs.

In California, he took up nature photographs as a hobby but found a willing market. Department stores bought them by the millions, and he made a ton of money, enough to quit architecture. The Butchers moved to Florida; Clyde almost went broke. Like his hero, the famous western landscape photographer Ansel Adams, he wanted to concentrate on black-and-white nature pictures, but everyone told him he had to shoot color to sell. "People wanted color photos that would match their shag carpeting. I wasn't inspired."

The tragedy happened in 1986. The Butchers' seventeen-year-old son, Ted, was killed by a drunken driver. Two weeks after Ted's death, Clyde's father died of what seemed to be a broken heart. Their nineteen-year-old daughter developed amnesia about her childhood. Niki was numb to the world. Clyde disappeared into the swamp with his camera.

He emerged with black-and-white photographs better than anything he'd ever taken. He says he realized that life was too short to do something he didn't want to do—take color photographs. He was going to take black and whites even if they didn't sell, and he was going to dedicate his art to his boy.

His work could hardly be more popular. It decorates the state Capitol and the mansions of senators, movie stars, and people who are moved by natural Florida. He wins art shows, and public television does documentaries about him. His photos are found in coffee table books. Art galleries adore him, and history museums use his work to tell the story of the Everglades.

It is hard to mistake a Clyde Butcher photo. His photos are full of mystery and passion. They tend to be large; some are nearly life-sized. "I want people to be stunned by the size. I want them to think they are actually walking into the scene. And it's going to be a black-and-white scene. Black-and-white, to me, stays with you. It can be haunting."

What Marjory Stoneman Douglas brought to the Everglades with the written word—she wrote *Everglades: River of Grass* a half century ago—Clyde did with visual arts. At their best, his pictures were worth a thousand words. "I want to celebrate the Everglades," he told me. "Every time I'm out here it's different. It's the wind, or the clouds, or the birds, or just the light. It's full of life, and it's totally unique. I never stop being inspired."

The sun was almost down, which meant the light was getting more promising for photography. With Clyde's friend Ron Jones running the airboat, we roared across the Everglades, the part known as the river of grass. This "river" is about sixty miles across and anywhere from a few inches to a few feet deep.

Squawking, great blue herons flapped out of our way. A snail kite, among the rarest birds on the planet, hovered over the marsh. Clyde nodded his head in approval. But he rarely photographed wildlife. He wanted to make a portrait of saw grass, but from a low vantage point, from water level. He wanted to shoot upward and capture the majesty of the sky.

He shouted as he saw such a place. The airboat glided in, stopping in a pond among a saw grass thicket. "We're in an alligator hole," Clyde declared. During droughts, alligators excavate holes, which become ponds, which gather fish, which feed birds, which in turn become nourishment for alligators.

We saw where a big alligator, probably a heavy male, had crushed the grass, but we didn't see the gator. "That's one of those good news and bad news things. Where is he?"

It was a question he always asks. On several occasions, as he has concentrated on his camera, alligators have cruised within inches. "They're curious, is all."

Sometimes they act as if their bellies are rumbling. One time, years ago in Central Florida, while waiting for clouds to enhance his photo background, he heard alligators hissing behind him. He had trespassed on their territory. It would have been nice to retreat, but Clyde was sunk deep in the mud. Only his head was above water. As the alligators drew closer, Niki failed to pull him into their skiff. She wondered if she was going to have to run back to the fish camp for a bigger boat.

"And leave me here with these alligators?"

Wallowing like a water buffalo, he managed to kick his way out of the mud.

"Well, I don't see the alligator," he said now. "I'm going in." As he set up his camera in the water, my job was watching for the alligator. Clyde took his time. He studied the saw grass. "I can even see some minnows! That'll be interesting." I waited for the alligator to ambush him. Clyde just waited. He waited for the sun to emerge from behind a cloud. Snap. A Clyde Butcher photograph. He hauled his body out of the swamp. "I wonder where that gator was," he said. "Oh, well."

❻ The Smallwood Store

Chokoloskee is modern now. It has a good concrete bridge and modern roads and acquaintance with air-conditioning. It has cable television and street lights. Tourists arrive in buses to take boat rides into Everglades National Park; later they fill canvas bags with souvenirs before going home.

But on a warm, breezeless afternoon, the tiny Southwest Florida village of Chokoloskee still seemed to be the last frontier to me. I felt the heat and the humidity and smelled the rotten egg smell of low tide and the mangroves. I felt the kiss of mosquitoes and the gentle touch of sand flies.

I love the Everglades, where I spent much of my youth fishing, hiking, canoeing, and contributing blood to the food chain. But I always wondered how the old-timers survived in the days before repellent and window screens.

The old Everglades folks were a tough breed. Ted Smallwood, Lynn Smallwood McMillin's grandfather, must have had a hide like a bull alligator. If he didn't, he could have bought one from the Everglades Indians. At his store, which he opened in 1905, he could have sold you a hide or corn liquor. And, if you had time and wanted to sit a spell, he'd have told you stories to curl your hair. He'd have told you, for instance, about the day Chokoloskee's menfolk got away with killing Mr. Watson.

Ted Smallwood was seventy-eight when he died in 1951, the year my parents moved from Chicago to Miami. My dad liked to fish, and we pursued bass in the eastern Everglades, closest to Miami. We never visited the Everglades region near Chokoloskee, the Ten Thousand Islands. To get there meant a two-hour drive across a bumpy two-lane wilderness road peopled mostly by Miccosukees who spoke no English, and by gun-toting squatters who cared nothing for civilization.

Had we braved the drive, we wouldn't have gotten to the Smallwood store anyway. We lacked a boat, and that was the only way to get to Chokoloskee Island. Civilization—the bridge to Chokoloskee Island—didn't arrive until 1956. That was the year Lynn Smallwood was born. Now she runs her grandfather's old store as a museum.

When I visited in 1997, the museum store was a dark, wild place, full of nooks and crannies and the ghosts of Everglades pioneers past. One ghost was Ted Smallwood himself. Walk into the dimly lit building and there he is. For an instant, you will be sure the stories of his death were greatly exaggerated. On second glance, you'll wonder if some taxidermist toiled overtime. Finally you realize you're looking at a very good Mr. Smallwood dummy. He was sprawled in a chair by the window, legs flung out, snoozing in round, Teddy Roosevelt–style spectacles. A walrus mustache hid a large mouth. He was tall and stocky, maybe a little stout, a man who had eaten his share of fried mullet and grits.

I wanted to ask him to point me to the alligator hides. He bought hides, alligator and otherwise, from the Everglades Indians—the Seminoles and the Miccosukees. They trusted him, an honest white man. "My grandfather was always fair to them," Lynn Smallwood told me. Seminole-Miccosukees who lived just outside Miami's city limits preferred to pole their dugout canoes the eighty miles to Smallwood's.

He traded sewing machines, cloth, and fish hooks for their hides. He paid in silver; the Everglades Indians didn't trust paper. In fact, the Seminole-Miccosukee people in the early twentieth century trusted very few white folks. Some of his older customers remembered the wars to remove them from Florida.

Ted Smallwood was different. He was interested in the Indian culture. He was one of the few white people who spoke their language. They'd arrive en masse and set up camp outside the store. If they planned to drink alcohol, they handed over their guns and knives to Smallwood, just in case the partying got out of control. They even trusted Smallwood with their silver money. He stored it, under lock and key, in a big wooden chest.

I saw the chest in the store museum. I saw his mildewed books, the deer antlers, the salt bottles, the nails, the coffee grinder, the grits bags, and the first Coke machine to arrive on the island, in 1945. Ted Smallwood sold Bibles, venison, pots, and pans. "His store was the original one-stop shopping place," said his granddaughter. It was the only store in the southern Everglades, the only store between Key West and Fort Myers.

Outside, he fixed boats and motors. If someone sick arrived in Chokoloskee Bay, he'd take them inside and doctor them. He was even nice to Mr. Watson.

Chokoloskee was, and still is, a rough place. At the turn of the century, the Ten Thousand Islands were wilder than any western frontier town. They were stocked by Civil War deserters, get-rich-quick schemers, plume hunters, and plain bad men. Watson was one of those. Ed Watson had fled to Florida from Oklahoma, where rumor had it he'd murdered the notorious woman outlaw Belle Starr. He settled on an island on the Chatham River, about a half day's boat ride from Chokoloskee.

By all accounts he was a good farmer, and he sent his tomatoes and avocados to the market at Key West. Workers to whom he owed money sometimes disappeared from the face of the earth. When he visited Chokoloskee, mostly he got along, though once or twice during arguments he lost his temper and tried to cut the throats of other men. At Ted Smallwood's store, he was welcome. He paid his bills on time.

On the day three bodies floated down the river, Watson naturally was the suspect. Watson denied the crime, but he said he'd be happy to catch the real culprit. Watson left in his boat and came back the next day saying he'd shot the real murderer and that he'd dumped the body in the Chatham River. Watson's excuse failed to satisfy the townsfolk standing on the dock near the Smallwood store. One man shouted for Watson to throw down his shotgun. Instead Watson swung it toward the dock and pulled both triggers. His shells were wet and the gun misfired.

Someone on the dock opened fire. The others fired too. A woman cried, "They're killing Mr. Watson." Watson, thirty-seven bullets in his body, fell dead.

Nobody in Chokoloskee ever stood trial. National Book Award–winner Peter Matthiessen wrote three novels about the Watson saga, *Killing Mister Watson*, *Lostman's River*, and *Bone by Bone*. Matthiessen is a regular visitor to the store.

Everybody who travels to Chokoloskee ends up stopping, be they German tourists, alligator poachers, Miccosukee Indians, or a woman complaining about a husband who is still in prison for drug smuggling. When

Everglades National Park eliminated commercial fishing, people naturally found other ways to make a living.

They took their skiffs out into the gulf to meet the marijuana ships. They brought the bales through the labyrinth of mangroves where nobody could catch them. The smugglers were people who had never had money before; some bought gold chains and Cadillacs. They were easy to catch, and the federal government sent more than a few to prison.

At the Smallwood store, life went on. Folks who didn't go to prison gathered to talk—about the mosquitoes, about the heat, about the rain, about the wilderness, about maybe building a new boat, say a boat about the size of a jury box.

7 Pictures of History

Phyllis Sheffield was an artist. She painted wonderful pictures in her day and won art-show ribbons all over the state. Well into her eighties, she never stopped working on her paintings. But I made a pilgrimage to her North Florida home because I wanted to talk about her photographs. Like her aunt Florence Randle, Phyllis was a pretty fair photographer too. During the depression, the two women began visiting the Everglades to photograph Miccosukee Indians. For Phyllis and Flossie, it was chance to make a few extra nickels during the hard economic times.

"Aunt Flossie and I never felt what we were doing was art," Phyllis said the day I visited her modest bungalow near the St. Johns River. "And we didn't tell ourselves that we were taking photos for posterity. We'd just look into the camera and think, 'This will make a nice postcard.'"

Their photographs did make fine postcards. Of course, those photographs are considered history now.

"Auntie was an adventuresome woman," Phyllis told me as we sat at her dining room table. Adventure was in her own blood as well. Phyllis took fly-fishing lessons, learned how to pilot small airplanes, and swam laps almost every day. People even now noticed her red hair, clear blue eyes, and quick mind and wondered if she had discovered the Fountain of Youth. "No. I think young." As we spoke she flipped through *Women Who Run with the Wolves*, a New Age text for women trying to connect with their primitive natures.

"I can relate to that book," said Phyllis. "Who wants to clean house?" Aunt Flossie, who loved the natural world, was not big on housework either. In her native Midwest, Florence Randle as a teenager strolled into villages of Indian people, alone and uninvited, to make photographs. In 1914, the Randle family boarded a houseboat in Minnesota and commenced a two-year journey down the Mississippi and across the Gulf of Mexico to South Florida. Along the way, Flossie Randle rowed ashore to photograph church socials, beaming children, and the occasional American Indian. She soon opened a studio in Miami.

Flossie's niece Phyllis was born in 1916. Miami, scarcely two decades old, was an exotic land, perfumed by tropical blossoms, salty air, and the ever present miasma of frying fish. The land was as trying as it was beautiful. People died of malaria and snakebite. The 1926 hurricane knocked the Randle home from its perch.

As a child, Phyllis dove for spiny lobster in Biscayne Bay, harvested coconuts, and ate snapper she reeled in herself. Even school was extraordinary: Phyllis once took writing lessons from a neighbor, *Miami Herald* newspaper columnist Marjory Stoneman Douglas, who later became famous for a book, *The Everglades: River of Grass*.

Until 1928, there were no roads across the Everglades. The people who lived in the cypress and saw grass—the Seminoles and their southernmost relatives, the Miccosukees—were among the most isolated Indian tribes in North America, chased into the 'glades by three nineteenth-century wars with the United States. They hunted deer, speared gar, and grew pumpkins. They slept in open huts called chickees. They celebrated their culture with the Green Corn Dance. Medicine people, who knew the magic of herbs and plants, healed the sick.

When the self-sufficient Miccosukees had a reason to trade with whites, they often poled dugout canoes across the saw grass and into the Miami River. Miccosukees often came ashore in Coconut Grove, where Phyllis, a teenager, was working in her Aunt Flossie's photo studio.

One day, a striking Miccosukee woman who was dressed in beautiful clothing walked into the studio. The strings of beads she wore by the hundreds made her neck look long and elegant. Her crow black hair, pulled over a frame made of animal bones, dipped toward a shoulder like the brim of a sun hat. Unlike most Miccosukees who came to town, she could speak a little English. She was selling palmetto baskets and mulberries. Did the white women want to buy any?

They did. They wanted something else too. Would the Miccosukee woman pose in front of their lights and camera for a studio photograph? The next time the Miccosukee woman visited, they made a gift of the photograph. The woman—Phyllis and Flossie came to know her as Squirrel—was delighted with the gift. A friendship blossomed, and Squirrel invited them to her village in the Everglades.

"Auntie was just as bad as me," Phyllis told me. "We weren't afraid of

Pictures of history. Photo by Maurice Rivenbark.

snakes or alligators. We weren't afraid of going into wild places by ourselves. We knew no fright."

In the early 1930s, probably the easiest way to visit the Indians of the
Everglades was by boat. Phyllis and Flossie loaded their little skiff with
the heavy 5-by-7 camera, film plates, tripod, food, water—and combs,
cloth, and even a sewing machine. They liked to arrive bearing gifts.

Initially, the Miccosukees seemed shy, almost afraid to look them in
the eye. Phyllis and Flossie hardly blamed them for being suspicious.
Some of them, they found out later, had never seen white people before.
And what the Miccosukees had heard about whites frightened them. The
most elderly had been children during the last bitter war against the
United States in 1858. The old people remembered how the American

government had deported Indian people to reservations in Oklahoma, and how the government took Indian children away from their parents and sent them to schools where only white culture was taught.

When Phyllis was a child, whites routinely treated South Florida Indians as if they were savages who needed to give up ignorant Indian ways. Sometimes, when Miccosukee women arrived in their dugout canoes near Phyllis's house in Miami, white preachers offered them a dollar to submit to a quick baptism. The women, who seldom understood English, would blink in confusion and try to comply.

"The preachers would pull the gals into the bay and kind of dip them back into the water," Phyllis said, bristling. "They'd be down a long time and come up terrified, gasping for air, not understanding what was being done to them." Waterfront ruffians hooted with pleasure, especially when the women's wet clothing became transparent.

On their first Everglades trip, Phyllis and Flossie saw a beautiful Miccosukee woman bathing her child in a canal. They stopped, climbed out of the boat, and set up their camera. They waved to the woman, who was too bashful to look at them. They took the photo. Instantly the woman stood, grabbed her child, and disappeared. On another trip, they cruised around a bend and encountered a Miccosukee man spearing fish. When he saw their camera, he snorted with displeasure and waved them off.

Phyllis and Flossie, with the help of Squirrel, made inroads during the next four years. They always brought photos and gifts. Miccosukee men continued to be wary, but the Indian women made them feel welcome. A very old woman cooked for them, offering meals of stewed possum or roasted gar. A prehistoric fish, gar was too bony and bloody for most white palates. Phyllis and Flossie found it delicious. "White people just didn't know how to cook gar," Phyllis said. "I tried to fix it at home, but I've never gotten it right."

The old Miccosukee woman was a healer. Sometimes, when the white visitors had headaches, she brewed a tea that cured them. During the summer rainy season, the old woman rubbed their skin with a plant that kept even mosquitoes at bay. "They were beautiful people," Phyllis said. "They were strong and healthy. They treated their children very well. We never saw them get cross with their kids; we never saw them scream at them or knock them around. The kids always seemed happy."

Miccosukees who got to know the two white women became willing models. When they saw the camera, they automatically posed. On their last Everglades trips, Phyllis and Flossie rounded a river bend and once more encountered the grumpy Miccosukee fisherman who had waved them away in anger a few years before. "Our boat was really loud," Phyllis said. "You could hear us from a mile away. He'd heard us coming and gotten ready for us." This time the man was dressed in his ceremonial big shirt, vest, and turban. When he saw the women, he waved them over. In sign language he told them to take his picture. Standing proudly in his canoe, brandishing his spear, he posed.

Many of their photographs became postcards. Some even showed up in history books. Many the two women threw into drawers and forgot.

Phyllis got married, had children, and put away her camera. Florence raised her own children, closed her photography studio, and got a job at another studio.

The Miccosukee people changed too. State and federal drainage projects damaged the Everglades and the subsistence culture of the people who had survived there for a century. To make ends meet they had no choice but to embrace the tourist industry, learn English, and send their children to school. By the end of the twentieth century, many of South Florida's Indian people no longer could speak their native language. Many lived in poverty. Phyllis got divorced, remarried, and gave up photography for painting. In 1975, she started giving Aunt Flossie art lessons. They had wonderful times together. Flossie enjoyed painting pictures of wildflowers and butterflies and even tried a few Miccosukee scenes.

In 1987, Flossie died. She was ninety-six. Phyllis grieved. They had been so close. She remembered their good times in the Everglades and suddenly had a desire to look again at their old Miccosukee photographs. They were better than she remembered. She had them reprinted and began selling the prints. These days they cost hundreds of dollars.

She became a regular on Florida's art-show circuit. She loaded her wares into her rusty van—the one with two hundred thousand miles on the odometer—and drove herself from city to city. Like her Aunt Flossie, she never lost her independent streak. "I'm not afraid to be alone," she said.

She and her second husband had been married for decades, though they got along best when they lived apart, in separate cities. His house was an hour away, in Ocala, but they saw each other regularly. One summer Phyllis vacationed, alone, in Russia. Against her husband's wishes she planned her next vacation, a cruise down the Nile.

"I haven't decided yet whether I'm going to overrule him," Phyllis told me. "He thinks a woman my age should settle down."

▤ Travels with a Bear Man

Looking for bear country in modern Florida, I drove past Steak N Shake, Bob Evans, Tire Kingdom, and the Office Depot on U.S. 19. I passed Chili's, a Publix, and Calendar Girls, a strip joint.

I pulled into the driveway of the Fun Center near the Hernando County line and parked behind the Dairy Queen. Mike Orlando was waiting—Mike Orlando, the bear man, who wasn't interested in soft vanilla ice cream. He jumped out of his truck, put together a weird antenna, pointed it at the woods behind Dairy Queen, and shouted: "Believe it or not, we got a bear *right here now!*"

She was known as Number 4. The previous summer, Orlando had captured her in a humane trap, tranquilized her, fitted her with a collar, and let her loose. The battery-powered collar beeps when he tunes a special radio. It was beeping now. From the beeps Orlando could tell she was hiding barely a football field away among the pines and scrub oaks. She probably could smell the stale waffle cones in the Dairy Queen dumpster. Her acute sense of smell probably detected Mike Orlando.

He was keeping track of Number 4 and seven other bruins that, by the end of the twentieth century, had the fortune—or misfortune—of living in what had become the most bizarre bear habitat in North America. Orlando's bears existed in a West Central Florida wilderness that was vanishing inch by inch and day by day. The bears were dwelling in woods and swamps west of U.S. 19 in a twenty-mile patch between Weeki Wachee and Homosassa. The bear wilderness was dotted by housing developments and golf courses and criss-crossed by roads that included the most congested in Florida. Heaven help the bear that tried to cross U.S. 19.

One dead bear in this area of the state represented about 10 percent of West Central Florida's tiny population. A University of Kentucky graduate student, Orlando was studying bears on behalf of the Southwest Florida Water Management District and hoped to learn how a wilderness animal copes with civilization.

He wanted to think more than eight bears still survived. But he didn't know for sure. "It's amazing we've got any bears at all in a place that's not even close to being desolate," he said as a Dodge Ram rumbled into the Dairy Queen parking lot. He was all too aware that many experts believed his population was doomed, that even a small bear population required a minimum of 400,000 acres to remain healthy. His bears were trying to make do with 370,000 acres.

He was a stubborn man. Mike Orlando was hoping his bears would prove the experts wrong. Perhaps bears and ice cream could coexist.

"I'm twenty-seven, and I get to catch bears," Orlando told me. "I have to think I'm the luckiest guy in the world."

With my weak stomach, I didn't feel so lucky. As we drove along he was looking for roadkill. He relishes roadkill, the more odoriferous the better. When he sees it, he stops his truck, shovels the decaying matter into a bag, ties it to the spare tire, and heads for one of his traps. Bears will eat anything. They like seeds and berries and plants and honey and sweets. But nothing gets them salivating like a nice rotten armadillo.

Orlando has baited traps with armadillo so decomposed that even he felt like gagging. But as much as he liked roadkill bait, most of the time he favored something less aromatic. "I work too close to civilization to use a rotten animal for bait very often," he said. "In a semi-urban environment, people in some of these housing developments would smell the armadillo and go nuts."

We were heading down U.S. 19 near Spring Hill and passing Honda dealers and auto body shops and the usual fast-food eateries. He whipped into the parking lot at Publix before we could encounter a dead armadillo. Inside, shoppers were filling their baskets with tissue paper and melons and hamburger buns and toothpaste, oblivious to the presence of bears in the woods just behind the store. Mike Orlando pushed his cart to the Publix bakery and strolled through a little door.

"Ah, the bear man," called the baker.

A twenty-five-pound sack of day-old doughnuts awaited. They included glazed doughnuts, powdered doughnuts, jelly doughnuts, and even a few bear claws. Sometimes Orlando ate one or two, but the treats were not for him. "Bears love doughnuts." He was hoping they'd step right into a trap to get one.

City people got upset when they heard that Orlando was trapping bears. They imagined an iron-jawed contraption crushing the bear's paw, and the bear suffering and maybe gnawing off its own leg. That never happened. He catches bears without harm. One trap is hardly more than a giant pipe: When the bear crawls in far enough to grab a doughnut or a dead armadillo, the door slams shut behind. His other trap was a snare. Orlando often attaches the plastic-coated cable to a tree and buries it. Then he spreads doughnuts over the sand.

When the bear grabs the bait, it also triggers a spring hidden in the middle of the snare. The spring closes the snare around the bear's paw. A plastic-coated cable does no lasting damage. Orlando checked his traps twice daily. When he captured a bear, he shot it with a tranquilizer dart, performed a quick medical checkup, fit the radio, then waited for the bear to wake. Easier said than done. The bear usually was less than thrilled at Orlando's arrival. It huffed and puffed, snapped its jaws, and lunged for him.

"If it got me, it would all be over. Nobody could help me."

Bear science is dangerous work, and not just because of the bears. Rattlesnakes coil in the palmettos, and lightning crashes above the pines. Orlando's thick arms were scarred from the bites of ticks. But biologists knew the riskiest part of their job was flying in a small airplane just above the trees. Twice weekly Orlando flew over his bear kingdom with radio receiver and kept track of his bears.

Only once did he see a bear from the air. But that one was special. It was bear Number 5. Number 5 was the bear that tormented the bear man. "I've never met a bear like Number 5," Orlando told me as we stopped to bait a track with a doughnut. He spoke from experience. As a University of Florida undergraduate, he had trapped bears in Osceola National Forest near Lake City and at the Eglin Air Force base wilderness close to Pensacola. He had always managed to get his bear. But not Number 5.

Unlike his country cousins, Number 5 was a man about town who knew the ropes. He learned from mistakes. He got caught once by another biologist and never forgot the humiliation and the stench of man. The time Orlando spotted Number 5 from the air. Number 5 was squatting on a road, eating doughnuts from a trap he had raided without incident.

On another occasion, Orlando was driving through the woods when he encountered Number 5 hunkered in the middle of a trail as if he had been waiting for his human opponent for hours. As Orlando's truck drew near, Number 5 rose and sauntered into the woods.

Orlando needed to catch him. The batteries on Number 5's old collar were wearing out. The bear man set multiple traps. He used doughnuts, raspberry extract, even roadkill. Number 5 figured a way to trigger the traps without getting caught. Then, of course, he'd wolf down the bait. Orlando set up remote cameras that pointed at the traps, cameras that documented Number 5 at work. After springing the traps, Number 5 often destroyed them.

"So now, not only am I having to fix traps all the time, he's wasting the film in my camera," Orlando said. We baited another trap and a trap after that one. He showed me an oak that a bear had used as a scratching post. He showed me bear dung. But mostly he talked about his long, fruitless hunt for bear Number 5.

July had become August, and August became September, and September, October. Orlando began thinking Number 5 was too smart. But bear biologists know a few tricks too. One morning Orlando caught a female bear. She was in heat, so Orlando collected her urine. He drove to Number 5's favorite woods and poured essence of amorous female bear into the snare trap.

As that guy in *King Kong* said, "It was beauty who got the beast."

When Orlando drove up to his captured prey, something was strange. Bears panic at his arrival, but Number 5 watched him calmly. "It was like he knew the procedure; he knew exactly what was going to happen."

Orlando likes to shoot his tranquilizer into the bear's hindquarters. Number 5 knew. He refused to allow his hindquarters to be a target. As Orlando circled with his dart gun, Number 5 pivoted his rear end on the ground, all the while watching the man. Then a mourning dove fluttered to the ground. Number 5 forgot himself and turned. Blam! Orlando fired his dart into prime bear butt. Number 5 fell sleep.

Orlando went to work. Number 5 was 350 pounds and almost three and one-half feet tall at the shoulders. "Lots of people have the impression that Florida bears are small," he said. A 350-pounder is a healthy bear, though in Florida black bears sometimes top 600 pounds. Number 5 had some growing to do.

Number 5 woke up. Orlando watched him lope off into the brush.

"I felt real sad after I caught him," Orlando told me as he baited another trap. "I felt let down, like there was nothing for me to look forward to. It was like when Sherlock Holmes caught his nemesis, what was his name? Professor Moriarty."

9 Torreya State Park

It was hunting season in the Florida Panhandle. I could tell by all the pickup trucks and the rifles in the rear windows. Camouflaged men dragged deeply from cigarettes, waiting for their baying hounds to run a deer out of the woods.

Gil Nelson and I were hunting too. I lacked his experience, so I left everything up to him. He hauled our weaponry in a small pack at his waist. He carried notebooks, magnifying glasses, rulers, and worn-out nature guides.

We were hunting plants in Florida's Garden of Eden. On the Apalachicola River, about ninety minutes west of Tallahassee, its real name was Torreya State Park. A crazy, mixed-up garden it was. The Creator must have scooped a hunk of the Great Smoky Mountains and dropped them in Florida, complete with the trees and shrubs and wildlife.

Changing leaves—I didn't believe it until I saw them—heralded fall at Torreya. Waterfalls spewed from steep cliffs. Copperheads lay coiled in the deep grass. "Can you believe we're in Florida?" Nelson asked.

Gil Nelson was among our state's premier naturalists, the author of *The Trees of Florida* and *The Shrubs of Florida*. He wrote the outstanding guides *Exploring Wild North Florida* and *Exploring Wild Northwest Florida*, which I carried in my pack. His words about this park had prompted my visit: "Few of Florida's natural areas rival the unique attributes of Torreya State Park."

In addition to cliffs and deep ravines and hills and river bluffs and mountain-region flora, the park was home to 120 plants that wildlife agencies listed as threatened or endangered. One tree, the torreya, was among the rarest on earth and probably doomed to extinction.

"I visit at any excuse," said Nelson, a forty-nine-year-old Tallahassee resident. For a living he taught computer programming, but his passion from childhood onward had been natural Florida. One year he hiked a thousand miles through the state's wilderness. His idea of a perfect day was driving to the Panhandle's coastal St. Marks National Wildlife Refuge in the middle of the night and walking until dawn.

"It's great at night," he said. "You see meteor showers and hear some great frogs. You know what's perfect? A cool October night. You get a chorus of leopard frogs so loud you have to yell. In February, you get those spring peepers. In August, you can hear those narrowmouth toads hollering."

On weekends, with more time, he liked driving to Torreya (pronounced "tory-a"). Sometimes he visited alone and sometimes led tours of elderly folks, naturalists, and even Boy Scouts. One trip was going perfectly until a scout picked up a venomous copperhead snake. "It turned out the snake wasn't very upset, and it didn't inject any poison. The boy was fine. But we do have to watch where we put our feet here."

I am a lousy botanist. Oh, I can bluff my way through the woods if I'm with a neophyte. Even though plants stay put, I find them harder to identify than birds. Many species look exactly alike. I lack the eyes and the patience. Nelson had both. When he was a rookie, he invited himself on hikes and learned from experts. As his interest grew, he set up camp in the woods, erected a card table, and spread out his library of plant books. He'd walk one hundred feet and snip the leaf of an unfamiliar plant. Back at the table, he'd take out his magnifying glass and his books and identify it. Torreya was among his favorite places to botanize.

"There are a number of parks in Florida I consider unique," he said. "Torreya is something special, something amazing. Botanists for two centuries have come here. For someone who loves plants it is a paradise."

Once there were people who believed Noah lived here because he built his ark from gopherwood, another name for the torreya tree. The late E. E. Calloway, who lived nearby in Bristol, developed a theory that Torreya was the Garden of Eden and that Adam and Eve were buried nearby. I told Nelson I'd settle for a torreya tree. A copperhead snake— I'd never seen one—would have me speaking in tongues.

I hiked behind Nelson, who was tall and bespectacled and bearded. He wore a long-sleeved shirt and long pants. In my shorts, in tick country, I felt like the rookie. We sauntered among ancient pines. "What you're seeing here is presettlement Florida," Nelson said. There were long-leaf pines. Once they covered millions of acres in the Southeast, but they were logged out and replanted with faster-growing slash pines. Today they're rare, though not in the park. Under them, wildflowers exploded from the grass—purple asters, golden asters, blazing star, blue curl, and wild buckwheat.

Gil Nelson and I slipped into ravines and crawled to the tops of small cliffs. Gazing at the treetops below, we felt like mountain men.

Torreya is the result of wonderful natural history. Ice Age glaciers during the last 1.6 million years pushed many northern plants south into the area. "It's a cooler climate here," Nelson explained. "And there are elevation changes of a few hundred feet that are dramatic by Florida standards. That adds to the plant variety. Torreya also is at the northern end of the subtropical zone and at the southern end of the temperate zone. So you get some plant mixing. The Apalachicola River is the dividing line for western and eastern plants, but there's some mixing. The Apalachicola originates a few hundred miles away in Georgia. Seeds float down and take root."

He plucked a leaf from a small plant. Crushing it, he said: "Smell that!" It was minty. "I don't think it has a common name. The genus is Dicerandra, but I can't remember the species. Sometimes I'll walk into an area that has a lot of them and I'll be completely engulfed by the aroma."

I noticed one of my favorite North Carolina fall trees, the tuliptree poplar. Its dying leaves were turning yellow. "In the next few weeks a strong cold front will get through," Nelson said. "Then you'll really see some color. The winged sumac will turn red. Sweetgum will be yellow. The sourwood trees, the same ones you'd see in the mountains, will be a rich crimson."

He touched me lightly on the shoulder to warn me.

"That's a rare sight, my man!" Nelson whispered. "What a nice copperhead."

The trail we were hiking should have been called "Copperhead Road." Walking past the snake, I heard a new sound in the bushes. Two copperheads were mating in the dried leaves. Or so it seemed to us. They lay entwined, then untangled and hissed and got together again. Eventually Nelson decided they were fighting. Hunkered five feet away, I jumped backward when one of the copperheads slithered my way.

At noon we reached the ridge overlooking the mighty Apalachicola River. We admired basswood trees and black walnuts, white oaks and eastern hornbeam. We were talking again about how foreign this environment feels to a Floridian.

"Hey, look here," Nelson said. "Know what it is?"

I guessed red cedar.

"No. You're looking at a torreya tree."

They were common early in the twentieth century, so common that residents used them as Christmas trees. A mysterious fungus began killing them in 1970. Scientists are still trying to understand it.

Nelson pointed to a brown spot on the trunk and said he expected the tree to die soon. He said he expected all torreyas to die in the near future. Extinction is supposed to be natural, part of evolution, but nobody has to like it.

It took nearly an hour to return to the truck. We shook hands and said our goodbyes; on the way out of the park I saw a young couple walking along the road, holding hands.

Pilgrims in the Garden of Eden, they reminded me of a postmodern Adam and Eve.

10 The Herlong Mansion

"What's going on in the bedroom?" Russ McCarty wanted to know. Carrying a small radio, he stopped dead in the middle of the room and read the dial.

"Two. Three. I got a five now," he said, watching the needle swing right. He crept toward the fireplace. "Six, seven. Whoa. Look at this. Almost a nine."

He was reading electromagnetic fields. In the upstairs bedroom of the spooky North Florida bed-and-breakfast called the Herlong Mansion, something weird was going on. Outside, of course, it was a dark and stormy night. Inside the three-story house, it was even spookier.

Russ McCarty shuffled toward the bedroom's rear wall. He stared, disbelieving, at his meter. "Here we go," he said. The needle on the electromagnetic reader jumped to 10. Something powerful—and invisible—was emitting energy.

It was a few days before Halloween, and I didn't know what to make of what I was seeing. All I knew was I planned to sleep in the old house, in the old room, all alone, tonight. Alone—unless Inez Herlong came calling.

Three decades ago Inez died. Most likely in this room. Some people swore she's still here.

When the sun was out, Russ McCarty studied prehistoric bones at the Florida Museum of Natural History at the University of Florida. After dark, McCarty drove away from Gainesville on black roads. Old houses in the country waited in the moonlight. Owls hooted. Floors creaked. Upstairs doors opened and shut—sometimes when nobody was home.

When night fell, Russ McCarty studied haunted houses. He had a partner, Jim Bosworth, who taught biology at Santa Fe Community College in Gainesville. They're mainstream guys who believe in scientific methods. They collect, analyze, hypothesize. Their daytime college work had nothing to do with their postsunset labor. Then they were the only investigators for what they called the Center for Paranormal Studies.

"We have open minds," McCarty told me.

Bosworth said, "There are things that can't be explained by mainstream science at this time." Like things that go bump in the night. Apparitions. Unpleasant smells. Voices. Furniture that moves by itself.

McCarty was fifty-six. Growing up, he had developed a taste for sci-fi comic books and weird tales. Bosworth was about the same age and had a similar background. In 1990, they got together to talk about the unexplainable.

They even found a house to investigate in the center of the state, Lake Wales. People had reported visions, sounds, vile odors. "The smell was awful—decaying meat," McCarty said. "I would describe it as putricine. Perhaps cadaverine." A putrid corpse. The ghostmen sucked up the stench with a vacuum pump and brought it back to Gainesville for scientific analysis. In the lab, the smell of decay was undetectable.

At the Herlong Mansion, heavenly smells came wafting down the halls and up the stairs. Sometimes it was owner Sonny Howard's gourmet coffee. More often it was one of his scrumptious breakfasts, maybe a bacon-and-egg quiche or Cross Creek grits.

Howard, sixty-one, was one of those southern renaissance men. Born in Alabama, he was all charm. He knew how to tell a story, cook a memorable meal, and, if he had to, unclog a toilet. He had made his money in the insurance business in Fort Myers, retired, and gotten bored.

He wanted to own a bed-and-breakfast and bought the Herlong in 1990. At the sale's closing, dining with the previous owners, he learned about the mansion's peculiar history. "I wasn't happy to hear about it," he told me once. "I didn't know anything about managing a bed-and-breakfast, and I knew I was going to have to spend every last cent to fix it up. The last thing I wanted was a ghost."

I didn't know Sonny then. If I had, I could have warned him about the ghost. In 1980, I had relatives who were caretakers at the Herlong Mansion, back when it was a dreary old house. Their job was keeping it from falling down while the owner decided what to do with it.

I slept there among the scores of doors and dusty rooms in dark that was foreboding. In the morning, I joked about having survived a night in

Something's not right at the Herlong Mansion. Photo by John Pendygraft.

a haunted house. My relative forgot to laugh. He told me that if he and his wife locked a certain upstairs bedroom, the door rattled all night. If they left it unlocked, nothing happened. He and his wife left the door unlocked.

Whatever was there stayed peaceful.

After he bought the house, Sonny Howard decided to add bedrooms to the third floor. The workmen slept in the living room. Some nights, they heard upstairs doors opening and closing. They heard footsteps. "They'd run up the stairs to see who was in the house."

Nobody.

A few laborers began carrying guns. There was no one to shoot. They finished the work but slept elsewhere.

Sonny moved in. One day he sat at his desk in the parlor and talked on the phone. He heard noises upstairs. He ran up. Nobody there. "It's the upstairs bedroom, just over the kitchen, that has all the action," he said. "The door makes a scraping sound. It's unique."

He began researching the history of the Herlongs. They came from Holland to South Carolina in the eighteenth century. In 1845, the Simonton family built a house in Micanopy. Zetty Clarence Herlong married Natalie Simonton. They moved into the Micanopy House in 1909.

Natalie was a beautiful woman with dark hair. Zetty was handsome and ambitious. He started a bank and raised oranges and livestock. He advised Florida governors. In fact, friends called him "The Governor."

He was a founding member of a mysterious club, established in 1892, called Hoo-Hoo. The number nine—the shape of a black cat's tail—figured prominently with Hoo-Hoos. Club dues were ninety-nine cents a year. Under the house, Herlong built a hidden room, nine by nine by nine feet. Club members met there.

The house remained in his wife's name. She died in 1950 and willed the mansion to all six children. That was a mistake, because they all wanted it. After eighteen fight-filled years, Inez Herlong Miller, the oldest child, finally got possession. She was sixty-eight, intelligent, and determined, a former schoolteacher and dress-shop owner.

On the big day, she walked into her new house, marched up the stairs and down the hallway to her childhood room. Suddenly, Inez fell. Hours later, someone found her in a diabetic coma. Within a month, she was dead.

The house lay abandoned for years. Big houses, especially old Gothic ones like the Herlong, inevitably attain reputations as haunted. Most don't deserve it.

Yet there is a postal carrier in Gainesville—a woman who wished to remain anonymous—who talks about visiting the Herlong Mansion as a child and watching furniture move by itself. She says she and friends saw smoke float up the stairs.

There is a former Herlong Mansion maid who was washing a tub in a guest bedroom. Stepping out, she slipped on the wet surface. Someone caught her. She turned toward her savior. Nobody was there.

"Thanks, Inez," she said.

Candy Lancaster was working at the Herlong Mansion when I first became a regular visitor. We often talked about ghosts. Alone in the house one morning, she was cleaning a downstairs suite when she heard footsteps upstairs.

"Hello," she called from the hall.

Nobody answered. A door opened and closed.

"Hello," Candy called again, goose pimples rising.

The door rattled frantically.

"Inez," she said loudly, "this is not how I want to meet you. You're scaring me."

A door slammed so violently the house shook.

"I don't know what to think of this place," Sonny was telling me one evening. "Nobody has ever been hurt. I'm completely comfortable here. If something is here, it's benign."

Tom and Nancy Bailey had rented Inez's old room for a night months before my visit. At breakfast, they looked disconcerted but said nothing to Sonny Howard. A few weeks later, Sonny received a letter from Tom:

> When we turned in for the night, Nancy was reading and I was trying to sleep. I rolled over and opened my eyes. There, in the mirror over the dressing table, was an apparition floating across the room. It couldn't be seen in the room itself, only in the mirror. It had a red shawl or hood over its head, and I couldn't make out the facial features, though I felt it was a woman.

Guests had been awakened in the middle of the night by a fine mist of water sprayed on their faces. Others claimed to hear a woman's voice, speaking ever so gently. One guest said she smelled perfume.

When I had business in North Central Florida, I often stayed at the Herlong Mansion. I enjoyed talking to guests at breakfast.

"How was your stay?" I once asked Andrea McClung.

"I'm still a little nervous," the Palm Beach Gardens paralegal said.

She said she had awakened before dawn and settled into the swing on the second-floor veranda and sipped coffee. Moonlight streamed through the oaks. She felt at peace. Suddenly she shivered, and goose flesh covered her arms. Andrea looked up. A mysterious woman stood watching her from behind a potted plant nearby. The woman wore a long blue dress with sleeves to her wrists. Her hair, brown and flecked with gray, was piled high on her head. Andrea could see the curve of the woman's pale cheek. The woman said nothing.

"I was so scared I spilled my coffee and ran back into my room," Andrea told me.

She regained her composure and ventured back outside for a second look. The woman was gone. How? Her only escape would have been through Andrea's room, a locked hall door, or a leap off the veranda. Now, as we discussed her experience, the sun was shining.

"You know, I have a very active imagination," Andrea said. "It could have been a trick of the light. But that wouldn't explain the goose bumps. I got those before I saw the woman."

"I don't know what to think of this ghost business," Sonny Howard said one dark evening. We were sitting in the parlor, barely illuminated by the dimmest bulbs I'd ever seen. "If you think the place is haunted, there's this psychological idea planted in your mind. You interpret ordinary events in that perspective."

One night he was awakened by otherworldly music. The musician turned out to be a guest. Impaired by wine and a disturbed mind, he was playing a harmonica. Out on the veranda. Naked.

Another morning Sonny heard a strange vibration coming from the back bedroom. The sound was coming from an old dresser. It stopped as he listened. But it happened again. Maybe it was broken pipes. "You don't need a plumber," said the mystified fellow with a monkey wrench. "You need a priest."

The sound happened again. Sonny attacked the dresser for the umpteenth time. In a back corner of the lower drawer was a beeper, one of those gadgets business people use to stay in touch with the office. A guest had left it, set to the vibration tone.

Sonny had been close to calling an exorcist.

The guys from the Center for Paranormal Studies I called up said they knew nothing about exorcisms. They weren't even interested. They told me they're interested in scientific facts about the unusual.

I asked if they believed in ghosts.

"My gut feeling is that things happen," Russ McCarty said. "We lack the science right now to figure it out. I imagine we'll find out these things have their own natural laws."

McCarty was reluctant to say more than that. He was a scientist, after all, and scientists require proof, proof, proof. If something couldn't be proven, it couldn't be real.

In some houses he had visited, light bulbs exploded. Doors opened and closed. In some houses, when the electromagnetic impulses were high, he had taken Polaroid photographs that captured ultraviolet and infrared images invisible to the naked eye. Sometimes white light showed up in the pictures.

I asked what could cause it. Solar activity, perhaps. When there's an explosion on the sun, houses said to be haunted suddenly become active. Why? If there's something in the house, maybe it needs extra electric energy to move.

"The solar activities may open a quantum door," Jim Bosworth said.

He looked almost embarrassed.

Sunset. There was a knock on the door. My ghostbuster, wearing shorts, a Hawaiian shirt, and Panama hat, had arrived. "Let's see what we have here," Russ McCarty said as I invited him into the room, the room where Inez Herlong had died.

He was carrying a briefcase. He took out his electromagnetic meter and looked around. There was an oak chifforobe, plush armchairs, a canopied queen-size bed, and a couch. There was an antique chest of drawers and a fireplace. The bathroom featured an antique claw-foot tub. On the door to the veranda hung a photograph of a turn-of-the-century couple unknown to even Sonny Howard. By their stern expression I guessed them to be unhappy. Wherever I walked in the room their eyes followed.

McCarty explored. He had lived in the Herlong Mansion for six months in 1970. Nothing unusual happened, he said, unless you counted his dreams. He had the most vivid dreams of his life. He saw children born into the world, saw lives lived, saw people die. Nobody he knew.

"Don't know if there's anything supernatural about that," he said. McCarty switched on the electromagnetic meter. It registered nothing. Standing in the middle of the room, at the foot of my bed, he cleared his throat as the meter twitched. It was picking up an electromagnetic field.

I felt nothing out of the ordinary. But if McCarty was impressed, I thought I should be too. I borrowed the meter and placed it on the bed. The meter twitched. Three. Four. Five. Six. I asked what was going on. "Hard to tell," McCarty whispered.

He told me he discounted nothing. Once he was called to North Florida to investigate a troubled house and a troubled family. Huge drops of water—they were slow-moving basketball-sized gobs—hung in the air. They'd fall, wetting furniture and people.

As he watched, an elderly woman was struck by a gob of water. Some water fell on the rug. McCarty dropped to his knees to study it. A big gob hit him in the back of the head. "I know this stuff sounds strange," he told me sheepishly. "I'm just telling you what I saw."

At the Herlong Mansion, we walked into the hall.

Near the top of the staircase, the needle on his meter shot far to the right.

"I don't know what to say," McCarty whispered.

About midnight, I went to my room. I climbed into bed and climbed out again. I'd forgotten to remove the cellophane from a box of chocolates, my gift to Inez. In life, she was diabetic. In death, she should indulge herself. I turned out the light, climbed back to bed, and drifted off.

What was that?

Was something standing at the side of the bed? I listened. Heard my own breathing. I pulled the covers over my head. What if there was something under the bed? I dozed, slept a fitful sleep. Had the oddest dream of my life: I'm watching birds with an expert. He has blond hair and buck teeth. My Lord, it's Tom Petty, the rock star who grew up in Gainesville.

He's an expert on hawks. Tells me to watch for a Northern harrier. I introduce him to a friend of mine, Lucinda Williams, another musician I admire. Tom and Lucinda hit it off.

I was grateful when morning arrived. At breakfast, Sonny served a fruit salad arranged to look like a happy face. The main course, hash-browns smothered in three different cheeses and eggs, went down easy as pie.

Before heading home, I drove through Micanopy down Whiting Road, which was all dirt and bumpy. On the left, a mile from the Herlong Mansion, through the oak trees, was a modest ancient house. Vastine Jehu Herlong, the last of the Herlongs at age ninety, lived there with his wife, Dorothy.

Sonny Howard had told me that Mr. Herlong probably wouldn't talk to me. He hates gossiping about his family. And he loathes surprises. He has run off uninvited guests with his shotgun. So I called first. Asked if there was anything he and Dorothy needed from town. White bread, Dorothy said. Merita. I brought it.

Herlong hobbled to the door on his cane and invited me in. He was affable, told stories about Micanopy and about his family. Inez, his oldest sister, was a terrific woman, he said. "A lot of people thought she was peculiar. Self-centered," he told me. "I don't think she was mentally perturbed."

I asked Mr. Herlong and his wife whether they've heard the odd stories about the mansion.

"I've heard them," he said. "I don't think they're true."

Dorothy, listening from her wheelchair, almost shouted. "A lot of old houses have stories to go with them! I don't believe in ghosts!"

Dorothy calmed down after a moment.

"I shouldn't have said nothing ever happened at that house. I don't know. Maybe they do hear strange noises at that house."

Maybe they do. If your travels take you to Micanopy, decide for yourself. Call Sonny Howard, tell him you want the haunted room, on the second floor, at the end of the dark hall. Bring your imagination, and maybe your Ouija board, and definitely your courage.

If something goes bump in the night, if your door opens without human assistance, tell yourself, again and again, the one important fact:

Though she left this earth before she could fully enjoy her home, Inez—at least the spirit of Inez—never hurt a soul.

11 Old Woman River

> I loved the Creek, I loved the grove, I loved the shabby farmhouse.
> Suddenly they were nothing. The difficulties were greater than their
> compensations. I talked morosely with my friend Dessie. I do not think
> she understood my torment, for she is simple and direct and completely
> adjusted to all living. She knew only that a friend was in trouble. She
> said, "We'll take one of those river trips we've talked about."
> —from *Cross Creek*, by Marjorie Kinnan Rawlings, 1942

Dessie Prescott, who taught her famous book-writing friend Marjorie Kinnan Rawlings how to hunt and fish, told me she could use a good river trip right now.

"I can't cast a plug anymore with an ordinary fishin' rod," she said. "Not since I boogered up my shoulder takin' a tumble. But I can still cast a fly rod. You use your elbow more than your shoulder castin' a fly rod. I would like to catch me some bass. This is a good time of year for them."

Dessie Prescott had turned ninety by the time I visited, and like Old Woman River, she still was rolling along. She was healthy except for that ailing shoulder, some allergies, and a knee sore from a fall in a boat. We sat on the back porch of her ranch in Citrus County; behind us, through the oaks and the cypress, the Withlacoochee River flowed toward the gulf like spilled moonshine. "Oh, there's big bass to be caught in the river," she said. She was sure that over the years she has tangled with world records, gape-mouthed bass likely to tip an honest grocer's scale past twenty-three pounds.

"Those big bass, they always broke my line swimmin' into the lily pads," she sighed.

Although Dessie was still passionate about her hunting, she no longer was comfortable firing a shotgun—the recoil was too great for her tender shoulder. Still, she slept next to her trusty 12-gauge and hoped never to use it. But give her a rifle and a quiet spot to sit in the woods, and she might like to shoot herself a wild pig—and do the butchering herself.

"I'm a tough old heifer," she said, daring me to argue.

Dessie had been an orange picker, a salad maker, a bus girl, and a waitress during her nine decades. She had killed and skinned skunks, and sold their hides. She worked as hairdresser and a real estate agent and sold cars. She was a municipal license inspector, a barnstorming pilot, and a military officer. If she were to describe herself as any one thing, it likely would be "sportswoman." And if people wanted to identify her as the late Marge Rawlings's best Florida friend, that was perfectly fine with her too.

As Rawlings described Dessie in *Cross Creek*:

She is an astonishing young woman. She was born and raised in rural Florida, and guns and campfires and fishing-rods and creeks are corpuscular in her blood. She lives a sophisticate's life among worldly people. At the slightest excuse she steps out of civilization, naked and relieved, as I should step out of a soiled chemise.

I first had met Dessie Prescott months before at the Marjorie Kinnan Rawlings Society's annual meeting. When Dessie ambled by, I was sitting in the orange grove at Rawlings's old house at Cross Creek and talking to Idella Parker, who had once worked for Rawlings as a helper in the kitchen. A vibrant African American in her eighties, Idella beamed when she saw Dessie, a dyed-in-the-wool Florida Cracker.

"Let me tell you about Dessie, honey," Idella told me, embracing her friend. "This here's a travelin' woman."

Dessie grinned. "I'm like an old bird dog," she said. "Open the car door and I jump in."

I asked Dessie that afternoon if we could talk in the future. "It had better be soon," she warned, sounding ominous. I wondered if she were ill.

No, she had a hankering for some traveling. She was going to Colorado to visit a gold mine she owned with one of her late husbands—she divorced or outlived six of them. Then she planned a North Carolina summer vacation. In the fall, of course, she would make her annual sojourn to Wyoming to hunt antelope.

"There's still light in her eyes," Jake Glisson once told me. An old friend of Dessie's, he lived next door to Rawlings as a boy. "As long as Dessie is alive, Miz Rawlings is, too. When you're talking to Dessie, you're talking to Miz Rawlings."

When Rawlings and her husband Charles first moved to the Creek, they were dreadful citrus farmers and had missed a few meals. Dessie knew how to survive. She was two when a man bludgeoned her father to death with a fence post. Her mother died of pneumonia when Dessie was twelve. Living with relatives, Dessie helped out by hunting and fishing, gardening, and picking fruit. She moved to Atlantic City for work in the hotel and restaurant trade. "My Yankee period," she called it. She had not reached her twentieth birthday when she moved back to Florida determined to build her own log cabin in the woods.

She picked the cypress herself by walking shoulder-deep into a swamp and marking trees. She found someone to cut them and haul them out with oxen. She found someone to lay a foundation and then found carpenters to build the cabin. She watched the carpenters set the first log and threw them off her property.

"Boys, pick up your tools and git goin'," she told them. "This is too painful to watch." She found carpenters who could do the work the way she wanted.

In 1928, a friend asked her to visit the new people at Cross Creek, the Rawlingses. They needed advice, and Dessie reckoned she could help.

On a late fall morning, I finally tracked Dessie down—she had finished her gallivanting for a while, thank you. Over the telephone, she gave crisp directions to her Crystal River ranch. "I'd be happy to talk about Marge Rawlings," she said before hanging up. When I arrived, she gave me a tour of her seventy-five-year-old house. Originally a log cabin, it had been fixed up over the years. Deer antlers and antelope prongs hung from the walls. She hunted in Africa, and one of her trophies included the head of a warthog. There was a stuffed bonefish from the Bahamas and a salmon from British Columbia. Nine tackle boxes, bulging with antique lures, were stacked in a corner. A lamp made from a stuffed largemouth bass lit the room. Watching over it all were two stuffed wild turkeys.

"I've always liked huntin' turkey," Dessie said. Wild turkeys are among the world's wariest birds, which makes them difficult to hunt. In the spring, when male gobblers grow amorous, they are more likely to become careless. Dessie liked to get into the woods before dawn, hide in the palmettos, and do turkey calls. She would imitate a female turkey looking for a mate, and the racket would woo a gobbler within range of her shotgun.

"One time I was sittin' in a windblown oak calling a turkey. Eventually I saw a man come creepin' across a clearing toward me. He thought I was the turkey. I stood to let him see me, and me standing scared the real turkey which was in a tree behind me. The turkey went flying, and the guy up and shot it. He picked up my turkey and run off. That wasn't very sporting of him."

Talking about turkeys made our stomachs rumble, and we decided to go for lunch. Dessie steadied herself on my arm we walked to my vehicle. "Nice truck," she said, when I opened the door. "What kind is it?"

I told her.

"I'd never buy a Japanese vehicle," declared Dessie, a World War II veteran. We could have taken her Jeep, I supposed. It had 140,000 miles on the odometer, but it ran, usually with Dessie behind the wheel. A few weeks before her last birthday, she passed all the appropriate tests and was granted a new driver's license.

"But I object at having to buy a six-year license," she said. "Hell, I could be dead next year."

I tried to picture Dessie behind the wheel on a modern Florida road.

"Oh, I'm fine," she said. "I don't like to drive in the rain or at night, but I do okay. Some friends of mine, they get nervous about me driving around by myself, afraid somebody will take advantage of me. So we dress up this big toy bear I have in men's clothing and put it in the passenger's seat. Looks like I got a hefty passenger with me."

We ended up at Dessie's favorite Dunnellon restaurant, the Dinner Bell, after a twenty-minute drive along curving, oak-lined back roads. "Watch it!" she called at one point, as I crept into an intersection that traffic had not quite cleared.

She backseat drove in the restaurant too. When she told me what she was ordering, and I said that her choice sounded tasty, she ordered baked ham, mustard greens, tomato and okra, and corn bread for both of us. As we ate, she carried on more than her share of the conversation. No, she had never killed a panther, but she had seen a number of them. She had killed a dozen bears, including one that tried to break into a little house she had in the Adirondacks in New York State. She had suffered three hundred skin cancers. "Hell, I didn't have a closed automobile or boat 'til I was forty-five." Now she protected her weathered skin by wearing long sleeves and any of her dozens of hats.

She was never bitten by a venomous snake, though only by the grace of God. No such luck with cats. A mad tomcat once sank its fangs and claws into Dessie's leg. "Aren't you going to get the rabies shots?" her nervous employer asked.

"Not yet," Dessie told him. "There are a few people I need to bite first."

"Marge and Charles, when I first met them, didn't know how to survive," Dessie said, back at her ranch after lunch. "They didn't have no chickens, no cows, no pigs, not even a garden. Marge and I liked each other right off. I asked her to go hunting with me. I had bird dogs that liked to point quail.

"Marge had a 12-gauge shotgun. I noticed every time she fired she flinched. The shotgun had too much recoil. I had a little LC Smith double-barrel 20-gauge with not that much recoil. I gave her that gun, and she started hitting quail right off.

"Anyway, I taught her to hunt. Then I got her a bird dog. We planted her a garden. Collards. Cauliflower. Rutabaga, turnips, radishes, cucumbers. I made her a little chicken pen. I told her she needed a hog. Hogs eat all your garbage and produce little hogs that you can sell or eat.

"I taught Charles and Marge how to fish. We went after perch in the lake."

Dessie asked me to fetch her a Tootsie Roll Pop from the table.

"Thanks. I ran out of saliva with all this talkin'. Where was I? Charles. Not enough is known about Charles. He was a tremendous-looking man, about six foot three or four and about three hundred pounds. But no fat. He wanted to write about the sponge divers over at Tarpon Springs. My husband was a doctor, and we spent a lot of time over in Tampa, and we knew people in Tarpon Springs. We introduced Charles to the right people, and he ended up writing for the big magazines.

"Marge was getting famous too. *South Moon Under,* her first book, was selling like hotcakes. Charles was hot stuff, too. The problem with Marge and Charles was they both wanted to be the big dog. One wanted the other to dance when the other one whistled. There was lots of friction, and I think their success is what destroyed their marriage.

"They fought like cats and dogs. Marge was very high strung, and she'd get more high strung after she had a few drinks. She had a mouth on her. Charles was normally pretty placid, but he could get riled after a few drinks. One time I came over and Marge was crying, cleaning the floor. She'd failed to season a crab casserole the way Charles liked it, and he threw it at her."

Marjorie Kinnan Rawlings sometimes shocked her Cracker neighbors. During a time when women were expected to be demure, she was opinionated and profane. She smoked more than one hundred Lucky Strikes a day and liked her whiskey straight. She could be a feisty neighbor, assertive to a fault.

Those were only the most obvious of Rawlings's qualities. She was also generous and soft, especially with children. By most accounts, she was a terribly unhappy woman, prone to periods of debilitating self-doubt. When she felt herself slipping into depression, she liked to call on Dessie, who seldom bothered with introspection. Dessie, though ten years younger, was Marge's rock.

"Young'un," was what Dessie called her older, volatile friend. In many ways, Dessie was Rawlings's mentor.

"Near the end of their marriage," Dessie told me, "she came over to my house on a beautiful, moonlit night. We had a few drinks, and we were talkin. She said, 'Dess, I need to get away to think.' That's when I said we could take a boat trip on the St. Johns.

"Next mornin', I got all our gear together and canned goods and my pistol and my .22. I went over to get her, but she had sobered up and changed her mind and tried to back out. But I wouldn't let her."

"Hyacinth Drift," about their ten-day journey on a wild Florida river, is the next-to-last chapter in *Cross Creek*. It would be impossible to improve on Rawlings's beautiful account. But Dessie's story is worth hearing too.

"Marge's job was to cook; mine was to make and break camp. We set up army cots with mosquito netting and didn't use a tent. We woke up the first mornin' with frost in our hair. I walked down to the river and killed a duck with my .22. That was the only time in my life I ever hit a flying duck using a rifle. Normally, you'd use a shotgun. We had him for supper.

"Another time we found a couple of netters who were illegally catchin' shad. Marge saw a fisherman drop a pack of cigarettes overboard, and we went over and traded a pack of cigarettes for a shad, fat with roe. If you haven't eaten shad roe, you haven't lived. By the way, you can still catch shad on fly rod in the St. Johns and in the Oklawaha Rivers.

"Our boat leaked. I'm not a good caulker, but I did okay. We were dirty and needed baths, but there seemed to be fishermen around every bend so we stayed dirty. Around noon one day Marge really had to wee, and we went ashore, and she found a quiet spot and pulled down her pajama bottoms, but there was a moccasin snake and she had to run off.

"Eventually, we reached the little town of Sanford and stopped at this dock next to a beautiful yacht. We needed gas. I stood and started strippin' off my Bowie knife and my pistol and looked up and there was this rich-looking, well-dressed, gentleman looking down at me. I said to him, 'Is it safe to go into this man's town without artillery?' But he didn't laugh.

"He volunteered to take us in his limousine to get gas. Just then his wife, who was dressed entirely in pink, come out. She said, 'You can't take them for gas! You got to take me to church!' He looked real embarrassed. He took Miss Pink Panties to church and came back and took us to get gas.

"Later, when we were leavin', he stood on the deck and waved. I said to Marge, 'I bet that son-of-a-bitch wishes he was going with us.'"

When *Cross Creek* was published, Marjorie Rawlings was already among the best-known writers in the world. Now she was even more popular. Few of her neighbors were happy to show up as subjects in her autobiographical new book. Still, they accepted that Rawlings was a writer and that writers needed to make a living too.

One neighbor, Zelma Cason, was furious with *Cross Creek*. She was the census taker, and an off-and-on friend of the author. Like Dessie, Zelma was a determined woman who took no guff.

Rawlings, in a moment she probably lived to regret, described Zelma in *Cross Creek* as "an ageless spinster resembling an angry and efficient canary. She manages her orange grove and as much of the village and county as needs management or will submit to it. I cannot decide whether she should have been a man or a mother. She combines the more violent characteristics of both and those who ask for or accept her manifold ministrations think nothing of being cursed loudly at the very instant of being tenderly fed, clothed, nursed or guided through their troubles."

Zelma Cason sued for invasion of privacy. The case, which attracted national attention, dragged on five years. Unable to concentrate on her writing, Rawlings produced only one book during the period, *Cross Creek Cookery*, which was mostly a collection of recipes. She drank even more heavily.

Dessie joined the military. She encouraged Marge to join her as a soldier. But Rawlings had fallen into a funk from which she never recovered. Rawlings's neighbors, despite their reservations at being the focus of her book, testified in her behalf at the trial. Dessie was delighted to be a witness too. She and Zelma, rivals for Rawlings's friendship, never had gotten along.

"I used to irritate Zelma on purpose," Dessie told me, full of mischief even now. "I'd drive by her house before dawn on a fishin' trip and blow my horn just to wake her. When she found out who it was, she called the game wardens on me."

At the trial, the judge asked Dessie whether Rawlings had quoted her accurately, cussing and all, in *Cross Creek*. Dessie agreed that Rawlings had caught the flavor of their conversations. And Dessie said she was not offended about reading her own four-letter words in print.

Rawlings lost her case. But the judge awarded Zelma only one dollar. Even so, Rawlings had spent $26,000 in her own defense and virtually had stopped writing. She produced only one other book after the trial, *The Sojourner*, which was set outside of Florida and considered a literary disappointment.

"Anything you could say about Zelma would be a compliment," Dessie told me, still holding a grudge after half a century. "She was a bitch."

When Marjorie Kinnan Rawlings died of a stroke in 1953, Dessie was just hitting her prime. She finally found the perfect job, managing the Withlacoochee River Lodge. She had thirty-six head of hunting dogs, as she puts it, for deer, bear, and hogs. She guided hunters to wild hogs, her specialty, and anglers to the trophy bass of their dreams. She'd take them out onto the river and soon have them casting Cripple Creek plugs or a Porter's Special at bucketmouths hiding near the lily pads. Sometimes Dessie cast too. She could make a lure dance on the water.

She married and divorced frequently—a husband often turned out to be a disappointing ball and chain for an adventuresome woman. But Dessie was proud she raised three sets of stepchildren and that she got along well with all of them.

"I've enjoyed my life. I still do. I'm going to try and continue to do what I want to do and have fun as long as I'm able, as long as it's no skin off some other fella's fanny."

We were standing in her kitchen at sundown, drinking apple juice, when I asked if she had any regrets.

"Not really. When I don't like the scenery, I move on."

Like Old Woman River, she continued to roll along. Still I wondered whether she had grown weary of Florida.

"It's been spoilt, but I like it, except in the summer. Air-conditioning has made me soft, and bottled me up, so I don't want to go outside when it's so hot. But Florida's as good as anywhere I know. I reckon I'm going to die here."

WINTER

12 Last Fish Monger

Buster Agliano was prepared, as always, for *Noche Buena*. His seafood store, the last in Tampa's historic Ybor district, had been ordering red snapper like crazy. On Christmas Eve, folks he sees every day and folks he sees just once a year would besiege S. Agliano & Sons Fish Co. at 1821 E 7th Ave. to buy makings for a holiday supper.

Buster expected to sell at least four hundred pounds. That's a lot of fish, though not like in the old days, when Cubans and Italians and Spaniards visited the store in droves to buy not only snapper but minnows and salted cod and even live eels on Christmas Eve.

"Those days are all gone," he told me. He was trying to be cheerful about the new, glitzy Ybor. The seafood store, which his grandfather established in 1915, was still hanging on in 2002. And so was Buster.

"He's the last of Ybor's institutions," said his old friend Ferdie Pacheco, who grew up in Ybor, was Muhammad Ali's physician, and later became an artist and author who has written about Buster's family in a cookbook.

Buster was a celebrity in Ybor. When he crossed the street to order Cuban coffee at La Tropicana, people mobbed him. He talked to friends in English, Italian, or Spanish. Judges and politicians and old Mafia guys kissed his cheeks and pumped his hand.

They wanted to hang on to him as long as they could. When I visited, he had just turned sixty-seven and had been diagnosed with cancer. The spot on his lung had diminished with chemotherapy. But so had Buster, down from 315 pounds to 273.

"For the first time in my life people are saying 'Eat! Eat! Eat!'" he said in a voice made raspy by the pressure of the cancer on his vocal cords.

He was tired—he so often felt tired—but he liked believing he was growing stronger by the week. He hit golf balls one afternoon; there is nothing like hitting a golf ball well to make a man feel alive. And at least

once or twice a week he was showing up where he belonged, at his odoriferous fish market, on his stool next to a very tall desk in a cramped office.
Forever he would be Buster the Fish Monger.

A seafood business on Ybor's most commercial street in 2002 stood out
like a church among bawdy houses. Years ago, when there were dozens of
little family businesses, a customer could walk from grocery to butcher to
baker to fish market and be finished with that week's shopping.

Now only the fish market remained. Its neighbors were a tattoo parlor
and a restaurant where one of the waiters wore yellow contact lenses that
made her eyes look like that swivel-headed kid in *The Exorcist.*

"Now your fish monger is the kid who sells you salmon at Publix,"
said University of South Florida historian Gary Mormino, author of *The
Immigrant World of Ybor City: Italians and Their Latin Neighbors in Tampa
1885–1985.*

You can buy a nice salmon fillet at a supermarket. What you don't get
is a lot of conversation. That sales clerk more than likely doesn't know
you, didn't know your mother or your grandmother, and doesn't know
your kids. That's what Buster represented, among other things, to Ybor.

"He embodies that old way of life of face-to-face relationships," Mormino said.

Buster's grandfather, Sebastiano Agliano, was the same. He arrived in
Tampa from Sicily a short time after Vincente Martinez Ybor moved his
cigar factory from Key West to Tampa and established the new community in 1886. Spaniards, Cubans, and Italians flocked across the ocean for
jobs. Spaniards and Cubans usually ended up in the cigar factories. Italians worked in the factories too, but often only long enough to save
money and start businesses, mostly in food. They grew vegetables,
opened restaurants, and caught fish.

Sebastiano Agliano caught fish and was selling them door to door by
1901. Then he opened his seafood market. If you were short of cash, he'd
give you credit. If you were broke, he'd slip you a fish head to make a
chowder. Buster was three when his grandfather died in 1938. His father,
Joe, and his Uncle Angelo took over. Buster spent many happy hours in
the store.

He was a growing boy, to put it mildly. Smoking did not stunt his
growth. He started lighting up hand-rolled cigarettes when he was four-

teen. "It was stupid," he told me. "You'd have tobacco all over the front seat of your car." He switched to Camels—unfiltered, of course—because Camels were macho.

In the first year of high school, he weighed 215 pounds. Down at the waterfront, he could swing a huge barrel of salted cod from dock to truck like it was a pound of coffee. He played football at Tampa Jefferson on the same team that starred Rick Casares, who became fullback for the Chicago Bears.

His best friend was a boy named Victor Martinez. When they meet now, all they do is tell old stories and laugh. In high school, Victor was the brainy guy who liked chess. Buster was the big-hearted guy who liked having fun. They were a good influence on each other. They went to the University of Florida together.

"Vic, the SOB, he could party all night and get A's the next day," Buster said as Vic roared.

Eventually, they got into a fraternity. Oh, the stories. Here is one I can safely print. It's about Buster's table manners. They weren't very good. "I'd pick up a steak with my hands and eat it." The frat established the "bad manners table" in Buster's honor.

All that changed when he met Mirtha Moreno. She was four years younger, a prom-queen beauty from Academy of the Holy Names. On their honeymoon, they headed to Miami to visit Victor, who was married and in medical school. From Miami, the couples traveled to Cuba.

In Havana—this was 1956—they headed for a night club, Sans Souci. The owner was Santo Trafficante Jr., the infamous mobster who had roots in Ybor. Buster didn't know him, but his father did. In the night club Buster introduced himself as Joe Agliano's boy.

That was good enough. Trafficante gave Buster and his bride and their friends the best table in the club and all the food they wanted. He also offered advice:

"Don't gamble."

"But we want to gamble," Buster protested.

Trafficante fished into his wallet and withdrew eight hundred dollars—two hundred dollars in gambling money for each of them. They blew every dime.

Later, in Ybor, Trafficante was a regular customer. He'd eat lunch at the Columbia and stroll over to buy a nice fillet of grouper.

"He always paid," Buster was saying. "He always insisted on paying. He was a very sweet man, a gentleman. You'd never have known about the other stuff."

Buster liked sports. People often were surprised, because a robust Buster could hardly see his feet, but he could whack a golf ball a city mile. He also liked to argue about baseball and football and boxing. He tried to promote a few boxing matches with Vic Martinez, his surgeon friend, but they barely broke even.

Buster enjoyed talking about politics even more. It's an old family tradition. Visit S. Agliano & Sons Fish Co. some Saturday morning and you'd see judges, city council members, and even members of Congress seeking counsel from the last of the fish mongers.

"He's one of those guys who has his ear always to the ground," said Pam Iorio, who became mayor in 2003. "He'll say, 'Pam, this is what I heard somebody say.' Or 'Pam, this is what people are talking about.' So that's why I enjoy shooting the breeze. Also, he's sweet and lovable. More than other cities, Tampa is a city of personal politics. To me he represents the best of that."

Jim Davis started visiting Agliano's in 1996, the year he won his seat in Congress. He was a Democrat, like Buster, but a more liberal one. "I talk to Buster as a reality check," Davis said. "I treasure directness, and he'll tell you exactly what he thinks." Ybor once was among the most liberal communities in America. But that was back in the first part of the twentieth century, when Tampa's big business community always was trying to crush the unions to which so many immigrants belonged. A lot of the working-class feeling continued in some quarters, but conservatives ran the show.

"I hate these corporate guys who run their businesses into the ground and then make millions," Buster said, sounding liberal. "That doesn't make any sense. Does it? What do you think?"

He always liked to know what the other person was thinking.

"But what do you think of welfare? I hate welfare," he said, sounding like Rush Limbaugh. "I hate that so many people are looking for handouts. That doesn't help them. People should work for a living." His daughter Aline, who worked in the fish market, had been eavesdropping. "Daddy looks out the back door and says 'Look at those bums!' and he sounds really mad. Next thing you know he's giving them food and blankets."

Aline had three sisters—Mirtha, Stephanie, and Stacy. They had given Buster and his wife four grandchildren. Mirtha and Aline enjoyed working in the market. They told their father he should change the name of the business to S. Agliano & Daughters.

Buster could have retired had he wanted. He had been offered piles of money for his seafood store, which, of course, would be torn down and most likely be turned into a bar. But he told people he wanted to keep it open. Most of his business was from restaurants and hotels throughout Tampa, but he refused to shut his doors to walk-in customers.

His walk-ins were the ones who liked to visit and talk about politics and the old days he so missed. "I'm an old-fashioned guy," Buster said. "I haven't gone to a movie in ten years. I hate the sex and violence. You know what I mean? It's bad for kids. But I also know that modern life is good. I'd be dead if this was years ago."

Over his shoulder, like the ghost of Christmas future, peeked the cancer.

Buster and Mirtha looked forward to the end of the year 2002. It had been that terrible. In August, Mirtha had gone to the doctor for a checkup. An X-ray showed a tumor on her kidney. Another X-ray showed something else: an aneurysm about to burst.

Bad enough for Mirtha. But Buster, fearing he was going to lose Mirtha, fell into a tailspin too. He stopped eating, the great pleasure of his life. Mirtha had surgery. The tumor surrounded the kidney like breading on a fried shrimp, but it came away in nothing flat. Next the aneurysm was repaired. Within hours, her kidney and her heart were doing fine. Buster, of course, was relieved. He told everybody how happy he was.

His voice sounded funny, though. Mirtha ordered him to the doctor. Vic Martinez, his surgeon friend, insisted as well. "Let me tell you a story," Buster told me. "I stopped smoking twenty years ago. I remember, I had this cough, and I looked at that cigarette and said 'screw you.' Some people say giving up smoking is tougher than giving up drugs. But to me, it was cold turkey and it wasn't that bad."

Two years ago he went through a bout of pneumonia. But his lungs showed nothing otherwise mysterious. In September, the cancer they found in his lung was about as big as a half dollar.

"If you don't fight this, I'll kill you," Mirtha told Buster.

When I met Buster, he was fighting for his life. After three months of chemo, the spot had shrunk to the size of a quarter. After chemo he would need radiation therapy.

"We're going to beat this," said his lifelong friend Vic Martinez, eyes glistening.

"Hey, that's my doctor talking," Buster said. "Sounds like good news to me."

Lung cancer can be tough. But miracles happen.

In Ybor, people talk about a miracle of sorts that happened at Agliano's during the depression. It's one of Ybor's most famous stories, told the best by Ferdie Pacheco and his wife, Luisita Sevilla Pacheco, in *The Christmas Eve Cookbook*.

By tradition, same as now, people with money bought red snapper for their *Noche Buena* suppers. But always there were poor people waiting in back. Buster's grandfather, Sebastiano, would try to save them at least a few scraps. Early on Christmas Eve, according to the story, the notorious mobster known as Tuto walked in and ordered the biggest red snapper Agliano had. But the boats hadn't come in. Tuto would have to come back later.

He returned at noon. Still no big red snapper. He promised to be back soon. It was a cold day. Agliano dragged a barrel into the alley in back and lit a fire. At least the poor people could be warm while hoping for a hand-out. Agliano passed out a few fish heads, and the line dwindled. Soon only the widow Maria and her small child remained.

The big snapper arrived. Where was Tuto?

Sebastiano Agliano wanted to close the store and go home to his family. But he didn't want to rile a mob boss. Fuming, he waited and waited. Finally, near dark, the neighborhood gossip, Pepe, poked his head into the store.

"You waiting for Tuto?"

Yes.

"It was on his collecting rounds—someone was waiting for him on Columbus Drive and blew his head off."

Sebastiano Agliano took the prize red snapper to the back of his store. The widow Maria's family enjoyed a fine *Noche Buena* meal.

13　Fruit Hog

Frank Wilson, fruit hog, jammed a fat cigar into his mouth and hauled himself up the ladder. He carried a large canvas bag and leaned deeply into the tree. His thin arms reached out like hands on a clock, and he started pulling. Oranges tumbled into the bag.

Wilson was going on eighty the day we talked. He told me he had been picking oranges for nearly six decades and had no plans to stop. The day before he'd picked eight thousand pounds—about three thousand pounds more than run-of-the-mill pickers. When he was younger and had more energy, he sometimes picked fifteen thousand pounds a day. He was what other workers called a "fruit hog." He was legend.

"The key is to keep your mind on what you're doin'," he told me, looking down from the top of the ladder, propped against a navel orange tree in a sixty-acre grove east of Bradenton. "If your mind gets to messin', you ain't going to get as many."

Men and women like Wilson, mostly of African American descent, were the heart and soul of Florida's citrus industry. They were the grove workers, the folks with strong backs who got their hands dirty for low wages. In a good year, they plucked about three hundred thousand boxes of fruit from nearly one hundred million trees.

"It's the onliest work I know," Wilson told me. He had picked tomatoes, beans, and corn and worked in a shipyard during World War II. He had laid rails for the Atlantic Coastline Railroad. "I helped build this country," he said, recovering from his modesty.

When I first met him in 1997, he was working for a variety of growers and packing houses in Manatee County. Ben Tillett, who owns the Citrus Place at Terra Ceia, valued Wilson so much he provided transportation to and from the grove. "There aren't too many people around who are faster and who work harder," Tillett said. "The very few who are a little faster are much younger men."

Frank Wilson's face was old. He had gray hair and a wispy gray mustache. His chocolate skin was creased by wrinkles, and his cheeks were sunken around bare gums. But up in a tree his body was supple and charged with energy. Twenty times an hour he ascended the ladder, filled his bag with fruit, and climbed down. He poured the fruit into a big bin, which holds about a thousand pounds. He filled a bin every fifty minutes and got about ten dollars a bin.

"It's better than minimum wage," he told me. "Five bucks an hour, it don't get you much. A pair of socks these days cost ten dollars."

As he perched above me on his ladder, I understood his concern about footwear. There was a hole in his left sock, visible through the hole in his boot. "You ain't gonna get rich doing this work," he called down. "But it's good, honest work. I don't believe in welfare."

Born in Georgia to a sharecropper and his wife, he was one of thirteen children. He was picking cotton by age nine. He hated picking cotton, and he had wanderlust, so he ran away from home. In South Carolina, he picked other crops. He moved to Tampa and did an assortment of jobs. He worked on the railroad. In the 1930s, he was walking along the tracks and passed a group of white men that included a sheriff. He said the sheriff hit him on the head with a blackjack for no good reason.

"I looked back at him and he put his hand on his pistol. I kept walkin'."

Talking, reaching for fruit, he leaned so far to his right on the ladder that the left rail came off the ground. "Florida could be a bad place for black men back then," he went on. "It's better now. Most of the time."

He told me he was healthy except for a bad hip broken when he fell from a ladder. Another fall years ago broke three ribs, but they had healed. He had been stung by bees and caterpillars and was so allergic he had to take the rest of the day off. He said he had avoided alcohol since he was a young man. "Drink will ruin you fast," he declared. "And I ain't worried about women at my age."

He never married. He said he had a girlfriend now, but she went her way and he went his way; they had no commitment and that was the way they liked it. He said his girlfriend was forty-three years his junior. "Women my own age are crabbish, too set in their ways," he explained.

His only admitted vice was cigars. He started smoking them as a teenager and later discovered hand-rolled Italians in Ybor City. He didn't inhale, just chewed. He said he could use a cup of coffee. Soon as he got home he'd fix a cup, then would make supper.

"I can eat anything I want," he said. His stomach was as rippled as a washboard. "I'll weigh 150 pounds when I take time off after orange season. But when works comes back and I spend days in the grove, my pullin' weight is 145."

Some pickers, anxious about falling, pluck fruit with one hand. Balancing, he pulled with both hands. He was, after all, a fruit hog.

Moving branches aside, he kept his eyes open for snakes. They're usually corn snakes and rat snakes, and they eat birds. They lack venom, but they'll bite a picker in self-defense. On the ground, in a grove with tall grass, he always watched where he placed his feet because of rattlesnakes.

"I don't even like to think of them," he said. "My sister was picking huckleberries in Georgia and didn't look down where she put her hands, and a rattler got her. She only lived a few days."

Descending the ladder, he dumped fruit into the bin. He refused to take a break and scurried up the ladder once more.

"Some groves are startin' to use machines now," he called down. "The machines shake the fruit off the tree. They tear the roots loose! People invent all kind of junk to make things easier, but you got to leave work for a man's hands."

14 Mister Citrifacts

Fidgeting came as naturally to Thomas B. Mack as drinking orange juice. Standing at his desk, talking on the telephone, he ran his hands through a crop of unruly white hair, adjusted his horn-rimmed glasses, hummed, whistled, played with a pencil, gazed out the window, tugged on his tie, shuffled papers, said "uh-uh, uh-uh" about a hundred times, and tried to make plans for the afternoon. He looked as if he was about to jump out of his skin.

Hanging up, he said: "When I retired, I thought I'd have some time on my hands. No! No! No! It hasn't worked out that way. I got more to do than I can possibly take care of!"

When I visited, Thomas B. Mack, professor emeritus at Florida Southern College, was poised to advise someone about landscaping, which was perfectly all right with him, because he remained rather good at it. When someone needed to know what kind of plants to grow in the yard, and where to put them, and what kind of fertilizer to apply, he was happy to oblige. But what he preferred was talking about citrus.

Citrus was Professor Mack's meat and potatoes, if you will, and in Florida he was sometimes known as "Mr. Citrifacts." At Florida Southern, he had taught all aspects of citrus farming and marketing for going on half a century. He wrote a monthly column for *Citrus Industry* magazine and was the author of *Citrifacts*, a book that could easily have been subtitled "Everything You Want to Know about Oranges, Grapefruits, Tangerines, and Limes But Are Afraid to Ask." He was founder of his college's Thomas B. Mack Citrus Archives, which was the Citrus Institute's museum of old photos, books, and records and celebrated Florida's five-century citrus history.

Mr. Citrifacts' home in Lakeland was painted orange, and the trim was painted a grapefruit yellow. "I guess you know I was voted into the Citrus Hall of Fame," he said. Alas, I hadn't heard. "I will be inducted by the governor in Winter Haven at the Nora Mayo Hall. By the way, I'm the only inductee who is still alive."

He looked about seventy.

"Yes, I'm seventy," he said. "And then you have to add a few years. I was born on October 27, 1914. My battery does start to run low at the end of the day, but as long as the sun is up, I am too."

Thomas Mack advised everyone to drink Florida orange juice. He said OJ keeps a person young. He drank a glass every morning, and no juice squeezed from a backyard orange ever passed his lips. Like most advocates of Florida's citrus industry, which sent 92 percent of its product to juice concentrate factories, he claimed that ever-improved commercial juice tasted better than the stuff people squeeze in their kitchens. I kept my opinion to myself.

"There are people who will tell you that fresh-squeezed is better than the commercial product," he said with a sniff, "but I don't think it is. We used to do a test at the college. We'd serve people fresh-squeezed, and we'd serve them the commercially produced juice. I think 95 percent of the time people couldn't tell the difference."

Although he was born in South Carolina, he thought it fate that the town was named Orangeburg. He was six when his parents moved to Central Florida, where citrus was a major industry and his father worked for a seed store. Groves sprawled across thousands of acres, and a future citrus advocate could stand on any hill and see orange trees stretching to the horizon.

At the University of Florida, he studied landscaping, but there were no landscaping jobs, so he ended up teaching citrus courses to returning veterans at a state agriculture school. He'd invite citrus industry leaders into his classroom to lecture, and he would devour their every word.

He grew oranges and sold them at roadside stands. He operated a roadside juice bar. He was a citrus broker, locating the best groves for the best packing companies, for a piece of the action. In 1951, he began teaching at Florida Southern. He taught citrus history, plant propagation, and soils and fertilizers. He told people, "I developed this program into the best citrus program in the country. It's not bragging. It's fact. I would like to believe we are teaching at this very moment the future leaders of the citrus industry."

When students visited his campus office, he asked them to take a seat. In front of them was his mind-boggling desk. If an empty desk is a sign of an empty mind, then Professor Mack was the Einstein of the orange. His desk had lost the war to books, notes, papers, rocks, shark's teeth, folders, rubber bands, pencils, paper clips, a magnifying glass, a shoe brush, and a bottle of Elmer's Glue. There was a sign that said, "The Older I Get the Better I Used to Be."

A good sign pleased Professor Mack. He pointed out another favorite: "They Shall Bend Their Swords into Plowshares and Their Spears into Pruning Shears."

From his bulging bookshelf hung a large envelope shaped like a Ruby Red grapefruit. Inside the envelope was his "Thought for the Day." Today's thought was "The Plan is the Thing."

I asked him to explain.

"You have to think before you act," he said. "Want to know my larger plan?"

I was all ears.

Professor Mack said, "One is nearer God's heart in a garden than any-where else on earth. I really believe that." He liked to tell people that the apple in the Garden of Eden was probably a citron, a citrus family member sometimes known as the Golden Apple. Was the citron his favorite fruit? He almost blushed when I asked. "I like them all," he stammered. I insisted on an answer.

"I would say a Sunburst tangerine is my personal favorite. I have to hold onto my tongue because I want to swallow my tongue along with the juice.

"Among grapefruits, my favorite has to be the Henderson Red. You're familiar with the Henderson Red? No? Well, inside the fruit is as red as this folder. Maybe a little redder. I mean, blood red. To me, there is no bitterness in a Henderson Red. I mean, the tang is gone. And it looks so beautiful on your plate."

When Professor Mack was a boy, he collected everything. He had rocks, butterflies, arrowheads, and sticks. He never threw away a book. As his interest in citrus grew, so did his collection of citrus memorabilia. Pretty soon he needed a room, and it became the Citrus Archives.

Over the years, he collected photos, maps, antique books, orange-crate labels, technical reports, and many pictures of citrus festival queens. He made it a point to visit citrus packing houses to beg for historical material. Recently, he traveled to an old packing house near Winter Haven and asked to look at old papers and photographs. When he opened the drawer, he almost wept when dozens of roaches spilled out. He even saw rat feces.

"Perry," he said to the foreman, "you've got to give this stuff to me. It's too valuable for this to happen." Perry said no, he couldn't give Professor Mack the records without permission. Two months passed, and Perry's boss said yes. Now the records took up two file drawers at the Citrus Archives.

Visitors to the Citrus Archives often got a tour led by Professor Mack himself. Talking to himself, humming, he scurried up ladders and retrieved huge scrapbooks, which he placed on the floor and examined with delight. As his finger trailed up and down the pages, he would say, "Yes! *Yes!*"

Catching himself, he told me, "I'm probably boring you. I'm sorry."

He leaped to his feet and cracked open another file. It contained stuff about none other than Professor Mack. There was an item about the time he met Bob Hope. Other clips talked about Frank Lloyd Wright. America's most famous architect, Wright designed the Florida Southern campus. Professor Mack knew him well. People always asked him what the architect was like.

"Oh, he had a big ego, kind of like Tom Mack. He liked all conversation to be focused on his architecture. I, of course, was interested in plants. I liked planting plants. He did not like plants covering the walls of the buildings he was so very proud of. He used to knock down the bougainvillea with his cane.

"Oh, my goodness. What time is it? You're kidding! Talking about citrus, I lost all track. I've got an appointment. Sorry, I have to go."

15 Miss Ruby

Ruby C. Williams owned a vegetable stand. Most of the time she stayed busy selling collards and turnips and rutabagas to customers who pulled off State Road 60 in rural Hillsborough County. One afternoon I stopped to watch her work.

"God bless you," she said to a motorist who had bought a sack of carrots.

For a few minutes there was peace. Miss Ruby—that's what everyone called her—retreated behind the counter, where her important work took place, the work she told me her God wants her to do.

She picked up a little tube of paint, dabbed some on a brush, and applied it to a hunk of wood. Sometimes a funny-looking alligator took shape. Or a young man and woman joyfully holding hands. Or maybe just the words, "I hurt so."

Another customer stopped in a Dodge van. Miss Ruby dropped the paints and hobbled out. She ladled the man some boiled peanuts. "You ready for the holidays?" she asked. He was. "Really?" she asked. "You mean you bought the wife a mink stole?"

She cackled. Where Miss Ruby lived was far from mink stole country. She lived in a land of cattle and citrus and strawberry fields forever. Turkey vultures glided above the highway looking for dead possums. In the tall weeds along the highway lay the refuse of the night, empty beer cans and broken whiskey bottles covered by red ants. Miss Ruby always found inspiration in this hard land.

"I paint when I feel like painting," she said. "When the right mood hits me, when I think I have something to say, I'll give it a try."

She was old enough to know better about telling her age to a stranger. I guessed somewhere between sixty and eighty, and when I asked for specifics I received a hard look. She wore a green ball cap, a green sweat shirt, black pants, and sensibly sturdy shoes. Her skin was the color of a Hershey's chocolate—bittersweet, just like she was.

Her great-great grandmother, a slave, helped settle Bealsville after word of the Emancipation Proclamation reached Central Florida during the Civil War. Growing up during the depression, Miss Ruby picked oranges and strawberries. She drove a tractor. She married, watched four children come into the world, and witnessed the sad end of her marriage. She moved to New Jersey and drove a bus, founded a church, and became an evangelist. She moved back to Florida, farmed, and opened her vegetable stand. She knew men and women couldn't live by food alone so she fed them the word of God too.

She became almost a fairy godmother to her community's poor. She outlived a son.

Sorrow and joy boiled through her. In the space of our afternoon together, she laughed and cried. So much emotion, Miss Ruby had. Thank goodness she had her art.

In 1988, a Lakeland folk artist, Rodney Hardee, drove by and saw the handmade signs at the vegetable stand. "Ruby's So Sweet Strawberries," said one. Another advertised peas. They were stylish signs inscribed with almost childish letters, colored blue and white and orange and filled with dots that could have been tears.

"You ever paint pictures?" Hardee asked.

"Not for a long time," Ruby answered. As a child, she liked drawing sunsets. Hardee gave her paints and plywood. He gave her a humble table to use as an easel.

She painted dogs and cats and pigs on the plywood. She painted a fish that had legs like a bird. Soon, people who stopped for eggplant were asking about her paintings. Her work attracted serious attention, especially when she began telling personal stories through her art. With their primitive figures, youthful letters, and bright colors, they looked innocent and happy. But underneath was an undercurrent of pain.

"Part of the rural Southern African American visual culture is autobiographical," wrote Jane Backstrom, a former Eckerd College folk art instructor who curated an exhibit of Ruby's work at the Polk County Art Museum.

"When Williams heard the blues sung as a young woman," Backstrom wrote, "she knew that the blues meant the world is a hard place to live in

Miss Ruby. Photo by Gary Monroe.

and some of her paintings today reflect the pain, troubles and yearnings of that genre."

"My husband broke my heart," was the caption of the appropriate painting. "It still ache."

No alcohol

Ruby C. Williams meant what she wrote on the sign. She tolerated no drinking near her stand, and no drugs. Nor did she permit loitering.

Zip-in. Zip-out. Can't you read, Buster? Buy a tomato, or a painting, and then kindly vacate that premium parking space.

"The 'C' in my middle name stands for contrary," she told me, cackling. She refused to give her real middle name.

Behind her was a painting of a blue alligator. "Tired of being the good guy," said the caption. The gator, I figured out, was a surrogate for the artist.

Miss Ruby sometimes thought her skin was as tough as an early season watermelon. But more and more it was becoming as delicate as a week-old strawberry. She needed tender loving care.

She grew up in the segregated South. Black kids, if they got an education at all, went to their own schools and were lucky to receive obsolete books. In the old railroad depot in nearby Plant City, children with the wrong skin color were unwelcome to use the regular washroom or drinking fountain. Years later, much to her satisfaction, Miss Ruby exhibited paintings at the depot.

Beyond racism, Miss Ruby remembered feeling plain different as child. She had six brothers and sisters who sometimes had little time for her. "They buddied up," she told me. "I was the odd kid. I learned to be alone. I'd fish, I'd hunt, I'd plant things to stay busy. I'd talk to the trees."

She felt a strong Pentecostal spirit. "My grandmother helped me come to Jesus when I was nine." Every Sunday, she and her grandmother sat in a pew at Antioch Missionary Baptist Church in Bealsville, established when slavery was still a part of America. "I knew I was saved."

Her grandmother helped keep her on the right path. She taught her important domestic skills and a sense of empowerment. "You have to be able to take care of yourself," Miss Ruby said. "You can't depend on anybody else except God."

She married a minister and had four children. She and her husband separated and divorced, bitterly. In her grief, Miss Ruby fled to New Jersey. She thought it would be a short visit, but it lasted twenty-eight years. She founded a mission that soon became the Spiritual Church of Love. She traveled and preached and traveled some more.

In 1983, she moved back to Florida to more or less retire. Some retirement. After she took over a piece of family land, her relatives and neighbors helped build the vegetable stand. Her son, Elrod, planted tomatoes and collards depending on the phase of the moon. Maybe it wasn't modern science, but it worked, and Ruby sold the produce.

She prayed and brooded. Finally, she painted. God works in mysterious ways.

She showed me her home, a humble trailer. Behind the trailer, clean clothes waved from a line. Her cows lowed and her chickens clucked. They seemed upset. One of Ruby's turkeys had pecked a hen to death minutes before.

We walked through her field, checking collards and turnips. She would sell her best vegetables to the public and feed her livestock the rest. She hated waste. Her grandmother Rose taught her that.

When she returned to Florida almost two decades ago, she worked like a woman possessed. When she picked vegetables, mister, she picked them as well as any man. If a field needed plowing, she hitched up the tractor. She lost herself in the hard physical labor.

"I'll *never* starve," she said, looking me in the eye.

Now she tried losing herself in the painting. Finding herself too. In one painting, a boy and a girl skip through a sun-kissed field. In another, a kid dribbles a basketball while his tongue twists out of his mouth in concentration. A boy and a girl hold hands, oh so innocently. But Miss Ruby knows about the plague and its impact on young people. "Watch who you sleep with now," says the caption. "I got the AIDS."

She worried about sexual promiscuity and created characters in her paintings who seemed as real to her as the young people who stopped to say hello. Like Mittie. "I love Jesus," Mittie says from a painting. Miss Ruby knows Mittie may love Jesus, and that Mittie may want to be good, but she hasn't been saved. Mittie's still taking her dress off for the boys.

"I like people," Miss Ruby said. "But some haven't got right with God."

"How could you take my husband?" weeps a woman in another painting. "He might have AIDS."

Between customers, between paintings, between my questions, she read her Bible. Proverbs 10:19. *Hate stirs up strife, but love covereth all sins.*

Sometimes rednecks drove past her stand and shouted the N-word. "I pray for them," she said. "You can take insults, you can take abuse, when God is with you."

Most people, whatever their race, were nice and polite and liked her tomatoes and her paintings. Some paid a dollar to look in the back room at her paintings. Some people bought them, paying fifty to seven hundred dollars. "You don't do this for money," she said. "You do it because the spirit moves you. I want to be like Martin Luther King. I want to leave something after I'm gone."

Brakes squealed. Miss Ruby looked up. It was the school bus. Six small African American children jumped off and ran to Miss Ruby, who crushed them in an embrace just like her grandmother, Rose, used to hug her. She gave each child a container of strawberries. She stood among them and let their love fill that empty hole in her heart. "Is there anything as innocent as a child?" she asked.

Her own, her youngest son, Roosevelt, passed away two Februarys ago. He was only fifty. It was his heart, the doctors said, but Ruby knew he was never right after he got out of the army a quarter century ago. Anyway, her son was gone, and the mother still grieved.

"Oh How It Hurts So," said the caption on the painting about her son. Her son is with Jesus now. Oh, Sweet Jesus, let us pray.

16 In the Footsteps of the Masters

Poor Michelangelo. Consider the sad genius, flat on his back lo those many years, painting the story of Creation with no chiropractor in sight. Pity poor Rembrandt. One sprawling masterpiece was hacked up to fit a narrow wall.

Artists know how to suffer. At least Christopher M. Still's Renaissance heroes never had to crush a cockroach crawling up their knickers while driving down the street.

Oh, Christopher Still. In his next life he will swap war stories with his beloved masters, Michelangelo and Rembrandt. They will tell him about perfectionist popes and cold-hearted bankers, and he will tell them about sketching cadavers at midnight, or about the one-armed fisherman who wanted to punch his lights out.

Finally he will tell the masters about his own version of the Sistine Chapel, how the state of Florida hired him to paint a million years of its history and, by the way, gave him all of eighteen months to complete it.

Pressure? A man who keeps his vehicle on the road while a cockroach tickles his thigh is up to any task.

Christopher Still, born in 1961, was a straw-haired Tarpon Springs resident who studied art in Europe and sold paintings that induced sticker shock even among the bluebloods who attended his annual shows. At a gourmet restaurant he might order pate; at home he slathered mayonnaise on a hot dog. He could explain painting techniques—how he used egg tempera and acrylics and oil, how he toned his canvases, how he glazed a final work—in perfect, refined paragraphs. Then he'd slip into an exaggerated Mississippi sheriff drawl while telling the story about the huge lawman who came to his studio after hearing a woman scream. Only it wasn't a woman; it was Still, responding to an unfortunate encounter with a large rat. The sheriff thought he was less than macho.

American Artist, a leading national magazine in the field, published a cover story about Still. He would be as thrilled if *Field and Stream* did a piece about his redfish and trout expeditions. He enjoyed those Saturday morning fishing shows on ESPN, the ones where grunting good old boys drawled, bragged, and landed bass to a banjo soundtrack. Then he'd drive to his studio and paint, humming along to a Mozart opera.

He was born, contrary to rumor, without a paintbrush in hand. That came a few years down the pike. In second grade, he was chosen to paint a mural at a fast food restaurant. He sold his first painting when he was fourteen.

He'd draw a battleship. He'd draw a plane above the battleship. Then he'd draw bombs dropping on the ship, and then he'd erase the ship and resketch it at the bottom of the sea. Maybe he'd add a couple of sharks devouring terrified sailors. He painted pictures of snook and tarpon and pelicans and ospreys. A Christmas tree, lying on the curb, infuriated him. "Such a waste." He tolerated no animal cruelty, and friends nicknamed him "Nature Boy."

In school, if he had to talk about Spanish conquistadors, his mother, Patricia, would whip up an appropriate costume for his presentation. His dad, John, was a well-regarded Clearwater High School teacher who would dress like Abraham Lincoln during lectures about the Emancipation Proclamation. He was pleased when his son gravitated toward the arts.

Chris was a bearded, long-haired, hippie drum major who once showed up at Dunedin High School dressed in a flowing white robe. "Jesus of Nazareth," sneered an administrator. He had a reading disorder: When he looked at sentences, he saw not black words on a page but the white space between the words. He got by using a bookmark under each line. Some teachers cut him slack, letting him paint rather than do homework.

When he was sixteen, he painted his first naked woman.

Ohmygod! he told himself. *I can see everything.*

In 1979, he was chosen the outstanding art student in Pinellas County. He won a scholarship to Philadelphia Academy of Fine Arts, then promptly kissed off the scholarship to travel Europe. He hung out with a fresco artist, ran out of money, worked as a gardener, and lived in a commune. He drank wine, loved life, and painted up a storm.

In the masters' footsteps. Photo by Scott Keeler.

In Sicily, painting a portrait of a volcano, he tried to roast a potato over the lava. The mountain rumbled, and he fled, still hungry. In Holland, he discovered the Dutch masters, Rembrandt van Rijn, Willem van Aelst, Frans van Mieris. They used vivid colors but also took advantage of dramatic shadow. At the Hague, he would stand in the galleries, study the paintings, and try to reconstruct how the artists did them.

He returned to Philadelphia, reclaimed his art scholarship, and lived in a YMCA with a bunch of winos. When he rented a dirty apartment, complete with mice, he fancied himself a young, struggling Vincent van Gogh.

Da Vinci and Michelangelo fascinated him. Captivated by the human form, they dissected corpses. Still talked a doctor into letting him make nocturnal visits to Philadelphia's Jefferson Hospital for Gross Anatomy. Soon he was a regular. He'd slice open a hand and sketch the tendons while comparing the dead fingers with his own live ones. One night he smuggled a friend into the lab. He cracked open a cadaver's chest and spread the rib cage. His friend looked woozy.

Thus ended his morbid period.

Still's work long had fascinated me. So when he invited me to accompany him on a trip, I jumped at the chance.

Driving with him through Tampa's rush hour traffic early one morning, I asked if we could stop for breakfast. He looked reluctant. When he is doing field work, he forsakes regular sustenance. In the back of the Ford pickup, he had packed his canvases and his easel and his paints. Sometimes he feels the need to pull off the road and paint a cypress swamp or a pine barren or a flock of sandhill cranes.

"Look at those colors," he shouted, pointing to a forest beyond a billboard on Interstate 4. "The trees are golden in this light, but they have a greenish tint. Nice maple. Morning light on a maple. It's tricky to get colors, because they're constantly changing."

I was relieved when we drove past a dead possum. I knew his story: If an animal is not too putrid, he takes it home, pops it into the freezer, and pulls it out when he needs a model. It was a skill he didn't learn in art school.

In 1986, when he returned to Florida from college, he decided he would combine his formal art education with his long study of the European masters and celebrate what he knew best, Florida. "I wanted people to understand what they have here. And what we could lose."

He created paintings of Cracker girls gazing out windows at livestock and collages of diving helmets and sponges. He painted seascapes and river scenes. In one sprawling work, now owned by the Museum of Florida Art and Culture in Avon Park, he captured the story of the Seminole Indians. Another major piece, *Hibiscus rosa-sinensis*, presented hundreds of blossoms in a vase.

"At first glance, Still's paintings appear to be an exact slice of life," wrote Eunice Agar, a critic for *American Artist*, "but like their European prototypes they're actually allegorical reconstructions of reality." Still wasn't sure he understood, but the critic's words sounded like a compliment.

His paintings have hung in the Smithsonian Institution, St. Petersburg's City Hall, and the White House. Hired to paint Lawton Chiles's portrait, Still was among the few people who ever told the late governor to sit up straight.

His latest project came about in 1999, when the state commissioned him to paint eight murals depicting its history. Each panel was to be ten feet wide and about four feet deep and hang in the House of Representatives.

"I'm completely overwhelmed," he said as we drove through the Florida countryside.

His wife, Evelien, was keeping him on track. He is emotional; she was calm. He is spontaneous; she liked to plan. At night, she relieved him of the remote; otherwise he channel-surfed, stopping at *Gilligan's Island* re-runs or anything starring Don Knotts. He loved *The Andy Griffith Show*. With red hair and a pale complexion, Still could have been Opie's big brother. His favorite Don Knotts movie was *The Incredible Mister Limpet*. "My dream come true," he said, "is a man who becomes a fish."

On their first date, Evelien climbed into his car and sat in wet paint. She led him back into the house, changed her clothes, and handed him her dirty ones. "Start cleaning," she told him.

She was born in Holland and came to Florida with her parents in 1980. She and Still married in 1987. Their daughters, Hannah and Esther, were already demonstrating artistic talent, judging by the Crayola portraits I saw on the refrigerator.

Still drove them to school every morning, then headed for his studio. At lunch, Evelien would provide the names of people he should call and people he should ignore. He has a problem saying "no" to anyone, so she did it for him.

Then he'd return to the studio and paint uninterrupted, spirits rising and falling depending on the quality of his work. When it was going poorly, he'd force himself to stay in front of the easel by promising himself a Coke if he could complete just a little bit more, or a bathroom break if he already had had a Coke. He'd come home at 7:30, exhausted. As he and Evelien ate, he rambled, his voice anxious, about what would come next.

"Chris," Evelien told him, "relax, breathe, taste your food."

She was his best friend and manager. She felt comfortable criticizing a painting. He trusted her to help price his work. Small paintings were about one thousand dollars. Big ones more than fifty thousand dollars. He sold his paintings only once a year, usually in a one-night gala at Ruth Eckerd Hall in Clearwater. The sale provided his income for the entire year. The Florida Legislature was paying him $150,000 to gussy up the House of Representatives. It sounded like a lot of money to me, but looking at Still's worried face, I didn't bring it up. I could tell he was suffering.

Eight murals had to account for a million years. An artist could get nauseated just thinking about it.

5 A.M. We were driving through Central Florida and looking for inspiration. Still hoped to paint a few studies. A study is a small quick painting that captures a moment. Later, in the studio, an artist uses the study as a model for a bigger painting. "I'll stop at the drop of a hat if we see something cool," he said. Practicing for his Florida Legislature murals, he had painted a study at a Civil War battlefield a few days earlier. He had painted a study of an old sugar mill and a study of an old railroad bridge.

At the Withlacoochee River, he once stopped to ask an African American woman who was fishing with a cane pole if he could paint her. She nodded yes and sang a song about Jesus as she fished for bream. While Still painted, a van rumbled up. Inside was a scary-looking guy who asked Still and the woman if they'd mind his kids for a few minutes. Startled, they said yes. The kids stood on the bank next to Still as the scary-looking man and his girlfriend made love in the van.

"Isn't Florida great?" Still said, remembering. "Anything can happen."

He told me that Florida was like the beauty and the beast. He loved it all. He loved the history, the culture, the tackiness, the seasons. He tells northerners who miss the seasons to shut up and pay attention. Florida has real seasons.

"I try to find inspiration from everything and everybody." I went with him when he interviewed an expert on the citrus industry. I tagged along on his trip to Gainesville and an interview with paleontologists. The experts wanted to share every detail of their lifelong studies with him; they wanted him to read their books and journals and scientific papers. "I don't have time," he told them politely. Thinking of his deadline, he asked them to tell him just the important stuff. They looked disappointed.

The first mural he painted for the state tells the story of prehistoric Florida. For models he borrowed ancient saber cat skulls, mastodon jaws, spear points, and pottery and posed them in his studio. He used a study from the Withlacoochee for the landscape and images of Crystal River in his depiction of Indian mounds. He invited Suzie Henry, daughter of a Seminole medicine man, to visit his studio because he wanted an authentic American Indian to pose as a Calusa, the tribe that lived here when Europeans showed up.

In the painting, she smiles a Mona Lisa smile at a crab escaping her basket. She is oblivious to what has appeared on the horizon. A Spanish ship. Genocide is on the way. How does one tell that story? Still doesn't want to be downbeat, so his Indian woman looks strong.

"But you can't sweep stuff under the carpet," he told me. "You have to figure a way to account for everything."

Normally Still liked to spend months or years on his big paintings. His legislative project was different. He was under pressure to crank out the most complex work of his career in a short period.

Pope Julius II gave Michelangelo Buonarroti four years to complete his painting of the Sistine Chapel. Christopher Still worried about disappointing the Speaker of the House. John Thrasher was not the pope, but he was close enough.

Tarpon Springs. 6 A.M. Still parked a rented truck in front of his studio. "One day," he said, "I'll do a painting small enough to fit into a regular truck."

Pete Hunter, an artisan in his own right, helped load the giant painting into the truck. Hunter had stretched the canvases for Still's art and built the frames. Hunter was going along to hang the mural in Tallahassee.

"I'm anxious about this, Pete," Still said. On the road, he was a bundle of nerves, worried about his reception at the capital. Traffic was heavy; the morning was foggy. Should have left earlier, he muttered, should have left earlier. Still's mood brightened with the appearance of the sun. "Look at the light on those palmettos," he called out.

I felt my foot reaching for an imaginary brake. Behind the wheel, Still was hazard. Delivering paintings, he once rear-ended a patrol car. Another time he ran over an empty boat trailer towed by a one-armed commercial fisher with a history of violence. He let Still off the hook.

An hour from Tallahassee. Would the bigwigs like his first painting? At first Rembrandt painted businessmen on commission and was anxious to please. But he improved, gained confidence, and worried less about their egos and more about his art. Rembrandt died in poverty.

The capital lay ahead. Still pulled into the garage, where workers waited to lead Still and Hunter through corridors, up elevators, and down thickly carpeted halls. They led the way to the cavernous House of Representatives, where other workers were preparing the chamber for the upcoming session.

Hunter hung the painting. Workmen applauded, but where was John Thrasher? The Speaker of the House ambled in. Still froze.

"Wow!" the Speaker said. "Man alive. *I love this!*"

The Speaker pointed to the Indian girl and the white ibis and the campfire on the painting. "I love the vibrancy. Thank you, thank you, thank you."

Blushing with relief, Still described plans for future paintings. One would show modern Florida and another would portray the Spanish invasion of the New Land. He'd account for the Civil War, Cracker Florida, the Seminole Wars, the beginning of tourism, Civil Rights, and the role of art and literature in Florida.

The speaker listened intently. "This is going to help make our chamber one of the most beautiful in the country," he said. "Hey, Chris, why don't you come back when the session begins next week? I'd love to introduce you."

Still looked horrified. "I don't want to hear a lot of compliments when my work isn't over," he said. "I don't want to be distracted."

The speaker looked surprised—and disappointed.

Hours later, heading home on U.S. 19 as night fell on the woods of Gulf Hammock, Christopher Still slapped himself upside the head.

"*Ding dong!*" he shouted. "What am I thinking? The Speaker of the House asks if I'll come back for the legislative session and I say no. No? *Ding dong!* Wake up, Chris! Wake up, Chris!"

Barreling into Tarpon Springs, he was wide awake. He had painting to do.

17 Smoked Fish

"How long has Ted Peters been dead?" I asked. The waitress known as Surly Shirley leaned across the counter, scowled, and pointed left.

"He's sitting next to you, mister." From his well-worn stool, silver-haired Ted Peters beamed with pleasure. He had big white teeth and eyes as blue as the back of a tuna. He was small, wiry, and wizened like a man who had spent many decades toiling in a smokehouse. In fact, he had. "I'm eighty-eight years old. And I'm tickled to death to still be standing above the ground instead of lying underneath it."

He swigged steaming coffee from a white cup.

"As a matter of fact, I'm still buyin' green bananas." Green bananas? "Lot of old people won't buy green bananas. They're afraid they won't live long enough for the bananas to get ripe."

Ted Peters, the monarch of mullet, the potentate of potato salad, the sultan of slaw, planned to hang around, maybe for another century.

Every morning he showed up at his restaurant, probably the best-known restaurant in Pinellas County, Ted Peters Famous Smoked Fish. He told stories between gulps of coffee and teased the folks who work there until they made him go home. Kinfolk were running the place when I dropped by, but the old man kept his leathery hands close to the till. The smoke that billowed out the chimney smelled like fish to me, but to him it smelled like something green.

"First of the month, I stop by, put out my hand, and say 'How about a little lettuce?'"

There was gold in them there fish. In 1947, Peters began practicing his piscatorial pulchritude—he won't reveal the ingredients of his secret sauce—on thousands of hungry diners Wednesdays through Mondays, 11:30 A.M. to 7:30 P.M. Like Bern's, the steak palace in Tampa, and Joe's Stone Crabs on Miami Beach, Ted Peters's little restaurant near the water became an institution. "I'd moved to Florida from New York after the war," he told me. "I'd been a plumber but I didn't want to be a plumber any more. So I'm drivin' down the road in Madeira Beach, and I see this broken-down little fish smoker on the side of the road."

Known as "Bear" to close friends because of his bruinlike habit of foraging in dumpsters, Peters plucked the fish smoker with the joy of a man who had come of age during the depression. Soon he was piling in the mullet, an underrated saltwater fish with oily flesh that is especially palatable when smoked over a bed of smoldering wood.

"Other people have smoked fish before," he said, "but most people smoked it in their backyard or in the woods. Not me. See, my claim to fame is I put the smoker right on the road where people could see it." He was never reluctant to promote his product. As traffic approached, he'd rush to the smoker, lift the lid, releasing the pungent aroma. Motorists veered off the road for a taste. Others called the fire department, mistaking his little smokehouse for a phone booth ablaze.

Peters tempted the hungry multitudes in Madeira Beach and Blind Pass until 1949, when he set up permanent shop at 1350 Pasadena Ave. S in South Pasadena. It was practically the only business on the block. Now it's jammed amid fast-food joints and condos. A jalopy in a sports car world, it was painted institutional green on my visit. The color-blind hungry needed only open their car windows and follow their noses to the parking lot.

On metal stools at the counter and at dozens of picnic tables sat attorneys in three-piece suits, nurses in hospital scrubs, a well-coifed secretary from the neighborhood synagogue, and a Catholic priest from St. Jude's. They shared space with sweaty lawnmen and commercial fishers wearing rubber boots. There was a burly greaser with a Metallica tattoo on his right shoulder and a wanna-be hippie chick with either pierced nostrils or a misplaced paper clip. We went home, one and all, with smoked fish on our breath.

Servers at other restaurants wear uniforms, talk nicey-nice, and call you "sir" or "ma'am." Some are students working their way through college. One day, they know, they'll find a better job. Ted Peters had a waitress named Dee Regan. As much an institution as the restaurant, she was known as Surly Shirley or Mother Superior.

She had heard so much bushwa, so much malarkey and flapdoodle that she wore the perpetual frown of a world-weary soul. But listen, she had been enthroned behind that counter for more than three decades and had no plans to leave. Occasionally, a shaken customer suggested Surly Shirley had lived up to her reputation. "She must really like you," Peters told them.

He tried to pick on her whenever I was there, but I got the feeling that she was more than his match. She called him the "Grumpy Old Man," and if he knew what was good for him he might have avoided further eye contact. She kept a baseball bat behind the counter.

Surly Shirley was a throwback to Ted Peters's other prominent matriarch, Matilda Peters, Ted's mother, who helped establish the restaurant. Matilda prized three photographs: professional wrestler Eddie Graham, wrestling announcer Gordon Solie—and Jesus Christ. Two photos were autographed. One night she got kicked out of a wrestling arena for throwing ice water on a villain. Another time she was arrested for assaulting a rude employee, after chasing her down the block, painful bunions and all.

Matilda stood four feet ten inches in heels. She could barely see over the steering wheel, which proved to be a disadvantage when she was required to stop. Instead of wearing out her brakes, she'd come to a halt by running into something—the restaurant, a curb, or an unfortunate automobile. Or she'd save herself the trouble and park thirty feet from the nearest space.

After a long day of fish mongering, her patience wearing short, perhaps anticipating a smoke-filled evening at the wrestling arena, Matilda Peters would board her 1951 Pontiac, roll down the window, and give traffic the evil eye.

"Get out of my way!" she'd roar and gun it onto Pasadena Avenue. She lived well into her nineties.

Ted Peters had his momma's genes. He drove a station wagon big enough to take on a tank. He was feisty too. Once, when his home telephone stopped working, he gave his neighbors bottles of Canadian Club whiskey for letting him borrow theirs. He deducted the cost of the booze from his next phone bill; when the phone company said "no way" he introduced the phone company to his lawyer. His whiskey bill was paid. "I've tried to have fun in my life," he told me. "And I've had good friends, and I've been very lucky. That's my secret."

He enjoyed a good round of golf. He had been a widower since 1992— he was married to his beloved Ellen nearly six decades—and faithfully visited the neighborhood American Legion club for a brisk evening of dancing with the younger ladies.

He still had the energy to climb into dumpsters and hunt treasure. "You'd be surprised at what people throw away," he said. If an item needed repair, Peters repaired and sold it. Sometimes he showed up at the restaurant in an outfit he had liberated from a trash bin. "I'm eccentric," he admitted. "They'd put me in an institution if I didn't have money."

At the restaurant, he liked to sell stuff he found in the trash. But his forty-eight-year-old nephew, who manages the place now, finally said no. Michael Lathrop grew up at the elbow of his Uncle Ted. "Ted Peters potty-trained me," he said. Lathrop helped his uncle harvest clams for the restaurant's famous chowder. He helped net mullet, chop wood, and carry water. He got to shoot pop bottles in the woods. All before he turned age six.

"One day Ted and my dad, Elray, glanced at me and looked real sad and said 'Well, I guess legally we have to send him to school.' So they did. I thought they were punishing me for something or other. I'd get in trouble with my teachers with my cussing. Of course, I learned that from Ted."

Now Lathrop managed the restaurant along with Ted Cook, Peters's grandson. They maintained the old traditions, with a few exceptions. No longer does Sugar Girl wander among the dangling feet of supping patrons. A portly pig, Sugar Girl was the restaurant's ever-hungry, always-thirsty mascot. Generous clientele poured beer into Sugar Girl's bowl—a hubcap—and she lapped contentedly. Then she'd sleep off her hangover.

Animal rights people might be grumbling if Sugar Girl were not already drinking her fill in porcine heaven. Environmentalists surely would mutter if Ted Peters were still harvesting buttonwood mangrove branches for his smokers.

"They'd put me in jail," he said. Mangroves are protected in modern Florida, and the restaurant had to make do with red oak. Current management considered installing natural gas smokers, but Ted Peters balked.

"Who ever heard of smokers that don't use wood?"

His restaurant was a dinosaur in a space-age era. Like a cave dweller, he had discovered fire—and the smoke it brought forth—and never needed anything more.

18 Winter Perfume

In the old days, when fewer cars had air-conditioning, the world was still a cool place, especially when the perfume of spring wafted through the Florida night.

"We'd pull off the road with the windows open," Russ Rouseff was telling me. "My wife and I would sit in the moonlight and smell the orange blossoms."

They'd park on U.S. 27 in the middle of the state and take sharp, deep breaths. The fragrance of the citrus flowers detonated in their nostrils, bombarded olfactory membranes up high, and was transformed magically from gas into liquid. Tiny hairs—cilia—swept the citrus mucus to the brain's olfactory nerves less than a quarter inch away. The Rouseffs' brains naturally broke into mighty grins.

"Ah! Orange blossoms," announced the brain core. "Isn't winter in Florida heavenly?"

Russ Rouseff was as romantic as the next guy when it came to singing the praises of the state flower. But he was also a University of Florida chemist whose specialty included not only the flavor chemistry of citrus but how humans perceived those flavors. A man with an educated nose took something as innocent as citrus blossoms more seriously than the rest of us.

When I met him, Rouseff was fifty-seven and working at the Citrus Research and Education Center in the middle of a huge grove of orange, tangerine, and grapefruit trees in Polk County. He told me he was confident that the lab's grounds were the sweetest-smelling place on earth. I agreed; it was blossom season.

Rouseff had been busy. In the winter, when scientists who work for the fragrance industries make their annual visits, Rouseff unleashes them in the groves. They saunter among the trees and take hearty gulps of air, hoping their olfactory nerves will not let them down. But sometimes they do.

"Fragrance is a very complicated thing," said Rouseff, who slowly chewed a bite of grouper and described in chemical terms what he was tasting when I took him to lunch.

Identifying specific citrus aromas—"volatiles," Rouseff called them—was his challenge. Humans could capture hundreds of different fragrances in a gulp of air; some fragrances were stronger than others, but even weak ones could be important. Fragrance industry scientists seldom trusted their own sense of smell. They carried machinery into the groves to collect citrus blossom aromas for later analysis. They were certain a blossom on the tree had a smell superior to that of a just-picked. Their task was finding out the right combination of chemicals and putting the essence into their perfumes.

Old-timey Floridians, of course, spent little time analyzing the perfume of winter. They simply enjoyed it. Of course, it was easier in the old days. Almost any town—even crowded cities such as St. Petersburg or Miami or Orlando—boasted hundreds of groves. A resident who stepped out the front door was overwhelmed by fragrance. At dusk, homeowners sat on their front porches—porches have become an endangered species in twenty-first-century Florida—and breathed in the glory of the nearest grove.

Wrote the poet Walt Whitman:

To my plain Northern hut, in outside clouds and snow,
Brought safely for a thousand miles o'er land and tide,
Some three days since on their own soil live-sprouting,
Now here their sweetness through my room unfolding,
A bunch of orange buds by mail from Florida

In 1927, a railroad line launched the Orange Blossom Special to the accompaniment of bathing beauties and orange perfume. The luxury train brought well-heeled tourists from the Northeast to Miami and St. Petersburg. A decade later, a homesick Florida boy, Ervin Rouse, tuned up his fiddle and wrote "Orange Blossom Special," which has since been recorded by hundreds of artists from Johnny Cash to Bill Monroe and his Bluegrass Boys.

When Rouseff got his doctorate from the University of Georgia and joined the Florida research lab in 1972, he thought he was working in a flowered paradise. The lab, built in 1917 near Winter Haven, was in the middle of Florida's citrus belt. Just down the road was a folksy attraction known as the Citrus Tower. From the top, tourists supposedly could see seventeen million citrus trees at once.

"Now almost all the groves around here are gone," Rouseff said. "You can go up the tower, but mostly you see golf courses and housing developments. I miss the old days."

After a series of freezes devastated groves in the 1980s, fair-weather growers put their farms on the market. By century's end, many of the groves were gone, replaced by pavement and St. Augustine grass. Hardcore growers migrated south toward Lake Okeechobee and began planting.

North Florida, where citrus once was king, had all but lost those perfumed winter nights. Central Florida was in the process of losing them. But not quite all. Rouseff still had 225 acres of groves behind his research center. And he had an ever-acute sense of smell with which to enjoy the blossoms.

To him, studying citrus blossoms and their fragrance was more of a hobby than real work. He spent most of his time trying to make orange juice concentrate taste more like the genuine nectar of the gods. When concentrate was invented during World War II, it tasted horrible. Over decades it slowly improved, but only an industry employee would insist that concentrate tasted as good as fresh-squeezed.

Rouseff and research assistants were unwilling to give up the fight. They spent hours sniffing citrus fragrances in hopes of finding the perfect chemistry. Rouseff had a machine—a gas chromatograph-olfactometer—that can measure odors. As it worked, a researcher did the same with his nose. The researcher breathed from a pipe connected to the machine and wrote a description of the scents.

"Humans can detect things machines can't," Rouseff said. "What the machine measures as significant may not be what the human nose believes is pleasant. There's no replacing the human nose."

A human nose knows what it knows. Or at least it thinks it does. One of Rouseff's researchers grew up in Alabama as a God-fearing Baptist. He recently smelled a musty citrus odor through the machine and described it as "old church." Another researcher, the staff romantic, described a delicate aroma as "perfume on a woman's neck."

Nobody who has spent any time near an orange grove in full flower would argue with romance. Most perfumes, in fact, are derived in part from citrus oil. They do everything but shout, "Come hither."

Citrus blossoms at one time were an important accessory in every society bride's wardrobe. An orange-blossom garland in her hair was a "must" when she marched down the aisle. Citrus blossoms were even considered a honeymoon helper—at least in the fourteenth century. The spicy parts of Boccaccio's *Decameron* had readers panting at the juicy passages involving orange-scented lovers and courtesans who seduced the rich and powerful after sprinkling sheets with orange perfume.

The amorous-minded Mr. Boccaccio might turn in his grave if he had to wade through Rouseff and company's recent scientific literature, including *2–Methyl-3-furanthiol and Methional Are Possible Off-Flavors in Stored Orange Juice: Aroma-Similarity* and *Using an Ion-Trap MS Sensor to Differentiate and Identify Individual Components in Grapefruit Juice Headspace Volatiles.*

On the other hand, he'd be glad somebody was treating the subject as important. He would surely appreciate that Rouseff and his wife liked to park in the moonlight and smell the blossoms.

Like Boccaccio, Rouseff was interested in the birds and the bees. Especially bees, which play a critical role in the pollination game. In the fall, when the first cold front barrels through Florida, an orange tree stops growing, setting the stage for reproduction. Rain and a patch of warm water inspire the creation of a bud.

Now here come the bees, those picky eaters, who prefer certain citrus blossoms over others. What gives certain orange blossoms the right stuff? Why do bees act as if Temple orange blossoms taste like leftover broccoli?

"It isn't the fragrance," Rouseff told me. It's the size. A larger citrus blossom is more visible. It also contains more nectar. To a bee, a big flower is a brewery, a small flower a shot glass of beer.

The information becomes important in the winter and early spring, when growers often import bees into their groves for pollination. Knowing bee preferences, growers can position hives so bees have to fly past small-blossomed trees first.

"Isn't the world wonderful?" asked Rouseff. "Isn't it neat to find out something new?"

When he took a deep breath in a grove full of orange blossoms, the left side of his brain, the analytical side, recognized linalool, esters, and maybe a dozen more volatiles. But the right side of his brain, the romantic's side, delivered a different message.

A woman's neck, perhaps.

19 Minding the Manatees

Wayne Hartley shoved his canoe off the bank and headed for deeper water. Stowing his paddle, he grabbed his notebook and wrote furiously. So began a winter ritual he had observed for almost a quarter of a century. At Blue Springs State Park, about an hour north of Orlando, his business was minding the manatees.

"Is that you, Destiny?"

She was found half-starved. Sea World removed the plastic she had somehow ingested and fattened her up with real food. Released at Blue Springs, she seemed to be doing fine except for the boat-propeller scars on her back. "Look over here," Hartley said to me. I felt the bump of a small manatee on the bottom of the canoe. "It's Bertram."

Separated from his mother when he was a young'un, Bertram became famished enough to eat unappetizing sticks instead of delicious grass. After time in rehab, he was ready for release too. Now Wayne Hartley wrote Bertram's name into his notebook.

Hartley, fifty-seven, felt he had the world licked. He had served in the army for a dozen years and later worked at Sears. Then he became a park ranger and the minder of manatees.

"I have the best job in Florida," he said. In the winter, as temperatures dipped into the sixties in the nearby St. Johns River, manatees took refuge in the seventy-two-degree water of Blue Springs. On a canoe voyage that lasted only a third of a mile, Hartley sometimes counted the noses of 150 of the warm-blooded creatures. The park was the easiest place in Florida to watch wild manatees.

In April, when manatees left the spring for the dangerous world beyond the ropes, Hartley was less sure he had Florida's best job. Like the parent of a teenager taking the car out for a night on the town, he felt that familiar gnawing in his heart. His anxiety lingered until the manatees returned in November.

"I'd say almost every one that comes back has a new scar or two," he said.

Some of his manatees never return at all. Asking boaters to slow down for gentle manatees might seem like a no-brainer. But it's not. Many boaters, fed up with speed restrictions and refuges where watercraft are unwelcome, wanted manatees off their backs as the twenty-first century began. Among other things, boaters who valued powerful outboard motors proposed taking manatees off the endangered species list. They claimed that manatees, plentiful enough, should not infringe on a boater's desire to have fun.

Manatees, which can measure a dozen feet and weigh more than a ton, are awesome animals. But they're also the world's most lackadaisical swimmers. They have no natural enemies beyond cold and disease. Born pacifists, they mind their business and manners. They float about the surface like giant sweet potatoes. When it would be prudent to crash-dive toward the bottom—say when a speeding boat is approaching—they generally poke along, oblivious.

Sometimes Wayne Hartley had to drive his truck across Florida to the state necropsy lab in St. Petersburg. Nothing bothered him more than counting one of his precious manatees as it lay dead on the steel examining table.

"Where is Jethro?"

Jethro was no longer as friendly as he once was. When Jethro arrived at Blue Springs in the fall, he bore fresh scars on his back from a boat encounter. Now he was nervous around even Hartley's canoe.

Hartley drew a sketch of Jethro that showed the new scars. Tracking the scars allowed him to tell manatees apart. As years went by and manatees collected new scars, Hartley added to his sketchbook.

"There he is."

Jethro seemed leery. For a manatee, fear of humans and their machines was a good life skill. At the beginning of the twenty-first century, nobody knew for sure if the state's manatee population was stable, growing larger, or decreasing. Counting them accurately was considered almost impossible.

One year, biologists in blimps and airplanes came up with 3,276 manatees—about a thousand more than the year before. Did that mean the manatee population was exploding? Or did scientists count some manatees twice because of turbid water or because they misidentified scars?

The most important manatee question of all has yet to be answered with authority. Does the death rate exceed the birth rate?

Manatees are slow to mature and to breed. Gestation lasts thirteen months, and many newborns survive only a few weeks. Cold weather or a sick or boat-injured mother can doom a calf. Some calves are abandoned or lose track of their mothers. "Some plain don't mind their mothers," Hartley said. "You know their mothers are calling them. But they'd rather play."

Manatees are a tourist attraction all over Florida. In winter, folks watch them cavort in the warm waters near power plants on both coasts. At Crystal River in Citrus County, divers and snorkelers love nothing more than swimming close enough for a brief commune with an endangered species. Some manatees tolerate the attention, but others don't. A diver never knows until the manatee flees.

At Blue Springs, manatees were also a tourist attraction. But hundreds of daily winter tourists did their watching from the boardwalk. Swimming was allowed only in places the manatees avoided. "We don't want the manatees to get used to people," Hartley said, paddling. "We'd rather for them to be a little scared of us. They'll remain healthier that way."

Hartley had joined the manatees in the water several times, and he and the manatees were unhappy about going nose to nose. In both cases, a sleeping manatee had awakened and surfaced for a breath. Right under Hartley's canoe. "If they slap your canoe with their tails you're in the water."

Like most middle-aged men, Hartley no longer was the svelte creature of youth. When his canoe tipped, he made a splash. The nervous manatees sprinted for the cold river. But seemed to hang around long enough to chortle. "Manatees all have different personalities. Some are so shy they hate it when we're doing construction near the spring and using electric saws. But some aren't scared of anything. They'll hug the canoe— or you."

Was that Arnold? Arnold was asleep in eight feet of water next to a fallen oak limb. "For years he was hanging out at a Cape Canaveral sewer plant. Then he showed up here. Arnold, you made a wise decision."

Hartley pointed out Eustis and Banks, manatees he named after Civil War generals. Brutus was lurking somewhere; Brutus started wintering at Blue Springs in 1974, when Jacques Cousteau filmed him and made him a star.

Hartley's newest celebrity was Stormy. Born in captivity in Miami, he spent most of his life in Tampa at the Lowry Park Zoo. Scientists wanted to give a healthy captive-born manatee a chance to experience freedom. He was fitted with a radio transmitter and released at Blue Springs. "We're not sure how he's doing."

Hartley and I watched with concern. Befuddled, Stormy swam in relentless circles, as if he were still confined to a tank, and seemed to lack the usual manatee social skills. Hartley worried; Stormy's back was gray and smooth. The price of his freedom most likely would mean a future encounter of the boat kind when left Blue Springs.

At the beginning of the new century, boat registrations in Florida had climbed to nearly a million. While most boaters seemed happy to cruise slowly through manatee habitat, some people who sold boats, or built waterfront properties, or rented marina slips were on the attack. Their hired lobbyists believed that additional speed restrictions and refuges were not only bad for business but unnecessary.

A hundred miles by car from the state capital, where the manatee political wars annually took place, Wayne Hartley floated in his canoe down the peaceful spring. "The worst injury I ever saw? That had to be the manatee I called Success," Hartley said, stowing his paddle and enjoying the drift. "She showed up in the spring one November looking like she was deformed. Her side had been more or less caved in by a boat. Her ribs were literally sticking out her flesh. She was gruesome to even look at.

"I don't know how she did it, but she survived. Her wounds healed. She gained weight. She mated. She even had several calves and raised them."

After the last calving season, she left the spring for the river and beyond.

Wayne Hartley, minder of manatees, hadn't seen her since.

20   What Lies Beneath

Notes from the underground: I switched on my headlamp, dropped through a narrow opening, and crept headfirst into the bowels of the earth. Swallowing claustrophobia, I slithered deeper while watching for the rattlesnakes that frequent cave entrances. Nothing fanged and cold-blooded showed up in the beam of my lamp.

The earth opened enough for me to stand. Not for long. Chasm ahead. I wedged my backside against one wall and propped feet against the opposite wall. By sliding a little at a time you can progress. But don't look down. It was a drop of a dozen feet or more onto sharp rocks.

"This cave isn't so bad," Tom Turner called from somewhere ahead or somewhere behind. In a cave, voices echo.

A Pinellas County landscaper, fit and tough at forty-two, he was known as "the Cave Hound." As a Boy Scout he joined an expedition to the Withlacoochee State Forest to explore a cave. After that he explored libraries for books about caving. When he was older, he began studying Florida topographic maps. They didn't pinpoint the location of the caves, but they gave him a place to look. He became a ridge walker. A ridge walker hikes in hilly areas likely to harbor a cave. On certain days, when air temperature and atmospheric conditions are perfect, steamy air might rise from one. A lucky ridge walker might have himself an expedition.

"Never go alone into a cave," warned Turner, who caved alone when he knew no better. He never broke a bone or got seriously lost.

On our expedition he brought along friends from the Florida Speleo-logical Society, out of Gainesville, and the Tampa Bay Area Grotto, a West Florida club to which he belonged. Four men and a woman, they were strong, flexible, and generally slender.

With my middle-aged paunch, I worried about holding them back. Imagine crawling under one of those muddy four-wheel-drive Dodge pickups. You might scrape your back on the chassis, but you'd pass easily beneath. Next, imagine creeping under a Plymouth Voyager van. You'd succeed, but find it more difficult. Now think about trying to squeeze under a Toyota Corolla.

"Cavers have a party game," said Tom Farnell, who was just as athletic, at forty-two, as Tom Turner. "Stick both arms straight in the air. Now get somebody to pass a wire coat hanger over your arms and down your body all the way to the floor."

If you're as wiry as Farnell, you might win the party game. Same was true for Tracey Matzke, a thirty-three-year-old house cleaner from Pinellas who recently had discovered caving. "You have to get dirty to find the excitement," she said. A moment later she contorted her body into a rolled-up pancake and squeezed through a hole like one of those snakes in *Raiders of the Lost Ark*.

"Let's turn out our lights," said Tom Turner, the cave hound. "We'll try an experiment." We all hit the switches on our helmets. It wasn't dark like in a bedroom closet. It was the dark of a tomb. I tried my own experiment. In the blackness, I pressed the illumination button on my wristwatch. The blue glow cast a shadow.

"Can you imagine getting stuck in here without a light?" asked Turner. "It would be pretty bad at first. But at least this cave only has about 1,500 feet of passages. You'd crawl your way out eventually."

Maybe he would. But most of us wouldn't. Few people even know Florida caves exist. Oh, they know about those underwater caves, the ones where divers drown. But the dry caves receive little press coverage. They're not in the league with those famous Kentucky and New Mexico caves, but few places on Earth are.

Florida's caves, created by millions of years of rain leaking through soil and limestone, can be spectacular enough. Some stretch for miles. Others boast a variety of formations and lakes full of albino crayfish, catfish, and other weird animals that evolved without needing eyes. Some caverns in Florida are big enough for a school bus or a basketball court. Some are so tall Michael Jordan might not be able to throw the ball all the way to the ceiling.

Of course, you couldn't drive the bus or carry a backboard into such caves. To reach the wide and high places usually requires crawling and creeping hundreds of feet, often past spiders, scorpions, and bats. The bats, vanishing species all, are harmless. Florida cavers, as a rule, avoid caves inhabited by large bat colonies. Nobody wants to disturb such fragile animals, and nobody wants to breathe dried bat guano, which can damage the lungs.

That's only one hazard. More worrisome is the possibility of getting lost or falling. It's more dangerous driving your car to a cave than exploring one, but cavers have been killed once inside. Caving clubs usually install padlocked steel doors at the openings of the best-known caves to protect beginners—and the foolish—from injury.

"And you want to know something?" said Dan Straley, the editor of the Tampa Bay Grotto's monthly magazine. "People who shouldn't be in caves still manage to get into caves."

Time to move. "Now we're going to have to crawl for a while," said a disembodied voice that belonged to Bill Birdsall, another cave hound of legend. He was ahead, in the dark, with Tracey Matzke, the human pancake. As a new caver, she was the most enthusiastic about trying to insert her body into tiny crevices.

Because I wasn't a human mole, because my years on earth exceed a half century, I expected to suffer. At first I walked on my knees, covered thankfully by pads. When the passage narrowed, I crawled, bumped my head, and thanked the gods for a borrowed helmet. I tried looking ahead for Birdsall's light but gave up. Not enough room to raise my eyes. I crept forward, nose in the mud.

"Almost there!" shouted Bill Birdsall. The passage had opened enough for us to sit, rest, and talk. Birdsall said he visited his first cave as a teenager. He had been a hard-core caver fifteen years. He was forty-seven, an old man in a young person's sport, but he was wiry and enthusiastic and knew this particular cave better than anyone. It practically lay in his Ocala backyard. He even carried the key for the steel gate.

Not that gating the entrance always mattered. Recently, cave club members had arrived to find their gate open. Somebody had broken the lock and removed the door. Vandals. They decorated the entrance with graffiti. "Pure Pimp," somebody wrote with spray paint. "We find all kinds of stuff in our caves," Birdsall complained. Beer bottles. Cola cans. Condoms. "We even found a mattress. Don't know how somebody dragged a mattress through these passages. Strange place for romance."

Birdsall said he loves caves for a different reason. "They're the last frontier," he said. His friend Bill Walker shined his light into my eyes. "Everything has been picked over and been seen on the top of the earth," he groused. Like Birdsall, Walker was a hard-core guy. At thirty, he was the editor of the Florida Speleological Society website and happened to be recovering from neck surgery unrelated to caving. Still, his bones remained a little tender.

"I should have worn my neck brace," he said. "But that would have made it tough to maneuver."

Bill Walker and Bill Birdsall often explored caves together. They had in common their ambition to find caves nobody had ever visited. "It's like leaving your footprints on the moon when you find one," Birdsall said.

Visiting an unexplored cave is especially dangerous for the careless. Birdsall, like Tom Turner now, always caved with other people. He taught himself to become an expert with map and compass. Every time a passage in a new cave turns, he stops, takes a compass bearing, and writes down the numbers. At home, he prepares a map based on his numbers. At other times, he sticks glow-in-the-dark markers on the cave walls. They reflect light on the way out. Nothing is more important than light. He has three different lights, independently powered.

He carried no ropes into this well-known cave, but sometimes he carried rope in other caves when rappelling became necessary. Not long ago, a couple of teenagers discovered a cave near Ocala. They carried a flashlight and a rope. They managed to get down the shaft, but when it was time to go home gravity was against them. Cave club members had to perform the rescue. Another teenager told his mother he was going to investigate the same cave. He didn't return home. Even the experts failed to find him. That's because he had changed his mind and gone to the mall instead.

The possibility of a tragedy, and the fruitless search and rescue effort, so frustrated the local sheriff that he ordered the cave entrance bulldozed shut. Cave clubs are negotiating to have it reopened. They plan to install a padlocked steel gate.

"It's a constant battle," said Dan Straley, a twenty-eight-year-old airline computer technician who teaches caving to Scouts and University of South Florida geology students. "We need to have access to the caves, but at the same time we need to protect the caves from people who might hurt themselves or damage the caves. So we operate in a shroud of secrecy. We don't want people to know where caves are."

"Caves can be spectacular," Tom Turner said. "I can hardly blame people for wanting to investigate. But it's dangerous if you don't know what you're doing."

He reached up and touched the ceiling. It was damp but clean. "People don't understand why they should care about caves," Turner went on. "You care about them because they're one level above the aquifer. If there's pollution in this cave—say there was a dairy right above us—most likely your water is polluted too."

Time to move. An extremely narrow passage loomed ahead. "I'm not looking forward to this one," said Dan Straley, muscular and flexible— but 190 pounds. "I'm very big for a caver." Last time here, he got stuck. He turned off his light to calm himself, breathed deeply, and managed to back out. He removed clothing and tried the passage again. He made it. Yes, he put his clothes back on.

Bill Birdsall carried a cigarette lighter. From time to time, he studied the flame. He hates to see an elongated flame. It tells him the cave's oxygen is low. He likes a modest flame. Our destination was a claustrophobic cell in which Birdsall once found a fossilized crab. Forty million years ago, Florida was under water.

"Crawl up that pipe," he advised me. "Then turn, twist, and see if you can get your head in that little passage. Put your right arm in first, then follow with your head. Keep the other arm at your side. Use your toes to push ahead."

Birdsall never knows what he will find. Usually it's fossils. He has never found contemporary bones. Humans, of course, have hidden in caves for eons. Tom Turner, the cave hound, once found shavings from rocks— evidence that prehistoric people were mining the caves to make arrowheads.

A few years ago he discovered an old gun and donated it to the Florida Museum of History in Tallahassee. The carbine once belonged to a federal soldier during the Second Seminole Indian War. Seminoles often hid in caves.

Bill Birdsall told me he buries people for a living. An Ocala funeral director, he sometimes worked nights, sometimes days. It hardly mattered to a cave explorer. It was always dark.

"You up for one more round?" He said it was going to be a little tight in there, tight like a coffin, but then it would open up and pretty soon the entrance of the cave—and blessed light—would loom ahead as a reward.

He shimmied away and turned out his light just to see if he could manage in the dark. He could. Like Turner, he was part mole and part bat. He likes to forge ahead of other cavers and wedge himself in a tight crevice near the ceiling. When other cavers catch up, he surprises them.

Experienced cavers don't scare easily. I was less confident. I was already anxious enough, having heard the names of famous Florida caves and famous Florida cave passages. Dead Man's. Pancake Squeeze. Mole Sewer. Knotted Hose. The Cemetery. My favorite cave name was given by a guy who liked to walk his dog in the woods. His dog had trotted ahead and tumbled into a sinkhole. At the very bottom of the sinkhole, waiting like a kitchen drain, was the cave shaft. The dog vanished into the shaft and fell sixty feet to its death. Drop Dead Cave.

Tom Turner was somewhere behind. Tracey Matzke and Bill Birdsall were somewhere ahead. I heard Birdsall direct Matzke to an especially challenging passage. Her voice was muffled but enthused. It helps to be an athlete, but not the kind I am. Above the ground, I swam, biked, ran, and considered myself fit. Under the ground, aerobic fitness should have been important. But more important, apparently, was the ability to control fear.

Crawl. Creep. On my belly like a snake. My chin scraped mud; my helmet raked the cave ceiling. I heard nothing but my own ragged, frightened breath. My heart pounded like in the last mile of a triathlon. Finally the passage opened. Birdsall sat waiting. "Catch your breath," he said. "Boy, are you sweating. But we're here. You've made it."

The entrance lay ahead. But it was on the other side of a four-foot-wide chasm that was a dozen feet deep. Once again I wedged myself between walls and inched my way forward. Gravity failed to help; I had to muscle my way up.

I could see the light at the end of the tunnel, but I wasn't strong enough to get there. My legs had turned to spaghetti, and my arms felt even weaker. I was sure I'd pulled a muscle in my abs.

Slipped. I almost fell into the chasm just then. It felt good to swear like a sailor.

"Hang on," called Bill Birdsall in front of me. "Take your time and you'll do fine." He grabbed my shoulder and told me where to place hands and feet. I breathed deeply to calm myself. Tom Turner was behind me in case I needed a push. "Don't worry," Birdsall said, in a calm funeral director's voice. "We haven't lost anybody yet."

Minutes later, when I stood in the cave opening, my head stuck out of the ground like a ripe cabbage. Crawling to the earth's surface, I gulped fresh air and gloried in the sunlight.

21 The Yearling Restaurant

I like standing next to the creek connecting Orange Lake and Lake Lochloosa at dusk, before the fireflies come out and the barred owls start hooting.

It's quiet on Cross Creek, except for the rustle of the oaks and the splash a bass makes chasing minnows. But stand long enough and you hear other things. A sandhill crane honks in the distance. Closer, a limpkin cries. Then the true opera begins. The frogs start quietly and build to a fevered pitch. The bullfrog shakes the earth with its basso profundo as little tree frogs delicately chirp. The pig frogs come in, singing in those sad oboe voices that touch your heart.

I am a terrible man. I love nature and I adore frogs, but every once in while I develop a terrific craving for a great big plate of their legs. Whenever I visit Cross Creek, whenever I drive over the bridge and stare into that black water, I dream of eating muscular-legged, deep-fried frogs, which I know have a hard enough life as it is, what with alligators, moccasins, and great blue herons already hunting them.

The Yearling Restaurant, a North Florida institution for four decades, closed in 1992. Like many other folks with telltale greasy chins, I mourned. Whenever I drove past the dilapidated building on State Road 325 and thought of the delicious frogs' legs the restaurant no longer would be serving, I mourned even harder.

When I heard The Yearling had reopened, I didn't know whether to laugh, cry, or say grace. But you could have knocked me over with a spatula.

Robert Blauer was one of those long-haired country boys who wore a cowboy hat even indoors. He was tall and had large dark eyes that took in the world through spectacles. He talked slowly and called just about everyone "sir" or "ma'am." He was born in Jacksonville in 1954, a year after Marjorie Kinnan Rawlings passed away. She was the most famous resident of Cross Creek, the community she memorialized in her book of the same name. Her novel *The Yearling* won a Pulitzer Prize in 1939.

Miz Rawlings, as everybody around here called her, prided herself on her cooking as much as her writing. The Yearling wasn't her restaurant, but it could have been. Many of her recipes, taken from her book *Cross Creek Cookery*, came to life in the old place.

Robert Blauer was a child when he first ate at The Yearling. It was a little expensive for country families, but they made a point to visit the Yearling for special occasions. Lots of people did; at one time, it was the place to go if you lived anywhere from Gainesville to Ocala.

The Yearling specialized in food rural Floridians had hunted, prepared, and eaten for centuries. It wasn't a place you frequented for a quick bite. Cross Creek is about twenty miles from Gainesville and the same distance from Ocala. It's a dozen miles from the interstate on lonely two-lane roads without street lamps. It's a destination, a place where you expect to sit a spell, chew the fat, and afterward clean your choppers with a toothpick.

The Yearling was good at country vittles. In the 1970s, it won a passel of Golden Spoon Awards, given to the state's best restaurants by *Florida Trend* magazine. But by the late 1980s, the restaurant was looking a little ragged. Some folks claimed the food wasn't as good as in the old days. Or maybe Floridians were just more health-conscious. The lines got shorter and shorter and then disappeared.

Like the most loyal customers, Blauer felt the restaurant's loss. He also wondered if its failure presented a business opportunity. He was a dabbler, one of those guys who realized you can catch a bigger stringer of fish with more than one line in the water. He sold cars and operated a business transporting Medicaid patients to their doctors. He sold antiques and old books. "I'm interested in anything that has to do with Florida," he told me, drawing cherry smoke through his ever-present pipe.

He grew up steeped in the work of Miz Rawlings. His father sold her books, and his brother even republished a few of her out-of-print ones. Blauer always enjoyed visiting the Marjorie Kinnan Rawlings State Historic Site down the road, and of course he couldn't help but drive past the old Yearling Restaurant and shush his growling stomach.

Six years ago, he saw the "For Sale" sign out front and made an offer. It was refused. A few months passed, and the sign remained. He made the same offer, and this time the owners accepted. "I thought I was going to open it pretty quick," he said in that slow way of his. "But the restaurant was pretty old, and it took a lot of work. It fought us the whole way. You'd go to hang a picture, and you couldn't find a nail. You'd find the nail, but you'd lost the hammer."

He put a lot of money into the place. How much? "In the country, we're private about that kind of information," he said, but with a blush. He opened his restaurant. It looks rustic and beautiful. Previous owners had covered walls with paper and tile; he removed them to find old wood. Previous owners had built a fake fireplace. He constructed a real one.

The ambience is old Florida: your basic hunting lodge or fish camp. If you're offended by stuffed bass, ducks, and alligators, you will be happier elsewhere. "I bought the restaurant for the reputation," Blauer said. "I always thought if I could just open the place people would probably come out of nostalgia. But I've been shocked by how many. I didn't expect that so soon."

A few weeks after the restaurant opened, 315 people showed up for supper on a Saturday. Blauer can seat only sixty at a time. Long waits commenced; grumbling customers sat at the creek and drank whiskey and whetted their appetites by listening to the frogs.

The restaurant, when I visited, was open Wednesday through Sunday for supper. On weekends, it also served lunch. The menu was vintage Yearling fare. A few healthy entrees graced the menu, but diners with high cholesterol who frown at fried food might want to choose instead one of those big-city restaurants that serve sprouts on their salads. "I don't think we have anything New Age," Blauer said, blushing again. "At least I hope not."

"Time to make hush puppies."

Junior Jenkins was talking as quietly as could be. You have never read about him in any cookbook or seen him on one of those TV cooking shows. If Emeril ever invited him, he'd probably say, "no, no sir. Ain't interested."

He was another quiet man. When I asked him a question, I could almost hear his brain working, as if his conscience was asking, "What makes me an authority?"

That's why January 28, 2002, the day The Yearling opened, was so interesting. The modest man walked through the front door, cleared his throat, and made a startling demand. "Give me an apron. I'm here to cook."

Robert Blauer didn't know what to think—until he learned that Junior Jenkins cooked at The Yearling during the period it was winning restaurant awards by the fistful. He grew up with country food, with soul food, whatever you want to call it. At fifty-one, he was as leathery as one of those gopher tortoises poor Floridians used to call "Hoover chickens" during the depression. His grandparents were Will and Martha Mickens, who worked decades for Miz Rawlings, who wrote them up in *Cross Creek*. Martha Mickens, in some ways, was Miz Rawlings's manager and conscience.

"Martha will have a finger in my pie beyond the grave," Rawlings wrote. Both women are in the grave, but Junior was still around, perhaps the finger Miz Rawlings was writing about. Grandma lived through him and family recipes.

In the kitchen, he wasted no words or motions. He got out his hush puppy mix—cornmeal and baking powder, salt and chopped onion, eggs and water—and without a word started hurling spoonfuls into oil so hot it spat at him in protest. He retreated for more mix and threw it into the oil. On a good Saturday night, he expected to fry up about a thousand hush puppies in addition to catfish and cooter turtles and whatnot, watched by Chef Robert Linebaugh when the chef was not already occupied by a pot of seafood chowder.

"It's Marjorie's recipe," Linebaugh said of the bubbling concoction. A newcomer to the Creek, he would be calling her Miz Rawlings before too long.

"I hold the theory that the serving of good food is the one certain way of pleasing everybody," wrote Marjorie Kinnan Rawlings in *Cross Creek*. Blauer agreed. He also admitted great fear. He owned a couple of Ocala restaurants years ago, and both failed. "We're getting people to come in here right now and that's important," he said. "But if they go home saying their food wasn't as good as in the old days, then we'll be goners. It's a very tough business. I live in Ocala. Ocala has four hundred restaurants. It's a different world now."

At Cross Creek, it's a different world too, a world older and quieter and slower than towns even the size of Ocala. The cabbage palms rustle, the moths bombard the restaurant's outdoor lights, and the whippoorwills sing.

So did Willie Green. He used to live in Ocala, where Blauer often saw him on the street. Green had no home, but he had a talent—singing the blues. Blauer gave him a place to stay at Cross Creek. When the restaurant is open, he drops by with his guitar and harmonica and performs for customers.

"I'm sixty-five, but I know I look older," he said. "I had some tough times, but God has led me here." His huge hands covered the strings as he picked out an old Jimmy Reed tune. Then he warbled an original, "Baby, You Mine." Cross Creek was always a melting pot of cultures, from African American to classic Cracker. Blauer intends soon to invite his favorite bluegrass band, the one with that skillful fiddler.

"Miz Rawlings was an amazing cook and entertainer," Blauer said. "But she can't do it anymore. I'd like to think it's up to us."

I am no food critic. In fact, some people would say I'm not critical enough. I like the filet mignon at fancy restaurants and also the chicken-fried steaks at those diners I frequent along the two-lane roads of rural Florida. I would rather eat grits than eggs Benedict. Sometimes I prop my elbows on the table and forget to take my hat off indoors.

Some folks, I knew, would plain hate The Yearling. For others, I knew just as well, a visit would be just what their cardiologists didn't order. They no doubt would eat with joy and diet tomorrow.

It was already dark outside when I relaxed at an old wood table overlooked by a painting inspired by the novel *The Yearling*. My backside was warmed by the blazing oak logs in the fireplace. A waitress with big hair called me "Honey" and delivered a heaping plate. The frogs' legs had been dipped in egg batter and deep-fried in sizzling peanut oil. They were piled high next to hush puppies and alligator nuggets and the soft-shell turtle the folks around here call cooter.

I didn't bother with a fork. I knew I could wipe my hands on my jeans later.

22   Black Seminoles

Like a Florida panther, Isa Hamm Bryant stopped dead in his tracks as he neared his prey. "This is the spot," he whispered. We were creeping through a palmetto-dotted clearing near the river. "They camped here. It's where they ate and where they slept and where they raised their children."

They also heard cannon fire along the East Florida waterway that the ancients called the Loxahatchee, the Turtle River. They died or watched their freedom slip away.

On the warm day I visited, Isa Hamm Bryant and I heard traffic roaring up Indiantown Road toward West Palm Beach. The interstate was minutes away and so was the state's most upscale shopping mall, the one with Macy's and Saks Fifth Avenue. Then traffic faded away, and it grew quiet except for the whine of mosquitoes. "Our warriors," Bryant said as one lit on his wrist. "They kept people away for years."

Even mosquitoes failed to stall modern Florida forever. In 1838, federal troops found the Seminoles camped near the Loxahatchee River. There was a huge battle and a truce and then a sneak attack that resulted in a tragedy and a black mark against the United States.

Isa Hamm Bryant, historian, author, and community activist, studied the tragedy. When I met him, he was trying to save the battlefield for posterity—and for his people. He traced his heritage to the Seminoles and to the black people who joined them ages ago. Together they fought for their freedom.

The Loxahatchee is among Florida's most beautiful rivers. Cottonmouth snakes hiss from cypress knees. Alligators ambush deer that come for a drink. It's easy to imagine a Seminole warrior slipping through the trees with a musket.

Instead, I saw Isa Bryant, a pinepole-thin man of fifty-three who was dressed in baggy pants and a baggy T-shirt bearing the likeness of Abraham, the late black Seminole scout. Bryant's dreadlocks fell to his shoulders. His beard and moustache were wispy like the Spanish moss hanging from the oaks. The oaks sprouted from a mound of grass and dirt. "I feel a spiritual connection to this place," he said, climbing the mound.

Nobody knew how long the mound had been around. Most people believed it existed even before the Seminoles arrived in Florida in the eighteenth century. They immigrated from throughout the South, Creeks and other aboriginals the Spanish called "Seminoles"—the wild people, the runaways.

Other runaways came to Florida too. Escaped slaves, they preferred taking their chances among the snakes and alligators to remaining on the plantations. The Seminoles usually tolerated them; eventually black people were allowed to have their own villages. They married into Seminole clans and fought alongside them.

On the banks of the Loxahatchee, they took part in an important battle in the longest and bloodiest Indian war in U.S. history. The Second Seminole War, as it was called, was fought between 1835 and 1842. The purpose of the fighting was to expel the Seminoles from Florida and to return escaped black people to slavery.

"Nice mound, isn't it?" Bryant asked me. The mound was in Riverbend Regional Park, seven hundred acres of wilderness purchased by Palm Beach County three decades ago. In 1990, an amateur archaeologist found a musket ball on the bank of the river. The word went out: Riverbend Regional Park was the site of the famous Loxahatchee battle.

An army of unscrupulous amateurs invaded the battlefield, determined to strip the ground of artifacts for private collections. Then gates went up, and fences, and "No Trespassing" signs. Guards patrolled night and day.

Now the county was developing the park. There would be a history museum. Isa Hamm Bryant liked the idea of a museum. If he had his way, nobody would ever build a shopping center or a tennis court on the spot.

> Away are the streets and memories of this place
> once a lamp of liberty
> in America's silence towards our plight
> Now we sleep the slumber of ignorance in paradise
> —by Isa Hamm Bryant, 1996

Poverty. That's what Bryant remembered from his Tampa childhood. He grew up malnourished and sickly from a diet that often consisted of bacon grease on a slab of bread. His sister carried him, a worm-infested child, to West Palm Beach to the arms of a grandmother and an aunt. His grandmother, a black Seminole, knew the old stories and spoke the language. She took part in the yearly Green Corn Dance to celebrate the culture. Sometimes his father visited. A Seminole, he taught his son about the history and instilled a sense of independence. As a teenager, Isa jumped a train and rode it to Okeechobee.

"Never knew such a sense of freedom," he said, "until I was arrested."

The judge told him to value religion and education. He also said he was going to let Isa go—because he was a good n——r. Emmett Till had just been murdered in Mississippi for whistling at a white woman. Bryant knew it was a bad time to be black and living in the South.

He studied technical illustration in the U.S. Air Force and attended Arizona State and San Francisco State. In California, he became an activist in the black community. He also was a radio DJ, plumber, carpenter, lifeguard, ditch digger, and drug counselor. Married twice, he had four sons.

In 1994, he returned to West Palm Beach to take care of his terminally ill father. "I promised him I'd keep our Seminole history alive," he said. His dad died before his son published *We Florida*, an account of Seminole life in Palm Beach County.

In 1995, he started the Florida Black Historical Research Project. With a small grant, he established his office in an old warehouse in downtown West Palm. He has a computer and a desk and a couch. There is no running water. When nature called, he used an old paint bucket for a toilet.

He was teaching people in his community how to grow their own food. He started a sailing club for inner-city kids, naming it after Leonne Trainor, a black man who taught him to sail when he was a teen. "Most of these kids today, all they know about their history is blacks chained in the bottom of a ship," Bryant said. "But there's another side."

Black people were mariners and pirates. Some former slaves escaped, by boat, to the Bahamas. Black Seminoles poled their canoes through the Everglades, lofted sails, and cruised along the Atlantic coast. "When I was a kid, the ocean was my babysitter," Bryant said. "I fished, I snorkeled, I'd spear something to take home to eat. Lots of kids today know nothing about nature. They don't know the real world."

Sometimes when he took kids sailing they insulted each other and used their fists. "Enough!" Bryant bellowed. "You're sailors right now. You've got to work together."

November 29, 1837. John Cavallo, a black Seminole, escapes from Fort Marion near Ocala and joins Chief Coacoochee. They head south toward the Everglades and rally their people. At Lake Okeechobee, they engage General Zachary Taylor, inflicting thirty-eight casualties. Then they flee to the Loxahatchee.

General Thomas Jessup tracks them. He marches his troops so hard they wear out their shoes. With machetes they cut their way through brush and swamp and woods. The battle commences. Jessup has brought seventeen hundred troops. The Seminoles have six hundred. Seminoles, ultimate guerrillas, camouflage themselves with Spanish moss. They fire, then roll their bodies to the side to avoid the returning gunfire. It's January 24, 1838.

Dozens of people from both sides are dead. Jessup is wounded in the face. Stalemate.

Jessup calls for a truce. He meets with the warriors. All they want is to be left alone. They swear they will cause no trouble. Jessup says he will consider it. Soon Jessup gets word from superiors. Under no circumstances are Seminoles to be allowed to stay in Florida. They have to go west like other Indians to a reservation in Arkansas (now Oklahoma).

At night, still under the flag of truce, Jessup attacks. He captures all but a few of the warriors, who escape south into the Everglades. Jessup marches his grieving captives west to Tampa. They are boarded on ships and taken to New Orleans. From there, they're marched to Arkansas. On the way, pirates attack, stealing black adults and children. They're sold as slaves. The trip west is now known as "The Trail of Tears."

"If we can't protect this spot," Isa Hamm Bryant announced to the trees, "we can't protect Florida."

John Street was listening. He was the director of Riverbend Regional Park. He was fifty-seven, white haired, an old-time Florida Cracker who spoke with a buttered grits southern accent. If you believed in stereotypes, he and Isa Bryant—a black Indian—shouldn't have gotten along.

But Street, like Bryant, was a history buff, and an expert on Seminole lore. He even knew how to build Seminole canoes. "This is an amazing place," Street told us. There were forty-two known archaeological sites in his park; no place in Florida had more. Some sites contained six-thousand-year-old artifacts.

He drove Bryant and me into the woods. We admired a huge cypress tree, what the Seminoles called a "grandfather" because of its age. Street leaned against his vehicle and imitated the cry of an osprey. An osprey answered.

"What happened here was epic," Bryant whispered. "People know about slavery. But they don't know what the native people did to survive. The story of the Seminoles is a story about survival. I'm in awe."

A produce truck roared down Indiantown Road, and a jet airliner headed toward the airport in crowded West Palm. Along the river, the afternoon breeze rustled the cabbage palms. Under our feet were sand and dirt and loam and the sacred bones of the old ones.

23 His Father's Voice

The voice, so deep and rich and wonderful, was alive only inside of Henry Aparicio's head. Henry had a way with words, but describing the voice to other people was next to impossible. "Oh, I wish you could hear my father telling a story," he said.

Like his late father, Henry was a storyteller. "You accumulate a lot of stories in eighty years," he said. He sat in his Tampa home, and his hands shook from the Parkinson's disease that had stolen his health. As long as a man can remember, as long as he can speak, he can tell stories. Yet Henry couldn't hear his father's voice, the soundtrack that should accompany so many of his best.

But he went on with the stories anyway, and they took me back into Florida history, back into Ybor City, where he grew up, where his father was a prominent man in the cigar business at a time when cigars in Tampa were *numero uno*. Henry's stories brought Ybor to life, helped me imagine how things were—what things looked like, how they smelled—so long ago. "It was so different then," he said.

He painted a picture of the world he knew, of the dark-haired people sitting on their porches, talking and laughing, drinking café con leche and playing dominoes. Children shot marbles and flew kites. The bread man stopped at every house and hung a loaf of Cuban on a front door spike. The afternoon breeze carried the music of softly strummed flamenco guitars, and the smell of roasting pork wafted over from Seventh Avenue.

In the factories of Henry's stories, hundreds of workers bent over their tobacco, rolling it by hand into fine cigars, all the while listening intently to *el lector*, the reader, Henry's father, the man with the wonderful voice. "Imagine this," Henry said. And so I tried to imagine: Señor Manuel Aparicio, known as "The Prince of the Factory," is sitting on a platform above the *tabaqueros*, the cigar workers, and reading to them. His voice is deep and stentorian when it needs to be, light and breathy in softer moments. Manuel Aparicio reads so dramatically! He brings words to life! Oh, how the tobacco workers love hearing him!

"Oh, I wish you could hear how my father read," Henry said. His father had been dead many years, and the golden age of the cigar factories ended seven decades ago. Modern Ybor City was a place where thousands of young people went to get drunk and listen to rock 'n' roll music.

Henry preferred the old days. Every once in a while he walked to his office and took out the cardboard package that contained the old long-playing record. The old record could be played only on a special kind of phonograph that was obsolete and he didn't own. Henry had never listened to the record. He did not know what was on it. But it belonged to his father; that's what counted. He said that the recording he would never hear contained a performance of his father telling a story.

"I wish I could hear him again."

Henry Aparicio taught trade-school drafting for nearly half a century and had a successful air-conditioning business, and he'll tell you about those jobs if you insist. But he would rather tell stories about Ybor's past and the role his father played in it. For years, Henry told people about his father every Saturday during the tour he led at the Ybor City State Museum. But he had to stop when he got sick. So now he told of old Ybor from his living room chair.

Cuba-born Vincente Martinez Ybor brought the cigar industry from Key West to Tampa in 1886. Within a few years, Ybor City boasted dozens of factories and ten thousand residents who built homes and restaurants, clubs and opera houses. They opened hospitals and newspapers. "What you have to understand," said Henry Aparicio, "is that Tampa did not make Ybor. Ybor made Tampa. When the cigar people arrived, the area was only good for snakes and alligators."

Manuel Aparicio, an eighteen-year-old University of Madrid student, came to Ybor to visit an uncle near the dawn of the twentieth century. Manuel walked into a cigar factory and noticed the respect that cigarmakers gave to their *lector*, their reader. He thought to himself, "I could do that."

The tradition of readers had been born in the mid-nineteenth century, in the Cuban factories where cigars were still made quietly, by hand. Cigar workers brought the *lector* tradition to Key West and to New York,

His father's voice. Photo by Bobby Sanchez.

and finally to Tampa. In Ybor, few cigarmakers had schooling. Many lacked the ability to read and write. Many were homesick for their old countries. The *lectores* were the most educated men, the most intellectual, the best teachers in the community. Each cigarmaker paid the *lector* twenty-five cents a week. A good *lector*, who might make one hundred dollars in a good week, was the highest-paid person in the cigar factory.

In the morning, the *lector* stood on his platform—imagine a lifeguard's tower on a factory floor—and read the day's English newspapers in Spanish to the workers. In the afternoon, he read the classics, perhaps Shakespeare, Zola, Molière, Cervantes. He might read something from the popular press, something amusing or something dramatic. The cigarmakers may have been uneducated, but the *lectores* made sure they were not ignorant. Thanks to the readings, the cigarmakers knew current events, politics, the arts, even fashion.

"My father was an actor!" Henry said in Spanish-inflected English. "They had no microphones in the factory, but my father did not need one. He could project so five hundred cigarmakers could hear him easily."

In Henry's quiet voice was the pride that sons have had for their fathers since the beginning of time. "My father liked to read soap operas to the cigarmakers," Henry continued. "You should have heard him. If the part he was reading was a woman, he would read in a woman's voice. You would swear he was a woman! If the part he was reading was a German—you would swear a German was in the room. In the late afternoon, he would stop reading, at a good part, where the characters were in trouble, and he'd shut the book. He'd say, 'to be continued tomorrow!'"

Por favor, Señor Aparicio! the cigarmakers would plead.

"No," Manuel Aparicio told them firmly. "*Mañana.*"

The people who owned the factories resented the *lectores* because they exposed lowly cigarmakers to radical new ideas regarding the relationship between workers and bosses. "Bolshevism!" cried the factory owners. "*Lectores* are troublemakers—We must get rid of them!" Whenever they tried, the cigarmakers went on strike.

The *lectores* were powerful men. "One time my father was giving a reading at the factory Garcia y Vega when the owner of the factory came in with friends," Henry Aparicio said. "What you have to understand is that the reader demanded respectful silence. The owner of the factory wasn't making a lot of noise, but my father heard him. My father closed the book he was reading and said, '*El que manda manda y yo me voy.*' That means 'Whoever is the boss is the boss, and I am leaving.' When he left, all the cigarmakers got up and left with him.

"The factory owner came running after him, '*Por favor, Señor Aparicio.*' My father accepted his apology and returned. And the workers followed him back."

After school Henry often visited the factory to listen to his father read through the open windows. So did the people of the neighborhood, including elderly women wearing flowing dresses and carrying parasols. At night, cigarmakers and the neighborhood people who had listened to a suspenseful soap opera knocked on the Aparicio family's door to beg for more of the story. "*Mañana,*" Señor Aparicio would tell them again. Then he would take pity and tell another story. He'd tell about Pancho Villa in Mexico, or about the Philippines, where mosquitoes were as large as horses.

Sometimes an illiterate cigarmaker might ask Manuel Aparicio to write a letter on his behalf to his mother living far away in the old country. Señor Aparicio would write something sentimental, something lovely—prose to make a cigarmaker's mother weep.

"What you have to understand is that the *lectores* were celebrities," Henry Aparicio said. His father, dark and handsome, looked and acted like a star. He had broad shoulders and did daily calisthenics to stay in shape. He spent money for good clothes and had a closet full of dashing suits. He was a good dancer. To the neighborhood women who waved to him, he threw kisses.

"The *lectores* were like movie stars."

For years, factory owners had tried to introduce new machinery into the cigar business. But workers, worried about the effect of mass production on jobs, always thwarted them with strikes. Finally, around the time of the Great Depression, the factory owners got their way. With mechanization came noise, and with noise came the end of the traditional reading in the factories.

One *lector*, lost without his job, took his own life. Some *lectores* moved back to Spain or Cuba. Some swallowed their pride, took whopping salary cuts, and became ordinary factory workers. Manuel Aparicio, a man of many talents, flourished. Sponsored by the federal government's New Deal, he established Tampa's Spanish Language Theater. He directed and acted and wrote plays. He read the news in Spanish at radio station WBNR in Tampa. He was the host and the star of a program called *The Spanish Storyteller*.

"You know how they have pay television now?" Henry Aparicio asked. "My father started pay radio. Of course, anybody who had a radio could listen for free. But for fifty cents a week, you would have a say in what my father read on the air. My sister Mary and I collected the money like on a paper route. My father had three hundred subscribers."

Henry always wanted to write a book about his father's life, which was rich even beyond his years as a *lector* in the cigar factories. Manuel Aparicio eventually moved to New York and became a translator at the United Nations. Later he worked for *Newsweek*; he interviewed Fidel Castro before the revolution and warned disbelieving countrymen that Castro was a communist. He died in 1975 at age ninety.

And what of the son? Henry Aparicio had a rewarding life too. His parents wanted him to work in the tobacco factories, but he became a teacher instead. A good teacher, he told me, has to be a bit of an actor, and acting, after all, was in his blood; his walls were plastered with testimonials from former drafting and geometry students. Henry married a woman from the neighborhood, beautiful Irene. They had been married fifty-eight years.

They lived in the same house, just north of Ybor City, most of those years. It was filled with mementos of their lives. There was a photograph of their only child, Henry Raymond Aparicio, a successful realtor who bore a stunning likeness to his grandfather. They had sketches of Shakespeare, a poster of Henry's cousin Julio fighting a bull in Madrid, and an antique painting of Don Quixote from Barcelona. They used to have a scrapbook of their family history, but it was lost in the mail, and they both grieved.

Henry walked gingerly to his office and returned with his most prized possession. It was bundled in very old cardboard and wrapped in rope. Inside the cardboard was the extraordinary long-playing record he had never heard, a record that was too big to play on modern phonographs. Before Henry got sick, he opened the Tampa phone book and called one radio station engineer after another to ask whether there was an old machine that could play his rare "transcription" record, as the huge discs are called. Nobody had one, and the people who promised to look for one never called back. Henry wasn't even sure whether they knew about the cigar factories, or the tradition of *el lector*, or about his father, or whether they cared about his own impossible dream. Nobody, it seemed to Henry, cared about the past. He gave up. At least he had his memories.

He asked if I could help. Sometimes people have the mistaken impression that reporters know everything. We're actually generalists who often know a little about a lot of subjects, but not too much about one thing in particular. About antique phonographs I knew *nada*.

But I told him I'd ask around, and for about a week, whenever I got a free moment, I did. A friend of mine, clever with computers, volunteered to do an Internet search for owners of antique phonographs. She located one good prospect, in Sebring, but when I telephoned, he said he didn't have the kind I needed. Neither did prominent antique phonograph collectors in Orlando or Kissimmee. A radio engineer in Tampa told me: "I don't think there's one of those old record players left in the state."

He was wrong.

Over in St. Petersburg, a man named Doug Allen started looking through boxes in his massive warehouse. He owned Bananas Compact Discs, Records & Tapes. His specialty was buying and selling used recordings. Sometimes, when he bought old records, he acquired old record players with them.

He told me he had a transcription phonograph, but he didn't think it worked. Days later he called back. The phonograph worked. I drove Henry and Irene and Henry's old record over. Inside the warehouse, surrounded by more than two million records in boxes and on shelves, Doug Allen warned Henry not to get his hopes up. Sometimes old records such as Henry's—his was more than sixty years old—fall apart the instant the needle touched them. We could destroy it by trying to bring it to life. Henry said to go ahead.

Doug Allen laid the record on the old phonograph's huge turntable. He gently rested the needle on the record. Henry, sitting on the warehouse's only chair, watched intently. There was a hiss as the needle touched the record. Henry leaned anxiously against his cane. He had been waiting so long for this moment.

There was a crackle as the needle entered the groove.

Suddenly, Manuel Aparicio, The Prince of the Cigar Factories, was with us in the room, telling a story, in Spanish. "That's him!" Henry whispered. "My God! That's him!" Behind him, Irene dabbed her eyes with a handkerchief.

"He's reading a short story," Henry said quietly. I didn't understand Spanish, but I didn't have to. Listening to Manuel Aparicio read was like listening to opera. The drama was in the voice, which caressed each word as if it were a precious stone. His voice rose and fell, cried and whispered. It never stumbled, never paused inappropriately. We were listening to a master.

Henry told me he thought it was one of the fifteen-minute recordings made of his father's radio show, *The Spanish Storyteller.* The radio station would send the recordings, on transcription discs, to Latin markets throughout America.

The story that Manuel Aparicio was telling us, I learned later, was about a prodigal grandson who has left the family home, breaking the heart of the grandmother who loved him so. The grandson becomes a criminal; now he is dying from a stab wound.

He crawls back to his *abuela*, to his beloved grandmother, to beg for forgiveness. She is old, propped in a wheelchair, dying herself. She welcomes him back with love. She tells him there is nothing to forgive.

The grandson's voice—Manuel Aparicio's voice—grows weak as death approaches. "A kiss, a kiss," he rasps, "and don't ever forget me. Good-bye—grandma . . ."

"Federico, my love!" Señor Aparicio's *abuela* cries. "Holy heaven, why don't you answer me?"

Soon the needle reached the end of the groove. All was silent in the warehouse except for the beating of an old man's heart.

"I told you! I told you!" Henry Aparicio whispered, wiping away his tears. "That is my father's voice."

SPRING

24 Coconuts and Alligators

On the day before I visited Tony Demaso to talk about his dog Co-coconut—a beautiful tawny dog with three legs, stitches on her face, and a newfound terror of alligators—I felt my old, seasonal urge to go picnicking.

In the spring, I like to load a basket with good Italian bread, black olives, beefsteak tomatoes, and sharp cheddar cheese and head for a wilderness park. I like to eat in the shade of an oak and look at the water and the birds and whatever else catches my eye.

As I picnicked, the alligators at Myakka River State Park near Sarasota looked bigger than Buicks. Invigorated by the fine weather, they cruised back and forth like passing freighters. They sunbathed, they cavorted, they lurked. From time to time, one would disappear under the black water.

I'm not afraid of alligators, but like turtles, garfish, and dogs named Coconut, I don't like to be surprised. Suddenly, as I nibbled an olive, I felt vulnerable. Where was that missing log-sized alligator? Was it creeping along the bottom toward me? Was it going to bolt out of the river, rush up the bank, and crash my picnic? And what was on the alligator's menu?

Of course nothing happened.

But that's how it is in the spring. In the spring, we Floridians stow paranoia in our tackle boxes and picnic baskets. It's not as if alligators are suddenly looking for a mouthful of picnickers, or even dogs, but the big lizards do become feisty.

They're hungry after the winter's somnolence. They're marking territories and fighting over mates. With all that reptilian drama playing out, it pays to keep your eyes open.

It doesn't mean we can't picnic or fish or even swim. But for heaven's sake, we have to be careful out there.

When I arrived at Tony Demaso's house in Tampa, he wasn't home yet, and his dogs let me know it. The big black one leaped, snarling, at the door. The smaller one, the pretty brown female, barked her head off. When she jumped at the door, I saw the fresh bandages.

Tony drove up. He was thirty-four, a Florida native, an FSU political science graduate who was looking for a job in government. He was muscular and athletic and low-key. He was unmarried but told me he would like to have a family one day. For the time being, his dogs were his kids. He doted on them. He took them everywhere. On warm spring days, he liked to find a swimming hole for them. Part labs, they're water dogs.

Last year he discovered the new artificial lakes in front of sparkling International Plaza, the ritzy mall in Tampa. He'd take Junior and Coconut to the lakes for a game of catch. Standing on the bank, he'd throw the ball as far as he could. Junior and Coconut would race into the water. One of them would paddle back with the ball. And then the game could start all over again. "I love my dogs," Tony told me as I sat in his living room next to Junior and the three-legged Coconut. "I'd never knowingly do anything to put them in danger."

Years ago, when I was a kid and Harry Truman was president, Florida's alligator population was small, reduced by decades of hunting and poaching. If you saw one, you were thrilled. With protection, the population slithered back. At the beginning of the twenty-first century, biologists were saying that our state boasted at least a million alligators. That was approximately one for every fifteen Florida residents.

I am delighted alligators share their state with us. They make Florida interesting to me. If alligators ever disappear, real Florida disappears with them. That said, I never forget that alligators are dinosaurs with big teeth and quite capable of making us their lunch. But generally we aren't on the menu. Alligator attacks on people happen about fifteen times a year. When I see an alligator, I don't go into the water. I am especially leery at dusk and never swim at night. I never feed alligators, knowing that it only teaches them to associate food with people. I never feed ducks or other aquatic wildlife, knowing that sooner or later an alligator will show up to eat the ducks.

When we dip our toes into a Florida lake or river, we are entering the wilderness. In the wilderness, we're not necessarily the highest link in the food chain.

The meal that got away. Photo by Ken Helle.

It happened after lunch on Good Friday. Junior, Tony Demaso's older dog, was tuckered out on the lake shore. But not Coconut. She was three, still girlish, and couldn't get enough of the game with the ball. As traffic poured into the mall, she paddled out after the ball. Tony snapped to attention. Coconut seemed to be struggling. Tony wondered if Coconut's legs were tangled in the weeds or stuck in the mud. Whimpering, she could hardly keep her nose of out the water.

Tony jumped in and splashed toward her. When the water got deep he swam. As he got close, he saw Coconut's gashed and bleeding face. Just before Tony reached her, the alligator surfaced. "I'm really afraid of alligators," Tony said. "If I'd seen that gator while I was still on shore, I can't honestly say I'd have jumped in the water. But once I was in the water and close to Coconut, I just acted without thinking."

Tony encircled Coconut with his right arm and swam like mad toward shore. He didn't look back because he didn't want to see what might be there. When it was shallow enough to stand, he dared a peek. The alligator, an eight-footer, was inches behind. He felt it brush his legs as he carried Coconut up on the bank. "I could hardly look at her. Her left leg was just dangling there by a thread. I put Coconut down real gently way up the bank and ran for my car."

It was parked near Dillard's. Tony drove back just in time. The alligator was creeping up the bank after Coconut.

"I parked the car between Coconut and the gator. That's when it went back into the lake."

Tony drove to the animal hospital in twelve minutes, running red lights and crying the whole way. The vets tried to save Coconut's leg but couldn't and had to do an amputation. A nurse wrote on the bandage "My Dad's My Hero" and drew a little heart.

Coconut seemed to be adjusting. Tony Demaso still had the shakes. She was learning how to walk and didn't seem to be in much pain. She liked to dig holes, but it would be hard now.

"I'll never go swimming again," Tony said as I petted Coconut. "My dogs won't either."

I drove to the mall and parked by Dillard's and walked to the lake where the alligator hurt Coconut. A state trapper caught the alligator only hours after the attack, but I wanted to see if there were more. I saw lots of ducks and turtles—good gator food—but no alligators. The place couldn't have looked more peaceful on a nice spring day.

The mall was busy for a weekday. I ate a couple of slices of pizza, then looked at the new whiz-bang computers at the Apple store. I bought a birthday gift for my daughter—a glitzy-looking clock—at Brookstone's, a store that also sells battery-operated nose-hair trimmers. The lake and its prehistoric animals seemed a long way off.

At Neiman Marcus, I visited the women's apparel department and checked out the alligator handbags, made by New York's trendy Judith Leiber. They cost $4,250. Matching shoes by Manolo Blahnik were going for $1,790.

25 Bartram's Travels Through Our Dreams

We met at the boat ramp on a sunny spring day when the clouds were piled high. Clay Henderson started the outboard of his thirteen-foot Boston Whaler, and we plowed into the river.

How was William Bartram equipped in 1773? He had a canoe outfitted with a sail. He had no charts, no binoculars, no guidebooks. He had a sense of adventure and his feelings of melancholy.

Bartram was North America's first native-born professional naturalist and first significant travel writer. His book, *Travels*, was published in 1791, and much of it was about Florida. It was full of solid, scientific fact. It was full of romance and beauty and mystery. The book influenced European poets, other naturalists, and the transcendentalists of New England, including Ralph Waldo Emerson. The book, still in print, inspires writers, poets, naturalists, and interested Floridians even now.

I am a Bartram fan. So was Henderson, the president of Florida Audubon, a man so enamored of Bartram he named a son after him. "I love this river," Henderson shouted above the roar of the engine. He wanted to retrace at least part of Bartram's route on St. Johns River in Northeast Florida and had agreed to take me along.

How had the river changed? How did it remain the same? Perhaps we would discover a new plant or an Indian mound or see a bear splashing through the shallows. What I was most hoping for—forgive my middle-aged need for an adrenaline rush—was an encounter with an alligator. An alligator charged Bartram, who wrote powerfully about the experience.

> As I passed by Battle lagoon, I began to tremble and keep a good look
> out; when suddenly a huge alligator rushed out of the reeds, and with
> a tremendous roar came up, and darted as swift as an arrow under

my boat, emerging upright on my lee quarter, with open jaws, and belching water and smoke that fell upon me like rain in a hurricane.

We should be so lucky.

"This is the time of year to respect alligators," Clay Henderson told me. I am usually comfortable around alligators except during spring. On edge, aggressive, looking for mates, they could be dangerous. "When I fish," Clay Henderson was saying, "I like to wade. I like to feel that water around me. In the spring I'll cast to movement ahead of me, and the movement turns out to be about ten feet bigger than the fish I was looking for."

Henderson would be a mouthful for any alligator. He was a burly six feet three and wore size thirteen sneakers. At Florida Audubon he was known as Big Bird. He grew up on Florida's east coast, in New Smyrna Beach; Bartram visited New Smyrna too. Henderson studied history and political science at Stetson University in Deland, Bartram country, and graduated from law school in Cumberland, Alabama.

Back in Florida, Henderson practiced environmental law. When he was elected to the Volusia County Commission he wanted to make sure his county preserved the best natural lands. He had read Bartram's *Travels* in college, but it never clicked. As a commissioner he read it again, and it hit hard. Bartram's book, written two centuries before, guided Volusia County's land-buying program along the St. Johns River.

Henderson owns a first-edition *Travels*, which cost more than two thousand dollars. He kept it at home, in his library. On the river, he carried a new edition that cost $37.50. Passages were checked and underlined. He liked to stop and read.

This world, as a glorious apartment of the boundless palace of the sovereign Creator, is furnished with an infinite variety of animated scenes, inexpressibly beautiful and pleasing, equally free to the inspection and enjoyment of all his creatures.

William Bartram was born on May 23, 1739, in Philadelphia. His father, John Bartram, was a famous botanist who worked for King George III. With revolution in the air, John Bartram was friend to Thomas Jefferson and Ben Franklin. He believed in public service and achievement. He considered his son a disappointment and called him, perhaps condescendingly, "Billy." Billy was a dreamer. He preferred walking in the woods and sketching flowers to a paying job. His father took him to Florida in 1765 and left him to manage an indigo plantation. Billy managed it into the ground and slunk back to Pennsylvania, a guilty failure once again.

The more he tried to please his father, the worse he felt. Although people today consider him a visionary—he was one among the first Americans to value nature for its own sake—he thought of himself as a misfit.

In 1773, a friend of his father's, a British physician, offered Billy another job. He wanted Billy Bartram to tour the Southeast and document plants, animals, and Indians. The war with England was imminent. A Quaker, thirty-five, Bartram did not believe in violence. He took his tour hoping to find himself by losing himself.

Over the next four years, he traveled thousands of miles on foot, horseback, and boat. Although there were no guidebooks to help him, he identified at least 358 plants, including 150 virtually new to science. He described for the first time many new animals, such as the gopher tortoise. He lived with the Creek Indians who had moved to Florida and were beginning to be known as the Seminoles. They called him Puc Puggy, the Flower Hunter. He documented their lives not with an imperialist's desire to steal their land but with an anthropologist's appreciation of their culture.

Yet when the book finally published in 1791, it was more successful in Europe than in the United States. In North America, most people wanted more to tame the wilderness than glory in it. Europeans considered the new world, especially reptile-infested Florida, a fascinating, wild frontier.

Scientists praised Bartram only grudgingly. They didn't quite trust him. (Years later, the bird artist John James Audubon would dismiss him as a "poet.") Although Bartram had scientific training, he did not think scientific language could sufficiently capture nature's majesty. He thought art was just as important a writing tool. Educated in literature, he wrote about nature romantically, which bothered scientists who value objectivity and pinpoint accuracy over emotion. But his romantic language captivated poets. William Wordsworth used Bartram's images in *Ruth*. *Travels* inspired Samuel Taylor Coleridge's *Rime of the Ancient Mariner* and *Kubla Khan*.

Finished with his book, Bartram stayed in Philadelphia at his family's estate, tending his garden. His travels were over.

We heard the osprey the instant Clay Henderson cut the motor and watched the big bird swoop down and grab a mullet. "I guarantee this section of the river has not changed since Billy Bartram saw it," Henderson said. He meant figuratively. Literally, the river near the end of the century could hardly have been more different. Powerful boats skipped by, pushing wakes toward us and the seawalls beyond. We saw channels markers and warnings about slowing for manatees.

"You're taking your life in your hands traveling with me here," Clay Henderson said. In court, he had represented the Save the Manatee Club in its lawsuit to protect the endangered species from speeding boats. A caller threatened his life, his dock was set aflame, and one night a marksman fired an arrow into his sailboat. But slow-down sections were set aside on the river for manatees.

At Alexander Creek, Henderson cut the engine. Seventeen miles away seventy million gallons a day of gin-clear water boiled out of the earth and headed for the St. Johns. Henderson put together his rod and tied on a fly he called "Bob." The night before, he had taken out *Travels*, turned to page 107, and followed Bartram's instructions about how to tie a lure to catch bass. His Bob featured three hooks, white hair from a deer's tail, and feathers from a chicken.

"Bartram was fishing for food," Henderson said, casting toward a submerged log. "I'm fishing for connection. Fishing is a way to connect with nature." Casting for connection, he hoped a fish would strike and he would feel its energy come flowing through the line and into his hands.

"I think the fish were more plentiful when Bartram was out here," Henderson sighed, admitting defeat. "And they weren't quite as smart as they are now."

We stopped to admire a giant alligator. Wild, leery of us, it dove for the bottom. But what of Bartram's alligators? They had almost no contact with humans, yet Bartram described them as fierce and as aggressive as dragons. Bartram's stories of his alligator encounters leave scientists shaking their heads. They concede the accuracy of his observations about plants and birds and even alligators. After all, he described alligator mating and nesting habits dead-on. But were alligators more dangerous than today? Bartram lamented that he knew readers would doubt his veracity. Yet he wrote:

> Behold him rushing forth from the flags and reeds. His enormous body swells. His plaited tail brandished high, floats upon the lake. The waters like a cataract descend from his opening jaws. Clouds of smoke issue from his dilated nostrils. The earth trembles with his thunder.

Bartram was proud of his illustrations. Virtually all of them are considered accurate today. But his drawing of an alligator shows a dragon. "It was an exaggeration," Clay Henderson conceded. "But his drawing, and his writing, captures the emotion of the moment. You have to think of it as a caricature of his first spectacular encounter with an alligator. He made it memorable."

Indeed, most people consider the alligator encounters their favorite part of Bartram's *Travels*. Henderson did. He liked to rent a houseboat and carry friends down the St. Johns to a place that contained many alligators. Then he would read to his friends the appropriate passages. Sometimes they laughed. That Billy Bartram! Taking liberties with the truth! They drank wine and went to sleep.

Insects hummed and owls hooted. The moon rose. Then the mighty roars commenced—male alligators were celebrating amorous intentions. Henderson walked on the deck with his flashlight. Pointed it. Reflected in the glow were hundreds of red alligator eyes. Henderson's guests knew what would happen if they fell into the river.

We arrived at Lake Dexter, Henderson's favorite stretch, at noon. He got out *Travels* and began reading. He was using the book as a guide to find a place on the west bank. We waded ashore, confident we had found Bartram's old campsite. The cove Bartram described was on our right. Before us was the bluff, high above the river. Bartram would have felt a little safer from the alligators.

Like Bartram, we stood among bald cypress, hickory, wax myrtle, and red cedar. Unlike Bartram, we looked down at a wet rug, a Budweiser can, and a Pepsi bottle. Real Florida, circa modern, was a scary place too.

Two centuries ago, Bartram had dreaded spending the night on the river. According to *Travels*, he built a fire before realizing he was short of food. Paddling his boat into the river, he used his Bob to catch bass. Alligators charged two at a time. He had left his gun at camp, fearing he might lose it in the water, and had to knock alligators away from his boat with an oar.

Followed by an alligator, he paddled back to camp, leaped from his boat, and got his gun. The alligator was mouthing Bartram's stringer of fish when Bartram fired a shot. The alligator sunk from sight. Feeling safe, Bartram began cleaning his fish. Something made him look up. A good thing.

> . . . raising my head, I saw before me through the clear water the head and shoulders of a very large alligator, moving slowly towards me. I instantly stepped back when, with a sweep of his tail, he brushed off several of my fish. It was certainly most providential that I looked up at that instant, as the monster would probably in less than a minute have seized and dragged me into the river.

We headed home in late afternoon, wind rushing through our hair in unbearable heat, our legs burned despite sunscreen, our mouths dry, our throats parched for water.

Garfish dimpled the surface; mullet jumped. An enormous alligator crashed off a log. A day in Bartram Country. At the boat ramp we said our goodbyes. The air-conditioning in my truck felt wonderful. Could I have tolerated Bartram's Florida?

Driving home, I thought about him back in his garden in Philadelphia, planting trees and drawing plants: The grand traveler was safe and content at home. Thomas Jefferson asked him to accompany Meriwether Lewis to find the Northwest Passage, but Bartram, in his sixties and feeling older, said no.

He was a sad man, according to biographies, prone to melancholy, or what we today might call depression. He brooded about his business failures as a young man, about his disappointments in love—he had never married—and his unfulfilling relationship with his father. Scientists had underrated his book. Few Americans bothered reading it.

Did he consider himself a failure? Did he learn self-acceptance? Did he dream of the smoke-belching dragons of the St. Johns?

On July 22, 1823, when he was eighty-four, he woke early and said his daily prayers. He needed a walking stick to limp into his garden, where it was his habit to record the temperature at dawn. He took out his notebook and jotted a few things down. He was sketching a plant when he fell over dead.

The following day, when he was laid to rest, the moon moved through the Earth's great shadow in total eclipse.

26 Idella

Idella Parker told me she visited Cross Creek as often as she could. She told me she drove over by herself, and sometimes with other people, who wanted to see the Creek through her eyes. There were few places in this world that elicited in her so many memories, both happy and sad.

I had talked to Mrs. Parker—"Call me Idella, honey"—at her home in Ocala. In her home, she seemed impatient about sitting and talking, and the only time I thought she was relaxed was when we stood in her front yard admiring her dogwood trees as I was fixing to leave.

It was only when I met her at Cross Creek that I realized it was folly to talk to her anywhere but on the North Florida farm where she and her late employer, the author Marjorie Kinnan Rawlings, spent so many years together.

Rawlings and Idella were close, probably about as close as any rich white woman and any poor black woman ever got in the heyday of Cracker Florida. In her 1942 essay collection, *Cross Creek*, Rawlings called her employee the "perfect maid," a description Idella treasured all the while denying its accuracy.

"I'm not perfect," she told people. "And neither was Mrs. Rawlings." Theirs was a complicated relationship. Idella was Rawlings's housekeeper and cook, cheerleader and friend. She knew the Pulitzer Prize–winning author at her best, but also at her very worst. Like perhaps too many creative people, Rawlings suffered from depression and alcoholism. Finally, caring for Rawlings became too much of an emotional burden for Idella, who left.

She once wrote a book about all of this, *Idella: Marjorie Kinnan Rawlings' "Perfect Maid."* More than just an account of her relationship with Rawlings, the book painted a vivid picture of the joys and trials of rural black life before integration.

Rawlings was only fifty-seven when she died of a stroke in 1953, and for many years, Idella could not bear to visit the Creek because of the most painful memories of their years together. But it is different now, and when I talked to her on her eighty-second birthday, at the Creek, she could remember the better days.

"Honey," she told me, "we had some good times here."

People are drawn to Idella Parker like bees to orange blossoms. At the Creek, sitting on a bench next to a tangerine tree, we were besieged by a crowd of people who treated her like a celebrity. Members of the Marjorie Kinnan Rawlings Society, a club that celebrates the author's life, they peppered Idella with questions and took her photograph. She sprang to her feet and posed. "Springing" came easily to Idella, who could have passed for an athletic woman three decades younger. She had smooth ebony skin and beautiful cheekbones and jet-black hair. She was small and lithe and walked ramrod straight with big strides.

"You look so young!" someone told her. "What's your secret?"

"I didn't drink Mrs. Rawlings's liquor!" she said with a belly laugh.

Idella Parker was born in 1914, the grandchild of slaves, and a distant relative of Nat Turner, who led the nation's most famous slave revolt, in Virginia, for which he was hanged in 1831. Her parents believed in education, and Idella and her sisters got enough to become teachers at black schools in the 1930s. Teaching turned out to be a poor living for Idella, who moved to West Palm Beach to cook for a wealthy white family. Trouble with an obnoxious boyfriend sent her home to her parents in Reddick, a little town near Cross Creek. One fall day in 1940, a white woman in a cream-colored Oldsmobile drove into her yard. The woman was chain-smoking and had unkempt black hair. She spoke so fast her words almost ran together.

"They tell me you're looking for work as a cook," Marjorie Rawlings said. A few weeks later, Idella loaded her bags into Rawlings's car and automatically started for the back seat. Black folks had learned to be cautious.

Idella's mother was nervous about her daughter going to Cross Creek, a community where black folks supposedly were unwelcome. Idella went anyway. She wanted a job, and there was something needy about Mrs. Rawlings. Rawlings was an unusual person, although Parker had never heard of her. A successful journalist in New York, Rawlings had repeatedly failed in her efforts to write fiction until she moved in 1928 to a backwoods part of Florida that lacked electricity and even running water. Inspired, she began chronicling in fiction the lives of its scrappy people.

The Yearling, which won a Pulitzer Prize in 1938, brought wealth and fame.

Rawlings stopped Idella Parker from climbing into the back seat of her car. "Sit in the front, Idella," she said. "Always sit in the front with me."

The Marjorie Kinnan Rawlings State Historic Site, with its rambling farmhouse, orange grove, cabbage palms, and stately oaks, is still beautiful, but it was different from when Idella Parker first saw it.

"My, oh my, yes," she told me, whirling in place. "Over there was the cow pen, for Dora and Ferdinand. Mrs. Rawlings had her own Gulf gas tank over by the barn. She had a windmill then, and the black people who worked for her had their own house back there by the cabbage palm. The road out there? It was dirt back then, honey. And across the road, where the oaks are now, was what Mrs. Rawlings called her young orange grove. My, how she loved those trees!

"That first time I drove in with her, everything looked so beautiful. She had a lawn that looked like a golf course, and pretty flowers everywhere. She had pecan trees and magnolias and oranges hanging from the trees. I wish I could describe all the colors, the pinks and blues and yellows."

When Idella told Rawlings just how pretty the yard was, Rawlings looked surprised. Thinking back, Idella believes Rawlings had never heard a black person talk lovingly about nature. Later, in *Cross Creek*, Rawlings wrote:

> There came to me, in answer to prayer, a reward for my sufferings, the perfect maid. She is well trained, as good a cook as I, well educated, with almost my own tastes in literature and movies. She loves the country, she loves my dog, she loves company dinners, she dislikes liquor and has no interest in men.

Idella, in fact, did have an interest in men. But pickings were slim out there in the country, and sometimes Idella felt she was living on a plantation in antebellum times, at the beck and call of a boss woman. Yet Rawlings was famous for her liberal views about race. Her black workers were paid more than the going wage for white laborers at other farms. Rawlings in speeches sometimes infuriated southern white audiences by speaking passionately about the plight of the black poor. She was generous to those in need. Once, when Idella asked Rawlings for a donation to a black college fund, Rawlings gave $150, a small fortune in those days.

Now, in the orange grove, Idella and I ambled back to the bench. A crowd waited for her. A tongue-tied young woman approached without speaking. Idella noticed something in the woman's hand. "Sweetheart, I see you got my book," Idella said. "You want me to autograph it?" As she signed, Idella offered the bashful woman some friendly advice. "My Mama always told me, when you want something, just ask for it."

Timidity was hardly a Rawlings trait either. She could be disconcertingly direct, and her emotions always seemed ready to boil over. She could laugh and weep in a short time span. She feuded even with neighbors who were close friends. She could cuss like a field hand, but she loved kids. Indifferent to fashion, she sometimes wore unmatched socks; her hair often needed a good combing. She enjoyed shooting a good gun and liked to hunt. When Rawlings was seething about something, she didn't walk. She stomped.

Idella had worked for Rawlings for months. She had never taken a day off, and Rawlings had never suggested that she take one. One Sunday, when Idella decided to rest, Rawlings ordered her to hem a dress. Idella complained about never getting to go to church. Bristling, Rawlings turned several shades of crimson. "I looked outside for the road," Idella told me with a smile, "just in case I had to run."

Rawlings grabbed the dress and stomped out of the room. She returned moments later, tossed her car keys to Idella, and swore. She apologized later. From then on, she lent Idella the car on Sunday.

A good place to talk to Idella Parker about Marjorie Rawlings was the kitchen at Cross Creek. "My, oh, my," Idella said. "We had some happy moments in here."

Rawlings loved to cook and loved to be around when Idella was cooking. A highlight of *Cross Creek* is the essay "Our Daily Bread." It was so popular with readers that Rawlings followed up *Cross Creek* with *Cross Creek Cookery*. She and Idella worked on recipes in the little kitchen, slaving over a wood-burning stove, running outside to pick something from the garden, or finding the right preserves in the pantry. Idella is credited with several recipes in the book, though she says she deserved much more credit.

"What's this?" she asked me, pointing at a glob of dough. A ranger earlier had whipped up a batch of hoecakes, a kind of corn pancake that was a staple at Cross Creek. Idella poked the hoecakes with a fork and frowned at the skillet. "Not enough baking powder," she said tartly.

Rawlings liked breakfast in bed, usually toast, jelly, coffee, and fresh-squeezed orange juice. Sometimes her Persian cat, Smokey, ate from the same tray. "We didn't have meals like normal people," Idella said. "Every night we cooked like we were having guests, even if we weren't. She'd want lamb chops, a baked potato. Broccoli she really loved, with hollandaise sauce. My, oh, my. I spent so much time in here, with the light coming through that window."

Rawlings would write after breakfast. Her typewriter was on a round table on the front porch. She'd ignite the first of dozens of Lucky Strikes and have at it. "For myself," Rawlings wrote, "the Creek satisfies a thing that had gone hungry and unfed since childhood days. I am often lonely. Who is not? But I should be lonelier in the heart of a city."

Beautifully written sentences came at a high price, and Idella knew enough to stay away when Rawlings was laboring. When things went poorly, Rawlings might jerk the paper out of the typewriter, ball it up, and throw it to the floor. Sometimes she'd stomp off the porch and march down the dirt road, two miles up and two miles back. Like many of her writing contemporaries, including Ernest Hemingway, F. Scott Fitzgerald, and Thomas Wolfe, she also soothed her pain with whiskey, often keeping a convenient bottle in a paper bag near her typewriter. Some days, Idella says, Rawlings would start the sipping early.

"I'd say, 'Please, Mrs. Rawlings. You have to stop.'" Sometimes, Rawlings wanted to unwind on a long drive, and Idella remembered fighting for the car keys. When Rawlings won, the drive was harrowing. One time, when Rawlings took a curve too fast, the car rolled over and broke Idella's ribs.

"I've thought about Mrs. Rawlings a lot," she said. "Who was that woman who was married to the man who ran for president? Dukakis? Kitty Dukakis! I remember she had a book out about her problems with alcohol. The thing is, she had people who helped her, and Mrs. Rawlings really didn't."

"She didn't smile much," Idella said. "I think she found it hard to be happy."

Rawlings struggled with her conflicting feelings about race throughout her life. In her early fiction, black people tended to be stereotypes and insignificant and were described in crude ways that are considered inappropriate in modern Florida. But her work evolved. Sometimes her Cracker characters used racial epithets, but she, as the narrator, did not. In parts of *Cross Creek*, she is condescending about black lives; in other parts, respectful and loving. In one of her later short stories, "Black Secret," a white boy finds out his favorite uncle has fathered a black woman's child. One of Rawlings's last works, *The Secret River*, is a delightful children's story about the adventures of Calpurnia, a wise and courageous black girl.

In public, Rawlings continued to fight for black equality: Once, she insisted that Idella accompany her to an Ocala movie theater where black patrons were allowed only after dark, and only in the balcony. The sun was shining, and the theater managers were angry at the impudent young black woman trying to see a show. Rawlings waded into them, cursing and intimidating, and dragged Idella into the theater. To this day, Idella can't remember the movie. Too frightened. Another time Rawlings wrote an angry letter to a Jacksonville newspaper columnist who had argued for continued segregation:

> How can I say it, how can I open your mind and heart, to the psychological and actual fact that "justice" and "opportunity," however far they extend into education, politics and economics, are a cruel and hypocritical farce, as long as the artificial barrier of "segregation" is maintained. Don't you see, can't you see, that segregation denies a man or woman something more important than "justice" or "opportunity," and that is self respect, freedom from being made to feel subtly inferior, from being, after all, and finally, an outcast.

At home, Rawlings didn't always behave so nobly. She'd curse Idella—and later shower her with gifts or the use of her car. Sometimes, when Rawlings and her second husband, Norton Baskin, hosted dinner parties, black workers had to troop into the house and sing for the white guests.

Rawlings entertained many famous writers at Cross Creek, including poets Wallace Stevens and Robert Frost and novelist Margaret Mitchell, who'd written *Gone with the Wind.* An infrequent guest was the black novelist and folklorist Zora Neale Hurston, the author of *Their Eyes Were Watching God.*

By most accounts, including biographies and personal letters published after their deaths, the two well-known writers were fans of each other's work. Idella has a painful memory regarding a Hurston visit to Cross Creek. The two authors, black and white, had spent the day together on the front porch, reading, writing, talking, and laughing. Now it was dark. Rawlings called for Idella and told her that Hurston would be staying for the night—not in Rawlings's empty guest bedroom, but in the humble black tenant house, in Idella's room, in Idella's bed.

"She didn't ask me. She told me," Idella told me with a sad smile.

Sometimes, when Idella talked about these things, some folks, both black and white, expressed outrage. They wondered how Idella could have stayed. "You don't know how it was," she tells them firmly. "You weren't there. Idella was."

There also are people in the Rawlings Society who like to think of Rawlings as a saintly Earth Mother, and they hate to hear anything even remotely negative about their favorite writer. "But I'd say most of us are fine with Idella," said Susan Woods, the president of the three-hundred-member society. "We're glad to finally have a more rounded picture of Marjorie."

Idella Parker told me she loved Rawlings, for all her faults. When they were alone, stopping the Oldsmobile along the road to pick dandelions, or admiring a cheese soufflé in the kitchen, they felt an easy friendship. They talked, and laughed, and shared important things about their lives.

Still, when Rawlings had guests, Idella would feel the walls—the racial barriers—going up. Rawlings suddenly acted distant, seemingly uneasy about appearing too friendly toward the people with black skin who worked for her. "I wish Mrs. Rawlings had lived to see integration," Idella said. "I think she would have loved it."

At Cross Creek, Idella Parker was still signing autographs and posing for photographs in the late afternoon. Then she ate a plate of fried chicken, baked beans, and collards, and washed the good food down with sweet tea.

In 1950, she left Rawlings for good. Idella found that caring for her employer was exhausting and frustrating and sad. Some mornings, she tells people, Mrs. Rawlings didn't remember what she had done or said the night before. Sometimes, she says, Mrs. Rawlings wept in her arms. Idella could only be so strong.

In 1953, Rawlings wrote her for the last time and asked her to come back. Idella didn't answer the letter. Two weeks later, Rawlings died of a stroke. Idella missed the funeral.

She went on with her own life. She married, worked in a beauty parlor, and taught home economics. Two decades ago, some friends brought her back to Cross Creek. She wept. Then she walked into the house and started telling her friends about Mrs. Rawlings. The rangers gathered in delight, happy to at last meet the woman they had read about in *Cross Creek*.

Since, she has been a regular visitor. She helped the rangers get the yellow curtains in the kitchen just right. They look so nice now. "I help them here at the house any way I can," she said.

On the spring day I was there, dark came late to the Creek, and Idella in the fading light was using her handkerchief to shoo away the mosquitoes. She was fuming about the insects when someone from the Rawlings Society stood next to the barn at a microphone and wished her a happy birthday. Everybody sang to her. She giggled with pleasure. Then she opened a birthday card. Inside were eighty-two dollars—a dollar for her every year.

"My, oh my," she said. A little while later she followed a trail lit by kerosene lanterns through the grove. She could smell the orange blossoms as she climbed into her car and drove away from Cross Creek, into the waning years of the century.

27 Mastry's Bait and Tackle

When I tire of modern life, I drive over to Mastry's Bait and Tackle Store on Fourth Street S. I don't fish much, but occasionally I like to be in the company of men who do. I like to hear the fishing stories and smell the fish smells. I like to touch the tackle and pick up a fishing rod and flex it as if I know what I am doing. I roll the fish sinkers around my palms, open tackle boxes, and paw through the plastic containers of flies, imagining the ones I'd buy if I were going after bass.

Like all classic tackle stores, Mastry's is big on pictures of men and the fish they've hauled in. Black-and-white photos of anglers long dead hang near the cash register. Others are taped to the wall next to yellowed newspaper clippings about the Mastry clan and fish they have landed, killed, or released. I never tire of reading them.

Starting at dawn, old guys in overalls stroll in to buy bait. Shirtless young slackers wearing shorts and flip flops cruise by at noon to pick up reels they left for repair. The only woman regular at the store is the proprietor's wife, though other women arrive after work and buy fresh fish for supper.

Although I consider myself reasonably sophisticated, I enjoy hanging out with men who probably don't subscribe to the *New Yorker* and hated the part in *The Old Man and the Sea* when the old man was dreaming about lions. Psychological phoo phaw! Let's talk about the marlin and those hungry sharks. When I'm at Mastry's, I want to hear: "The kings are running at the Whistler Buoy," or "There are trout on the flats on a rising tide at the clam bar if you got white bait," or "Man, I got me a nice snook on a Rattlin' Chug Bug."

In Florida, especially coastal Florida, there used to be hundreds of places such as Mastry's. Many are gone. Like the family hardware stores squeezed out by Home Depot, they couldn't compete with the sporting goods megastores of modern Florida.

More than a quarter century old, Mastry's clings to life. Much of the success probably is due to well-stocked shelves and Mastry expertise. Part of it, though, is the ambience: old, smelly, authentic.

Larry Mastry and Dale Mastry, middle-aged brothers, own the store. Their father, Mike, pushing eighty, works there too. Larry's wife, Nancy, usually lurks behind the counter. A bunch of family friends perform odd jobs.

Mastry's is small and cramped. On a busy Friday, when anglers are planning a fishing trip, I can't turn around without bumping something or someone. Sometimes it is Larry Mastry I back into. Tall and tanned, he is seldom without an unlit cigar in the corner of his mouth. He has almost mastered the ventriloquist's skill of talking without moving his teeth.

"Now whatcha you want is either a 358 Daiwa or a four-ought Penn Senator." The customer, who needs a reel for a grouper rod, listens as if he's getting word from the burning bush.

Like other Mastrys in Pinellas County, Larry grew up on the water. He caught his first tarpon—a corpulent silver fish prone to gill-rattling leaps and bounds—when he was six. He has since won fishing tournaments galore. His daddy, Mike, was a fearsome tarpon angler in his prime. Anglers in the know bow their heads when whispering about Larry's Uncle Johnny, who died of a heart attack while fighting a tarpon. Dale Mastry is no fishing slouch, but he prefers hunting. Photographs all over the store document his prowess.

"Now that's an elk I got with bow and arrow," he said of one murky photo. "I bugled him in—I pretended I was another elk with an elk call—and got him close enough for a shot. That was Wyoming."

Mastry's is not a politically correct place. Folks who patronize it for the most part have come to terms with the blood on their hands. They like providing their own vittles. At the new sporting goods department stores of modern Florida, you usually can't find a stick of beef jerky or a jar of pickled eggs. The person selling tackle may be a kid with a summer job, dressed in a uniform, polite as all get out. He or she may or may not be an expert. That's okay if you are the expert, not okay if you want a trout rod and end up with a grouper pole. At the shiny new store you probably won't hear the same kind of stories, stories with dust on them.

"Did I ever show you these pictures?" Mike Mastry limped to the counter with a scrapbook. "Here's a picture of me and Babe Ruth. In 1934."

In the photo, Mike was about sixteen. He used to go to the dime store and buy a dozen baseballs for a quarter. Then he'd hightail it to Waterfront Park, where the Yankees trained in spring, and hand his box of balls to the Babe. "Here, Keed," the Babe would say, autographing every ball. "Hey, Babe," some grouch would complain. "The kid is selling those balls and makin' lots of dough off you."

"I grew up poor," Babe would reply. "I appreciate a keed that works."

During my visit, Jimmy Kelley ambled into the fish-market section of Mastry's. Jimmy is in his mid sixties. He and his dad, the late Papa Jack Kelley, ran a bait store on the downtown pier for more than a half century. When it closed, Jimmy caught shrimp for a living and tarpon for fun.

He fishes little now—it got too high-tech with tournaments and egos for him. But he enjoys the old-fashioned fish talk too. He toils part-time at Mastry's but says he'd work for free if he had to. "You want snapper?" he asked an old lady at closing time.

She wasn't sure and wanted to look more. Mastry's keeps all the fish inside eighty-gallon coolers. Mullet lie in that one, shrimp in another, sheepshead, grouper, grunt, and bream. You'll have to clean them yourself. Most Mastry customers are not repelled by the thought of cleaning a fish. Some even take advantage of the Mastry inventory and purchase ingredients for hush puppies and grits. In today's sushi world, Mastry's is a fried-fish kind of place.

When Jimmy Kelley was a shrimper, he worked all night, which got in the way of tarpon fishing during the day. Or would have, except he figured out a solution. Jimmy cast out his tarpon baits and napped. Suddenly, a bite, and a bark. Jimmy's dog, Sugar, was trained to wake her master when he had a tarpon on. Sugar was a West Florida legend.

When the Mastry brothers were kids, Jimmy Kelley was their hero. They had others. Old Baldy, at Betts Tackle Shop, knew his onions. Pork Chop—a heavy, short guy—could catch kingfish in a bowl of grits.

"There's a real generation gap now," Dale Mastry said. "A lot of the old-timers are dying. Then there are people my age who still like to fish. There are younger guys, in their twenties, who fish hard, but not like in the old days. And the big thing is you don't seem to see as many kids coming in the store like when I was a kid. Now there are just too many distractions. Soccer. Computers. Stuff like that."

Dale's brother, Larry, agreed so wholeheartedly he ripped the cigar from his mouth.

"When I was a kid," Larry said, "I couldn't sleep the night before a fishing trip. Your typical kid now, even if you're going fishing in the morning, you got to wake him up."

Outside, on a Friday afternoon, the rain battered a parking lot full of pickup trucks. The weather was supposed to improve by morning. Maybe the wind would die. Maybe the kings would bite.

▉▉ Barren Beauty

It is easy to take natural Florida for granted. We have no mountains or canyons or the wonders that make people in other places gasp with pleasure. We have amazing swamps, of course, and wonderful springs. But most people avoid swamps and are ignorant about springs. Much of real Florida is lost on them.

Sometimes real Florida is lost even on real Floridians. Steve Morrison grew up fishing for bass and hunting arrowheads in Central Florida. His parents, leading environmentalists, loved Florida. He resisted. "I thought Florida was ugly," he told me. "I wanted to get out the first chance I got."

After college, and an art degree, he relocated west, to the mountains of Montana and Washington. He loved the high country, the crisp air, and the rugged people. But he missed his family and moved back to his old state. When he did, a funny thing happened. He fell in love with Florida, ugly parts and all.

Morrison met me in Central Florida, in Lake Wales, at the Nature Conservancy office. He wanted to show me around a 4,800-acre conservancy wilderness, Tiger Creek Preserve, a place I had longed to visit.

At forty-six, he was Tiger Creek's caretaker. In other words, he did everything. He set some fires and fought others. He planted good trees and killed bad ones. He counted birds, snakes, and mammals and learned to identify the rarest plants. He kept bees; eventually he grew immune to their stings. He had less patience for game poachers and arranged for their arrest. He was one of those self-reliant men that are a vanishing species. If something needed building, he was good with a hammer. If somebody showed up with a guitar, he could accompany on fiddle. Just for the record, he knew how to sculpt things using a chain saw.

We rode his decade-old Dodge Raider into Tiger Creek Preserve and boarded a John Deere vehicle with fat tires that can handle sand. We needed it. Tiger Creek was part of an ecological wonder known as the Lake Wales Ridge. The ridge contained Florida's rarest, and least-known, habitat. It was a wet desert, desert that received more than fifty inches of rainfall annually, a desert home to scrawny plants, tortured trees, and animals found nowhere else on Earth.

There were eight-foot-high oak trees that might be a century old, brownish grasses that happened to be among the world's rarest plants, and weird lizards that swam through the sand. Eastern diamondback rattlesnakes awaited in the shadows of green palmettos. Hikers had to watch where they stepped, not because of fanged serpents but because prickly pear cacti were tucked around every corner.

"Years ago, I would have called this ugly," Morrison told me. When he returned to Florida in 1971, Morrison went hiking with his father, Ken, the former editor of *Audubon* magazine and manager of Bok Tower Gardens. They were enjoying the father-son outing at Tiger Creek when they discovered a ramshackle cabin in the woods. "I wanted to live in that cabin," Steve Morrison said.

Months later, they found the owner and bought the cabin. Steve moved in. It was miserably hot in the summer and surprisingly cold in the winter. It was also very small. He built a tree house and slept there when he had visitors. In the cabin, there was no running water or indoor plumbing. Spiders lurked in the outhouse, and scorpions scurried in the dead oak leaves nearby. Outside his door, tawny-colored Tiger Creek flowed by as moccasin snakes slithered along its banks.

The solitude and opportunity for self-reliance was what Morrison craved. He grew his own food and harvested honey from his own bees. He raised earthworms and his own fish bait. He kept a herd of dairy goats and a flock of ducks. One day, the Nature Conservancy offered him a fifteen-hour-a-week job as a warden. He was horrified.

"Fifteen hours seemed like too many hours," Morrison said. "It felt like it might impinge on my freedom. And I didn't want to be a game warden. That seemed kind of authoritarian."

He settled for "caretaker" and accepted the job. The Nature Conservancy sent zoologists, botanists, ornithologists, and herpetologists into the preserve to document flora and fauna. Morrison accompanied them, and the more literate he became about Tiger Creek, the more he appreciated it. The job evolved into a full-time career. Suddenly, Florida seemed less ugly.

We strolled onto blackened earth. "Your shoes are too clean," Morrison joked. "Let's get dirty. I love to drag people into charred areas." He recently had burned this area on purpose. Years ago, when Tiger Creek was privately owned, fire was considered an enemy. But the woods changed for the worse. Areas that were supposed to be grassy soon sprouted pine trees. Areas that were supposed to have scrawny oaks suddenly grew larger ones.

Like other modern ecologists, Morrison used fire to manage Tiger Creek. Fires open pine cones and spread seeds. They burn the underbrush and clear the ground for new growth that wildlife devours. In the scrub, the rare desert area of Florida, fire keeps the vegetation low and the ground open for its unique plants and wildlife.

Morrison set a number of controlled fires every year. It will take decades for Tiger Creek to be the way he wants it, full of scrawny plants and those weird scrub lizards. Until then, most of Tiger Creek would remain a place of mostly large trees and lovely trees. Too lovely for him, because in this place, lovely should mean scrawny.

We drove into a hammock, a shady area dense with oaks, cabbage palms, and bay trees. Hammocks are my favorite Florida haunts. Morrison liked them too. But not here. "I may have to kill some trees," he said, eyes twinkling behind gold-framed glasses. "The hammock is what most people think of as 'beautiful.' Killing oaks won't necessarily make the area look prettier. But those big trees don't belong here."

We explored another area, where he showed me his idea of beauty. He admired short, scrawny plants, dead trees, and lots of white sand. "Now this is beautiful," he said. "This is what a scrub should look like. But most people would consider this kind of ugly. I know I did."

A scrub is a strange world, full of alien beauty. Tiger Creek sheltered fifteen endangered plants of global importance. But they were not the kind of plants that casual naturalists got excited about. Some looked like weeds. Most were brown. Blossoms were tiny. Once there were two hundred thousand acres of scrub in Central Florida in a one-hundred-mile area from Lake Placid to Lake Wales. Now most of the scrub was covered by subdivisions, golf courses, and citrus groves. Fewer than twenty thousand acres of scrub remained.

"Here's one of our sexy plants," Morrison said. He introduced me to *Lewton's polygala*. Most Floridians, living in subdivisions among green lawns, would have mistaken *Lewton's polygala* for a weed and plucked it from the ground. But it is found only in Central Florida's scrub lands. I knelt and admired it.

"You're probably going to get bit by some chiggers down there," Morrison warned. Chiggers, near-microscopic insects that burrow into the skin, love the scrub. After a day or two, the agonizing itching commences. Mr. Paranoid, I stood. "I always like to get my guests at least a few chigger bites," Morrison said.

Heaven or hell? Tiger Creek was a little of both, and both could be beautiful and ugly, at the same time, if the eyes of the beholder were truly open.

29 Tom Gaskins

I once knew a man named Tom Gaskins. He was one of those fellows who had a million stories. He could talk about bears, about turkeys, about venomous snakes, about how going barefoot was good for your health. He knew Real Florida, and he was a true eccentric. Sometimes he wore a large bowl, fashioned out of a cypress log, as a hat.

Cypress, the dominant tree of southern swamps, was his life. When he talked about them, there was romance and adventure in his voice. "Cypress trees are beautiful to look at," the old swamp man would say with a sigh. "They're mysterious. They're nature's art."

In 1951, he founded the world's only museum devoted to cypress trees in a swamp on Fisheating Creek near Lake Okeechobee. He called it Cypress Knee Museum. A cypress knee is a root that pops out of the base of a cypress tree. Most roots look something like a witch's hat. Gaskins collected weird, gnarled roots that often resembled famous people. He had one that was the spitting image of the late French President Charles de Gaulle, down to the prominent nose.

"You just don't see places like this no more," Gaskins told me. He was right. And now he's gone. He died a few days ago at the age of eighty-nine. His son, Tom Jr., vows to keep open the little museum near Lake Okeechobee on U.S. 27. I hope he can, but we're living in a different kind of Florida now. Most tourists are afraid of rural roads, and they race past places like Cypress Knee Museum on their way to Walt Disney World.

Old-fashioned roadside attractions are as endangered as Florida panthers. They're unprofitable and unfashionable; the modern Florida visitor is looking for a five-star resort and state-of-the-art entertainment. The most successful tourist destinations today are generic "anywhere USA" attractions that seldom have a relation to the region in which they're located. I'm talking about the Magic Kingdom, of course, but also about attractions such as Sea World and Busch Gardens. The old-timey attractions, on the other hand, depended on the region and a sense of place.

"Sense of place," of course, is another vanishing species. Few modern Floridians have it or even know what a sense of place is. Who could blame them? Most of our cities look the same. Like our malls, they have the same stores and restaurants. People value consistency over the surprise of new experience. That's why the parking lots at any McDonald's overflow while the lot at the wonderful Desert Inn, near the Florida Turnpike's YeeHaw Junction exit, is empty.

Most folks have lost their taste for adventure too. It was different in the Florida of my youth. Adventure, once you got away from Miami Beach, was all Florida had to offer. On the outskirts of any respectable town, you'd pass gas stations with snake pits in back. You'd pass attractions where a farmhand collected a dollar and let an ostrich haul you around in a cart. Any Seminole village offered alligator wrestling.

Such places are politically incorrect today. No right-thinking person wants to admit he'd enjoy something that might be construed, you know, as animal cruelty. I was curious as a kid, and I am a curious adult. I did, and I do, enjoy the animal weird. I guess it's the prospect of seeing something totally unexpected. At Mouseland, every moment is scripted.

Nothing was scripted at Cypress Knee Museum. Old Man Gaskins was 90 percent of the show. What kind of a mood would he be in? Funny? Angry? Would he hanker to tell stories? He had interesting theories about staying healthy. He'd stand hours on his head to increase the blood supply to his brain. Back when people thought exercise was to be avoided at all costs, he did hundreds of push-ups a day. Even when he was in his sixties he ran ten miles every morning, along a creek, barefoot.

"It's an easier life without shoes!" he once told me while chewing tree sap, his vilest habit. "If I have to go to a funeral, I'll wear 'em. Otherwise, no. Shoes and socks, they're expensive." Even getting to Cypress Knee Museum was fun. As you approached Palmdale on U.S. 27, you'd start encountering his signs. Growing up in the era before professional billboards, he preferred the Burma Shave approach. He'd tease you for a hundred miles with rickety signs made of cypress limbs:

"Lady, If He Won't Stop, Hit Him on the Head with a Shoe."

Last time I stopped, his son took me aside. "Dad's not himself," he said. "He's got Alzheimer's disease. He doesn't know." The old man still had the physical energy of ten whippersnappers. He took me on a wild tour of his cypress swamp on a boardwalk he had built with his own hands. The swamp was dry, and it was an eight-foot fall if we slipped. The boardwalk was narrow and lacked hand rails. I was sure I'd impale myself on a cypress knee. I suspected he had no liability insurance.

Gaskins sprinted along the boardwalk on his callused feet. Every once in a while he'd scurry down a piling like a monkey and run off in the swamp, confident I'd follow. I did, but slowly, because I lacked Gaskins's simian virtues. As he talked, he'd frequently repeat himself. "Did I tell you that already?" he asked, looking puzzled. "My mind is not what it used to be." He knew something was wrong.

Eventually, his family had to take him away from his beloved swamp and move him to Miami. Only a big city could offer the medical care he required. When he passed away, another piece of Real Florida died with him.

30 The Guru of Fly-Fishing

My dear friend Carl Hanson died on a Sunday morning. He was cantankerous and warm, profane and gentle, impatient and patient both. He was a great fly-fisher and a teacher of fly-fishing. He was my teacher and years later taught my son. He was the Lord of the Flies.

Esther, his wife whom he called "Momma," was with him at the end. They watched TV and then headed for Bob Evans and Carl's favorite breakfast, blueberry pancakes. "I'm going to take a nap, Momma," he said when they got home. Then he quivered and his heart stopped and he fell like a wind-blown pine. He was eighty-four.

I met him at his famous free fly-fishing clinic in 1977. His tiny house was bursting with men wearing suspenders and smoking cigarettes and pipes. Carl sat at his dining-room table and held court. He loved to argue. "A fish is too valuable a commodity to be caught only once," he thundered. "Understand?" And men who liked to come home with a bragging stringer of fish nodded like schoolboys.

When he felt the tug of a fish on his line, he was sure he was shaking hands with Mother Earth. Before anyone used the word "conservationist," he was one. "There is an evolution to a thinking fisherman's career," he once told me. "At first you want to catch as many as you can. As you get older, you want to catch the biggest. Later, you want to catch big fish in the most sporting way. Finally, you don't care if you catch a fish or not."

For years I fished every Sunday night with Carl and Esther under a bridge that crossed Boca Ciega Bay in Pinellas County. Esther and I caught lots of fish. Carl too, I guess. But he was more interested in the fellowship and casting his line well. Fly-fishing is to most kinds of fishing what ballet is to marching in combat boots. It takes timing and grace. Carl was an artist. I'd stand, self-conscious under his glare, and try to drop my fly in front of a hungry ladyfish or snook.

"What the hell are you doing?" he'd roar. I'd sputter, try to figure out just what he was asking.

"You're making it look too damn hard!'" he'd shout. Then more gently: "You're overcasting. You do not have to be a big strong man to cast a fly." He'd come behind me, hold my casting elbow to my side, forcing me to cast using only my forearm. My line suddenly rolled out into the darkness.

He had eyes the color of the Gulf of Mexico and the biggest hands I'd ever seen. How could they tie something as delicate as a fly? He had white hair and a Hemingwayesque beard and seemed larger than life and was completely intimidating.

For years he worked at Bill Jackson's, the high-tech outdoors store in Pinellas County. He had this "bite-the-hand-that-feeds-me" attitude that was refreshing not only to his customers but to the Jackson family as well. They never complained, other than rolling their eyes, when Carl discouraged a customer from spending too much of money.

"What the hell you think you need an expensive rod for?" he'd snap at Mr. Moneybags. "You don't need a two-hundred-dollar fly rod. This thirty-dollar rod will do fine. I don't want you to spend more than twenty dollars for a reel either." The customer, totally confused, would obey. And then he'd reach for a two-dollar package of Carl's flies.

"This is going to be an expensive hobby for you if you have to buy flies," Carl would growl. "Hell, come to my house on Tuesday night. I'll teach you how to tie your own flies."

Carl held his first clinic in 1950. His final clinic was five days before his death. He never missed the appointed night, even if it was Christmas Eve. If one person showed up, there was a clinic. Sometimes there'd be thirty cars parked along his street's curb. Men, and more recently a few women, would practice casting in his front yard. Inside the tiny house were tables overflowing with fly-tying equipment and wanna-be fly-fishers. Carl would be tying and talking and growling. My son, when he was a teenager, attended on summer Tuesdays. He was the youngest person and a quick study. The old man loved him. Peter would come home and say, "Dad, Carl really cusses."

Carl and Esther were married eighteen years. I attended their wedding at Freedom Lake Park in Pinellas Park. Before the ceremony the bride and bridegroom fly-fished for bream. We guests brought our flyrods and arched them over Carl and Esther as they walked to the preacher.

Carl was in ill health in recent years, and they fished less than they wanted. But they did go last week to Myakka River State Park. Esther caught a big fat bream, and Carl got nothing. He didn't care. "Who the hell needs to catch a fish to have fun?" he shouted into the phone when I called for a report.

There will be no ceremony to mark Carl's passing, which is how he wanted it. His body will be cremated. His ashes will be cast upon the waters so he can sleep with his beloved fishes.

31 Marjory Stoneman Douglas

I had the last "come in, sit down, would you like something to drink?" interview with Marjory Stoneman Douglas. It happened in 1992, and I was as nervous as a kid reporter.

Mrs. Douglas was one of my heroes, the person who had done the most to try to save the Everglades, a place I had loved and explored since childhood. Her landmark book, *The Everglades: River of Grass*, was considered the Bible by people who cared about natural Florida, including me. Still, the aristocratic Mrs. Douglas could be daunting. Blind and virtually deaf, she already had entered her second century on the planet, and she was notoriously cantankerous.

Often she admonished reporters who asked "stupid questions." She might sniff, "Read the book!" when she sensed a journalist had failed to do necessary homework about her 'glades. People in my profession develop thick skin, but I couldn't stand the thought of being treated roughly by someone I so admired. I ended up spending a delightful afternoon at her home in Coconut Grove, a suburb of Miami. She was alert and friendly, and she snapped only once, when I asked two ambiguous questions in a row. "Oh, mercy!" she stormed, throwing up her translucent hands in disgust. Mrs. Douglas valued clarity.

But she liked a gift I had brought, a rug, and she answered questions about the Everglades in perfect paragraphs. She made me feel at home by asking questions about my life and my children. I stayed three hours, and she even gave me the run of her house, inviting me to poke around, to jot down things I might use in the story I was preparing.

Now Mrs. Douglas has left us. When a 108-year-old woman dies it hardly is a shock. Everyone who loves the Everglades long has known this day was coming as surely as dusk. Still it stings more than I thought it would.

She was our Joan of Arc. Tiny and frail, a straw hat upon her head and pearls around her neck, she could be counted on to stand up and defend the Everglades. She spoke with the moral authority of someone who knew herself, who knew what was important and what was right, and didn't care what anyone thought once she had made up her mind. The Everglades were worth saving. And that was that.

As a young woman, she enjoyed driving out the new Tamiami Trail with friends and picnicking where the highway ended in the saw grass. But she was no sportswoman. She didn't hunt or fish or canoe or camp. She hated the heat and the mosquitoes, much preferring the sound of ice rattling in a glass of scotch.

Yet she valued the 'glades for the beauty, for the birds, and for the water, the lifeblood of South Florida. A talented reporter who learned her craft on her father's newspaper, the *Miami Herald*, she was the perfect person to write a classic.

"There are no other Everglades in the world," was the first line in her memorable book. The year was 1947, and the federal government had just opened the national park. At the same time, federal engineers, at the urging of the state, were beginning a huge project to drain the 'glades forever. Another federal project was in the works to floodproof the beginning of the Everglades system, the meandering Kissimmee River, by straightening it into a canal.

The importance of Mrs. Douglas's book was that she recognized the Everglades as more than a "swamp." Swamps are easier for politicians to destroy than "rivers," a word that connotes moving water and life. Educating the public about a unique river of grass was a public relations coup.

Yet it took several decades—and Mrs. Douglas's personal involvement in environmental causes—for her lessons finally to sink in. In 1968, Dade and Monroe counties proposed building a huge jetport in the middle of the Everglades, already drying up because of roads and 1,400 miles of drainage canals. Land speculators rejoiced, for a jetport surely would open more of the 'glades to development.

Mrs. Douglas, already seventy-eight, formed an organization, the Friends of the Everglades, to oppose it. Eventually, the jetport proposal was killed by President Richard Nixon, and a few years later the federal government began buying up the Big Cypress to protect the western flank of the Everglades system.

Mrs. Douglas stayed on the case, focusing attention on the need to provide the Everglades with a steady supply of clean water. Other environmental groups took up her cry. She especially dismayed the sugar barons and the politicians who represent them. She was a public relations nightmare for opponents who found it nearly impossible to criticize a true icon.

Today the Everglades is considered a world treasure, and politicians from both parties like to publicly fall all over themselves in declaring their love and support for it. Several federal projects costing billions of dollars have been proposed to restore the damaged plumbing system.

Mrs. Douglas, I am sure, would urge skepticism. She always said the times to be most alert were those moments when everything seemed to be going well. Where's the money for the restoration? And who are the experts here? Those likely would be among her legion of questions.

Who can replace her? She survived her two most important, and younger, allies: the ecologist Arthur Marshall, who saw all parts of the Everglades as interrelated components, and George Barley, a businessman who had taken on the sugar industry during the 1990s.

It is impossible to say who will step forward now that she is gone. I'm tempted to say that she is irreplaceable, though to that she probably would say "poppycock!" a word with which she was comfortable. Of another era, she also got through life without owning a car, air-conditioning, or a television.

I tried to keep in touch with Mrs. Douglas after our first meeting, sending her Everglades-related stories whenever I wrote them. She always answered promptly, through her secretary, who read my stories to her. Mrs. Douglas often offered something encouraging, and once in a while sent a personal message.

I don't know what happens or where people go when they die. Mrs. Douglas told people she didn't believe in an afterlife. "The soul is a fiction of mankind, because mankind hates the idea of death," she once wrote. "I think death is the end. A lot of people can't bear that idea, but I find it a little restful, really. I'm happy not to feel I'm going on. I don't really want to. I think this life has been plenty."

Her ashes are going to be scattered across the river of grass. I hope someone remembers to toast her with two fingers of Desmond & Duff, her favorite scotch.

32 Builder of Boats,
Keeper of History

Nobody ever could sneak up on Glen Simmons. Not in the old days when he was building his famous boats, growing bananas, and hunting alligators. Nor in the present, when one dog patrolling his yard answered to the name "Rotten."

All his dogs, but especially Rotten, alerted Simmons when he had a visitor. Four of them, barking frantically, were waiting by the fence when I arrived at his gate in Florida City, near the eastern border of Everglades National Park. The Belgian shepherd, tail wagging, seemed the friendliest. But when I tried to sweet talk Rotten, he bared his teeth.

Simmons hobbled slowly through his yard. Almost eighty, he had thick white hair and leathery skin. As he opened the gate, he took my measure with a hard-eyed squint. "Don't pay no attention to them dogs," he said. "They won't bite."

Out where wild Florida collided with civilized Florida, an old Everglades man sometimes felt more comfortable with four-legged critters than the two-legged ones who showed up with reporter's notebooks. He wondered why in the world anybody wanted to talk to him. "I ain't done nothing special," he protested. "But I tell the truth if you want to hear some stories. I ain't one of them blowhard fellas."

He was born in 1916, when wilderness began just outside Miami's city limits. Florida City, his home, the mainland's last outpost, was a village in the Everglades. When he was twelve, kinfolk taught him how to make the boats that have won him the small measure of fame he can't understand. They are called Everglades skiffs, and you might say they helped tame the river of grass. Patterned after the dugout canoes built by the Seminole Indians, the skiffs were used by white settlers to eke out a living. Standing in the tippy boats, they shot deer and alligators and plume birds. They gigged frogs and cane-poled fat bream. Cartographers used them while mapping the Everglades. Scientists used the skiffs for exploring.

When the airboat arrived in Florida after World War II, the demand for Everglades skiffs began drying up. Fifty years later, two of the last lay on their sides in Glen Simmons's yard. He was the only master Everglades skiff builder left on Earth. "The thing is, the skiffs was so common in the old days," he said.

I watched a mosquito land on his cheek as he stood in his yard under the weight of a merciless sun. He didn't strike the mosquito; the trick for an Everglades man was not minding. Nor did he complain about the heat. That's why big-brimmed hats—his had an alligator tooth on the brim—were invented. Sweltering, I begged for shade.

His yard was a wonder, filled with storm-tortured fruit trees and what rude folks might describe as old-fashioned junk. There were two power-boats, a bicycle, a trailer, pipes, tires, bottles, tools, nuts, bolts, lumber, a water fountain, and, lying in the weeds, a kitchen sink. There was a vast shed full of geegaws stacked nearly to the rafters. Spring had arrived, but not the urge to do spring cleaning.

"They was the perfect boat for the Everglades," he went on about his skiffs. "Now, the dugout canoe of the Indians was great, but they was heavy and you needed lots of water. I had two of them, and one was twenty-six foot long! Hard to maneuver in tight spots.

"The Everglades skiff is smaller, sixteen to eighteen feet, and much lighter, sixty pounds when I started making them with plywood, and easy to get around in. It goes right through the saw grass. If you have decent water you can travel anywhere. You don't paddle them. Good God Almighty! Paddling will kill you! You take this pole, fifteen foot or so, and push yourself along. One push and I could go a hundred yards."

The Everglades, when he was young, came up to his doorstep. Alligators dug deep holes in his backyard. During dry season, the holes contained water and provided a living area for everything from catfish to herons. The piney woods to the west and the east held deer and turkey. The saw grass had plenty of otters. When you poled out of the saw grass, you entered the mangroves and finally unspoiled Florida Bay. No road connected mainland Florida to the Keys, but there were train tracks for Henry Flagler's Overseas Railroad. At night, American crocodiles crawled out of the water and lay on the sand of the railroad bed.

Now most of this world was gone, and the people who remembered the world were either dead or feeling their age. The Everglades had been drained and ditched and polluted. Florida Bay, scientists said, was dying for poorly understood reasons. Fish were contaminated with mercury. At dusk and dawn, flocking birds no longer blotted out the sun.

Glen Simmons's sixteen acres of fruit trees were surrounded by farmers' fields that went on forever. When the wind was blowing, he could smell pesticides. The Florida Turnpike was only a couple of miles away. Crocodiles were an endangered species, but there were more people living in South Florida than he could believe.

Hurricane Andrew had leveled his town and his house. He rebuilt. So did Florida City, a shinier, newer, more prosperous-looking place than it had been before. One of those big outlet malls now sprawled along U.S. 1. It was snagging tourists on their way in and out of the Keys.

"This place is not a good place to raise children now," Simmons said. "Nothing for young-uns to do. No birds for them to see. No woods to ramble in."

When he was growing up, everything was different. "I'd go into the woods with them old fellers and listen to what they could teach me. I guess today they'd be called homeless. They lived in little old shacks and lean-tos. They lived on coons and coon grease, mainly. Any money they had they would drink up, surely, just like alcoholics do today. But they was interesting fellers. They knew a lot about the woods, about the game, the gators, the birds, and how you did everything.

"Anything you could grow or kill you could sell. Everybody did. My granddaddy freighted buttonwood to Key West in the 1880s. He raised eight young-uns doing it. He done all right.

"Listen, folks done whatever they had to back in them days. People who weren't here during the depression wouldn't understand, but those times was so hard. There was no work, hardly. You could go to the county yard every day and most likely you'd be turned down for a two-dollars-a-day job."

Yet nobody went hungry.

"Good God Almighty, there was lots of curlew, which people now call white ibis. Tens of thousands! We ate them all the time. They're scarce now. In Florida Bay, I used to net mullet and cane-pole trout."

The Everglades, nature's miracle, were re-engineered in the name of progress.

"There was big storms in '47 and the government started draining everything. Then the park took over. They absolutely mishandled everything. They couldn't help it. They come in here from the North and didn't listen to anybody. The birds is gone now. You don't even have the snakes you used to see."

He kept an oak barrel in the back of his Model-T just in case he encountered a snake crossing the road. He made money selling them to zoos and scientists. Eastern diamondback rattlesnakes came into his yard and killed his dogs. One morning he saw a big one on his porch. He killed and ate it. Snakes had their little victories too. One rattler buried its fangs into his left hand. His wife—Maxie and Glen had been married more than half a century—insisted he see a doctor.

"The old doctor we found got mad! I got him off the golf course, Good God Almighty! He give me a full dose of antivenin. The antivenin like to have killed me. Everything on me swelled. They had to treat me for that.

"Alligators? It's only tame alligators that will grab you. Wild alligators ain't no trouble. I had the hell knocked out of me now and then, though. You'd be messing with one and that great big head would swing around and like to break your leg.

"I killed crocodiles too, though not as many. Crocodiles never was too thick."

Eventually, alligator and crocodile hunting became illegal. It didn't stop him. He hunted them throughout South and Central Florida. He almost got caught once near LaBelle, but the game warden failed to look under his truck, where he had built a secret box for the hides. He was even luckier the time somebody hired him, of all people, to guard a swamp against alligator poachers. The fox was in charge of the chicken coop.

Ah, the stories. He had a dog that used to jump out of the skiff and attack alligators, who were so startled by the bold hound that they fled. He had a dog that attracted alligators the instant it entered the water.

Simmons waited until the alligator was lured into shooting range. Then he'd take a head shot.

"Never lost a dog to an alligator."

What was the biggest alligator he ever killed? "I ain't gonna say. If I tell you, there's always some blowhard feller down the street who's gonna tell you he got one bigger." Inside his house, hanging from the living room wall, was the likely answer. Over the mantle was the skull of a fourteen-footer. Next to it is a skull of a thirteen-foot crocodile.

His house almost got blown away by Hurricane Andrew, which scored a direct hit on Florida City. His home quivered and shook when howling winds surpassed 150, 175, maybe 200 miles per hour. His biggest trees fell on the house, and windows caved in and the door flew open and the wind hurled rocks that peppered the walls and soaked everything with water. When it was over, he had to cut his way out with a chain saw. He wore out a couple of chain saws. He had no insurance, but he rebuilt the best he could. He refused to complain about his misfortune. "It was just as bad for everybody else," he said.

He had fewer trees than he once did. But some of them came back strong. I saw mango and sapodilla and coconut palms. I saw papaya and lychee, guava and sea grape. I ate a banana from one of his trees.

Sometimes, at night, dishonest people braved his dogs, even Rotten, and climbed over his fence and tried to steal his fruit. Alerted by the dogs, Simmons calmly picked up his gun, walked outside, and started shooting.

"Haven't killed anybody yet," he said ruefully. One night, when he was gone, it was wife Maxie's job to discourage fruit theft. She was no stranger to Smith and Wesson. "It must have scared them," Simmons said, "hearing them bullets go ripping through the leaves. They went a-running. Left the bananas. Left their knives, too."

⛓ No Such Thing as a Dead Gator

Columbus White had been a farmer, and he had packed fruit. He manufactured juice cans for a spell and always liked fishing and frogging. When people like me sat in his North Florida yard, under his splendid oak trees, we didn't ask about okra, oranges, speckled perch, or pig frogs. We asked about giant, toothy alligators.

Columbus White was the grand old man of alligator trapping. Semiretired, he told stories about nasty dog-eaters and about the bad boys that chomp naive swimmers and careless trappers who included, over the years, his own self. He told about gators that hid from him under cars or fled him on golf course fairways or ate a farmer's unfortunately thirsty calves.

Of course, he told me the hair-raiser about the time he caught what was the largest officially documented alligator in Florida history and showed off the stuffed monstrosity of a head, a souvenir that could have been a prop in *Jurassic Park*.

"People keep trying to buy that head," he said, scratching his brow under a dirty ballcap. "I'm going to hang on to that head."

He started hunting alligators when he was thirteen. He was seventy when we chatted, and he looked forward to his next alligator hunt. Officially he had hung up his harpoon, hatchet, steel noose, and gun five years ago when his heart started misbehaving. "Then they did two operations and slapped a pig valve in me," he said, blinking blue eyes behind horn-rimmed glasses. He felt better now, and sometimes got a hankering to go out on moonless nights with his son-in-law, the one who took his place as a state alligator trapper in North Florida. Columbus White would go along with the boy, offer advice, and maybe point out likely spots to look for alligators the state wanted removed.

When he directed his son-in-law with his left hand, his pointer finger was about two inches shorter than it once was. If you didn't know Columbus, if you were to bump into him in the hardware store, you probably would have assumed he had gotten careless with a band-saw. I did, until he leaned over, shook his head, and touched my knee.

"Ain't no such thing as a dead gator," he said.

Columbus White over the years wrapped his nine fingers around many an alligator, about three hundred a year during his heyday. He took them in lakes, rivers, and ponds. He got them in garages, and once under a shiny new car parked at an Olive Garden restaurant in the middle of Gainesville.

"The feller said, 'Please don't hurt my car.' A gator, he goes crazy when you try to pull him out, and I thought he would chew up the bottom of that car sure as anything. But we coaxed him out with a pole, and the car was okay."

He was born in Alabama but moved to Lochloosa, a hamlet near Cross Creek, when he was six. His mama died young, and his sisters helped raise him. It was the depression, but his family never missed a meal. There were quail in the palmettos and ducks in the marshes. Catfish bit on trotlines, and speckled perch swam into seines. He was barely a teenager when he took his first gator, for the hide and the meat.

He joined the navy, sailed up the Seine River in Paris, saw the Egyptian pyramids, and eventually visited a grim Hiroshima. After the war, he married his sweetheart, Mertie. They had two sons. Columbus farmed string beans and okra during the day; at night, out in Lochloosa, he caught fish, gigged frogs, and hunted alligators. Connected to the rhythms of nature, life was simple and beautiful.

Alligator hunting became illegal in 1962. Environmentalists said alligators were disappearing, and Columbus had to make do with other work. No other job he had was as satisfying to him as killing alligators.

By 1977, Florida again was crawling with alligators; too many, according to state biologists. Gators were showing up in suburban swimming pools, eating poodles at lakeside developments, and biting, or worse, the occasional swimmer at riverfront state parks. The state began looking for people who knew how to catch alligators.

Columbus did not think he would get a job, because he had once been arrested for illegal fish trawling. "But I don't drink, and I don't smoke, and I don't abide taking the Lord's name in vain," said Columbus, who was wearing a T-shirt embossed with the words "Christian Soldier" when we spoke. He became the first trapper hired in North Florida, and the first trapper to legally take an alligator again.

Alligator trappers sell the meat and the hides. They keep 70 percent of the profits, and the state gets the rest. Next door to Columbus's modest tin-roofed house was a smaller building, home of "White's Meats." Alligators were a lucrative business, though White didn't like to advertise the money aspect.

Gator trapping has always been controversial in certain quarters. Some environmentalists believe that commercializing wildlife can lead to depletion, and some animal protectionists loathe the idea of cruelty to alligators and absolutely hate that somebody might actually enjoy hunting them.

Most Florida residents have mixed feelings about alligators. They are both fascinated and repelled. They enjoy the novelty of having prehistoric animals living so close. At the same time, they fear them. The state dispatches trappers to remove a few thousand so-called "nuisance" alligators a year.

"The biggest thing people can do is not feed gators," Columbus White muttered. "But these people from up North, they treat gators like a friendly house pet. The more a gator is 'round people, the more dangerous it is. It's hard to educate these northern people that gators is wild animals."

Inside of gator bellies he discovered dogs and even cats. He encountered partially digested otters, turtles, and at least six species of fish. He dug out fishing hooks, fishing line, and fishing bobbers. Occasionally when he opened a gator, Styrofoam chunks floated out. So did pieces of metal, tires, and bleach jugs. "A gator will eat anything."

A nine-footer caught a boy in a creek near Gainesville. The boy recovered, but the gator didn't recover from an encounter with Columbus White. "It was a skinny gator, real poor, real hongry-looking."

Another time, a University of Florida sailing instructor did something foolish at a lake near Paynes Prairie. "He was teachin' a class. One of his students turned over in a boat, and he swum out to help. The other students saw the gator—it was about ten feet—comin' up fast behind him. They started yellin', but the gator got holt of his arm. The other students was scared, but they wrassled their teacher into their boat. The gator followed the boat to shore, then veered off into the swimmin' area."

In his shady yard in Lochloosa, Columbus leaned back on his chair. Then he leaned forward and tapped my knee before continuing. "Everybody out in the water piled onto the dock. The gator hid under the dock. That's where he was when we got there. Our plan was just to go out on the dock and shoot him through the slats. But the state didn't want us to kill him in front of everybody—it upsets some people. So we had to wait for dark."

The student survived. No such luck for the alligator.

Columbus White lived in alligator country, minutes from Lake Lochloosa, which was connected to Orange Lake by Cross Creek. They are big lakes, and big lakes produce large alligators.

"The gator was in Orange Lake, hangin' around a fish camp, where people cleaning fish threw the guts and heads in. Now the gator was wary, and he only come out when he took the notion, which was at night. But he was a big 'un and had folks worried.

"I went out there with my son and my son-in-law one night fixin' to shoot him. But when we got there, the gator never come out. So we headed home, in the middle of the night, and on County Road 318 we got hit by a logging truck. Part of our truck got sheared off, and the boat got messed up pretty good. My son Danny almost bled to death, and his back got messed up bad. Only thing happened to me was the rifle in the back window flew up and hit me 'cross the neck. We all was lucky not to get killed."

It was fall, 1988.

"That accident set us back some. It was four months before we come back to Orange Lake. That big gator, he was still there. Somebody new had bought the fish camp, and some fellers were fixin' up the dock. They was in the water and there was that gator again. We had to get him.

"Now the first night out, we didn't see nothing. Second night, we brought the airboat. Somebody told us the gator was in a hole on a little old island about a hundred yards from the camp. We got the airboat up on a plane and jumped the island and slid into the hole in the middle. The gator was there, and we was able to put a harpoon in him."

The gator dived for the bottom.

When Columbus was a young man, he did reckless things. Sometimes when he shot an alligator, and the alligator sank, he'd jump overboard and feel around for the alligator with his feet. Then he'd dive and grab it. He was cured of the habit by a supposedly "dead" alligator that surfaced next to him, quite alive. Fortunately, his son managed to shoot it for keeps.

On Orange Lake, with his harpoon attached to a very large alligator, Columbus had no plans for a late-night swim. "I just stuck a pole down there to feel exactly where he was. When I found him, my son-in-law, Bobby, stuck in another harpoon. Then we started pullin' on the rope. Well, we couldn't budge him. He was that big."

When they backed the airboat, the taut rope towed the thrashing alligator to the surface. It came close enough that Columbus's son, Danny, managed to hit the gator in the head with a bangstick, discharging a shotgun cartridge into its brain. Divers use bangsticks against sharks.

"The bangstick didn't kill him. Danny hit him with another round. That killed him."

Columbus's airboat was twelve feet long. The alligator looked bigger. "Not only was he long but he was fat! We couldn't pull him out of the water; we could hardly budge him. I pierced his jaws and run a rope through. We tied the rope to an ax handle. Bobby and I would pull back on the ax handle as hard as we could, maybe get a couple of inches in, then walk toward the gator and wind in the slack. We winched him a little at a time that way. Took almost three hours. We never did get him into the boat, but we got part of him over the bow. He weighed the front of the boat down so much I was afraid he'd sink us.

"At daylight we called the state biologist. I said, 'Bring your scales. This one is special.' They came with their scales, which they attached to a winch, by a chain, to the side of their truck. When they lifted, the chain done snapped. I called my grandson, who drove over in his tow truck. We got a heavier chain and lifted him up with the tow truck. He weighed 1,043 pounds. Measured out he was thirteen feet, ten inches long."

Officially it was the heaviest and the longest alligator ever documented in Florida. It took thirteen men to lift the alligator to the skinning table at White's Meats. Columbus got 294 pounds of usable meat from it, and removed a hide that when stretched reached sixteen feet. He sold meat and hide for $2,500.

A few months later, another trapper got an alligator two inches longer near a fish camp on the Apalachicola River. Relatively puny, it weighed 750 pounds.

"Mine had a lot of meat on him. He ate good."

Columbus White loved the alligator business. He made a good living at it, and he never had to work in an office. He was his own boss and depended on his own resources. Killing alligators took muscles and smarts, especially the big ones, which generally were too wary to approach. "There's just something about messin' with them," he told me, and once again I noticed that missing finger.

One morning his telephone rang at 3:30. A big alligator was lying on a major highway, State Road 20, east of Gainesville, near the creek that connects Newnan's Lake with Paynes Prairie. Could he pick it up? There is little traffic early in the morning, but there is some, and a big alligator could cause an accident.

Columbus roused his son. They got into the truck and drove. The alligator lay on the highway. Columbus reckoned it was about eleven feet long. As law enforcement officers lit the scene with powerful lamps, Columbus's son took out a .22 rifle. He approached carefully and fired a hollow-point slug into the alligator's poker-chip sized brain. The alligator shuddered and lay still.

Columbus approached, gingerly, from the rear. He planned to reach over the alligator's head and grasp the jaws, holding them closed, while his son tied them shut, just in case.

"There ain't no such thing as a dead gator" is what he forgot to remember.

"Just as I was reachin' for him, he come alive and got me by the left hand. It ain't no fun to be gator-caught." An alligator can bite down with tremendous force, about twelve hundred pounds of pressure per square inch. The alligator crushed Columbus's pointer finger to jelly and fractured the middle finger in three places.

Columbus got his hand back. The gator lunged for the rest of him. Columbus took to running, with the enraged gator inches behind him, jaws snapping. "He missed my leg, but he caught me by the dungarees. My son said the deputies took to runnin' the other way at that point, but I can't say for sure. I only know my son shot the gator again and this time killed it dead.

"I was bad hurt. Now, a gator has just about the dirtiest mouth in the animal world. You can get bad infections easy. But at the hospital they gave me the right antibiotics. I lost most of the finger, but I healed up nice. I kept those torn britches for a long time, as a souvenir."

Handling alligators is primitive, brutal work, and sometimes the men who do the work were primitive and brutal as well. But not an alligator hunter who wore a "Christian Soldier" T-shirt.

"My biggest concern was not being able to play the guitar no more. I always played in church and now I couldn't play a chord. But my wife bought me a nice Dobro. It's like a guitar, only I hold down the strings with a steel bar."

On Sunday mornings, last I heard, you could find Columbus, and his Dobro, in the choir at Lochloosa Methodist. Folks tell me he plays like an angel.

34 When Trees Talk

Another hurricane season was around the bend, and Jack Kepler could hardly wait for a big blow. Soon he would be tuning his television to the Weather Channel and his radio to hourly tropical forecasts. Driving down U.S. 1 through the Upper Florida Keys, he would flash a "thumbs up" to friends who professed to understand his peculiar obsession. Jack Kepler was known as the chairman of the board. He loved wood, everything about it, from its weight to its texture and even its smell. He believed wood talked to him, whispered, shouted, and even begged.

He built things out of the rare tropical hardwoods that grow in the Keys. But since it was unlawful to harvest living trees there, he had to wait until they were dead.

They often were killed by tropical weather. In 1992, hours after Hurricane Andrew roared through South Florida, he placed a classified ad in the Miami newspaper. In a single morning, he answered thirty-seven calls alone from Ocean Reef, a wealthy community in Upper Key Largo. Homeowners begged him, "please, take the mahogany that crushed my Mercedes."

Kepler loaded his chain saws and mounted his sawmill on a boat trailer. For weeks he cut trees and turned them into boards. When he was finished, he had collected the fifty tons of lumber stored under his stilt house on Plantation Key. When I visited, he had about thirty thousand feet of lumber left, more than enough to build a pretty good home or hundreds of the exotic wood sculptures and furniture for which he is famous. But to his eye, thirty thousand feet of lumber looked skimpy. A wood addict always wanted more.

"Last hurricane season was very disappointing," he said. "On the first day, I mean June 1, there was something tropical out there that looked like it might develop into a hurricane and hit the Keys. But then it spun out into the Atlantic. We didn't have anything worth talking about the rest of the year."

His mouth puckered as if he's bitten into a key lime.

Kepler, who was about fifty, was not a celebrity. Jimmy Buffett was a celebrity. But Kepler was the real Keys deal. "Jack is weirdly, wonderfully Keysian," said novelist James W. Hall, who lived part of the year in Key Largo and set many of his mysteries in the Keys.

Kepler looked at life with a true eccentric's eye. He was a bearded ex-hippie who always wore a Miami Dolphins cap over his bald pate, a chain smoker who avoided red meat. He made a lot of money but could have made lots more, except for his habit of turning down customers whose values he did not share. He knew the Latin names of hundreds of tree species but sprinkled his conversation with the word "ain't."

A few years back, Hall had made a pilgrimage to Kepler's home to research how somebody might build a house from salvaged tropical hardwoods. Kepler was such a perfect fit he became a character in Hall's next novel, *Tropical Freeze*. "Jack's a very cool guy," Hall told me. "I call his house 'Mr. Natural's cathedral.'"

The Kepler cathedral featured winding staircases, magnificent decks, and doors that weighed hundreds of pounds. Patterns on his wood swirled and danced. What other builders considered ugly—a knot or a bump—he saw as beautiful. He carved loggerhead turtles out of imperfection.

He started building the house in 1979. "It's not finished," he said, but it probably never would be. When a new storm came along, he knew that ideas would pop into his head about what he might do with another load of wood. "I am known as 'Have Chain Saw, Will Travel.' I'll go anywhere, any time."

Years ago, after reading about old homes in West Palm Beach scheduled to meet a bulldozer, he sped up the turnpike to salvage the lumber. Dade County pine, so hard it thwarts termites and even nails, was used up by the middle of the twentieth century. But the wood from the old houses became the floor in his new house.

He read about a problem at the Port of Miami, where ships from Asia arrived with yachts encased in giant wooden yokes made from tropical forest trees. The port was paying fifty dollars to anyone who'd haul away a yoke. Kepler became a frequent visitor; he happened to be looking for exterior walls for his house at the time.

The man who talks to trees. Photo by Lara Cerri.

For most of his construction he depended on the Florida Keys hard-woods—the gumbo limbo, wild tamarind, ironwood, and mahogany. Have chain saw, will travel. A terrible fire, sparked by the old Flagler Railroad, had swept Key Largo in 1915. Blackened dead trees stood in lonely desperation for decades—until Kepler volunteered to take them. Behind the burnt bark was perfectly aged Jamaica dogwood. It made a pretty exotic bathroom wall.

Scavenging in the devastated forest, he harvested a small collection of lignum vitae, perhaps the most valuable tree in the Keys. He used the wood in his shutters and in his drawers. A thunderstorm knocked down a spalted Indian tamarind in his neighbor's yard. He built kitchen cabinets.

He disliked nails. His boards were held together by homemade wooden pegs made from the ironwood tree he recovered in that burned-out forest. His house probably was worth millions, but he was not even curious about it. After all, he had gotten the wood for free and done all the work himself. He had no intention of moving. He lacked insurance.

"Don't believe in it," he said. "I built the insurance into this house. It's built with the hardest woods on earth. If a storm is tough enough to knock down my house, well, my house ain't going nowhere. If it does, I'll just have to find it and bring it back in one whole piece."

"I tell my wife: 'Just keep me healthy. I can build anything, fix anything.'"

Working with wood was part of the Kepler genetic code. He was born in Illinois but grew up in Wisconsin, where his father was a prominent builder and his mother was known for her woodworking. At thirteen, he was making seven dollars an hour as a carpenter; at sixteen, he designed a house his father built; as a high school senior, he taught drafting to freshmen. He built his first house when he was eighteen. "I didn't go to college," he said. "What did I need that piece of paper for? I knew what I wanted to do."

So he moved to the Upper Keys—where his parents had owned a winter home—and worked as a carpenter and bartender. When he saved some money, he moved temporarily back to Wisconsin in order to marry Phyllis, whom he had met at a birthday party when they were teenagers. He brought her back to the Keys, where they lived in a trailer in a wild, buggy tropical hammock. Jack worked as a handyman, Phyllis as a nurse and cheerleader who didn't mind sawdust in bed.

Wood called his name. It called to him from the beach next to the Channel Five Bridge. It called to him from construction sites in Marathon. The Coast Guard called about an eighty-four-foot gum tree it had towed from a shipping channel and left on the beach. Later, he traded lumber for an air conditioner and began building the air-conditioning ducts. In almost every house on earth, air-conditioning ducts are metal. His were made from the Coast Guard's gift tree, which Kepler thought toppled into the Mississippi somewhere north of Missouri, flowed with the current into the gulf, then somehow drifted over months or years toward Florida, to the Keys, to his sawmill.

He had no desire to build a house for somebody else. But he was paid handsomely for custom cabinets, window frames, furniture, and giant vases onto which he carved tarpon scales. On the stairway he built for a millionaire, he carved parrots, mangroves, and a moray eel. In his mind, the stairway was a tropical isle. His bill? Fifteen grand.

Kepler was one of those people who hated sleep. He rose at 3 A.M. and walked to the Marlin convenience store for coffee and a quiet read of the *Miami Herald.* At sunrise, he hit a hundred golf balls to focus his mind.

Then he got to work. He might be building an altar for a local church or a door for the friend who had given him yellowtail snapper filets. Kepler sometimes preferred bartering to a paycheck. He built kitchen cabinets for a chiropractor who treated his bad back for a year.

A bad back came with the job. The hardwoods of the Keys are extremely heavy. Take ironwood. An ironwood board, twenty-four inches long, eight inches wide, and one inch thick, weighed approximately twenty pounds. "Don't grab if you're in a boat that's sinking," Kepler joked.

He traded his beloved sandals for steel-toed shoes after he accidentally kicked a wild tamarind and ended up with an eight-inch splinter in the arch of his foot. "You have to be very careful when you work around saws and heavy wood," he said. "When I make a mistake, I quit for the day and write myself a note: 'Jack, that was very, very stupid.'"

When he sawed mahogany he wore a ventilator mask. Its dust made his throat swell shut. He stopped harvesting poisonwood; poisonwood sawdust had prompted another trip to the emergency room. Watching him work, I had to slap mosquitoes constantly; he left them alone. He had trained himself to spare even the giant, quite poisonous scorpions that inhabited his woodpile. He believed in karma. The only time he squashed a scorpion, he was stung hours later by an even larger one.

There were creatures in the Keys that were more dangerous than scorpions. Fortunately, some of them made noise. Unfortunately, he was hard of hearing after years of listening to chain-saw symphonies. "Hey, Jack, move, will you?" hissed a neighbor one afternoon. Kepler had failed to notice the rattle of the big Eastern diamondback that slithered out of his woodpile.

"I don't kill rattlesnakes, either," Kepler said defiantly. "Why should I? They eat rats, and they have the same right to live as I do."

He thought of himself as an environmentalist. He said he was against logging in tropical forests. He said he was happy whenever he heard that a wood thief had been apprehended at Dagny Johnson Key Largo Hammock Botanical State Park or Crocodile Lake National Wildlife Refuge or John Pennekamp Coral Reef State Park. The preserves contained the last of North America's tropical hardwood forests and had become a magnet to wood rustlers. "We think of Jack Kepler as a good guy," said Jim Duquesnel, the biologist for the Keys state parks.

The parks kept Kepler's name handy, in case they needed him to remove a foreign tree that doesn't belong in a Florida Keys hammock. A scientist's trash was a wood addict's treasure.

"He absolutely hates waste. Loathes it. Can't tolerate it," said Hank Gilpin, a prominent New England sculptor who bought lumber from Kepler. "He loves trash. It's wood that other people typically haul to the landfill or to the woodchipper. To Jack, it's treasure. He looks at a pile of discarded wood and sees dolphins leaping out of it."

Kepler told me he hated answering the phone. But sometimes he was glad when he did. Ken King, owner of Golden Bough Tree Trimming in Key West, called while I was visiting. King was another tree addict. His wife was threatening mutiny over the mountains of mahogany piled in the backyard. King had permits to remove mahoganies threatening to damage a house and another permit to cut down a diseased mahogany, one of the largest in Key West. He wanted to do business with Kepler.

Of course, Kepler told King he'd be right down. Kepler, who drives an old Ford F-150 pickup with a forest of chain saws in the back, loved road trips. "Sometimes I'm driving and I'll get a gut feeling to drive down a side road, and there will be a pile of lumber just waiting for me." He remembered the time he acquired a wild tamarind killed by lightning during Hurricane Floyd in 1999. Wild tamarind always has pretty grain, but this one had spectacularly wild grain. "When I sawed open that tree, I realized the lightning had scared the tree to death. I had never seen grains like that, zigging this way and zagging that way. It was like the tree had seen the face of God." Out of it he built the grandest fish aquarium I had ever seen. It was as long as a car, and he intended to sell it for sixteen thousand dollars.

As we drove toward Key West, he never stopped talking about wood. He told me he wished the Keys had saved more of the old bridges, especially the bridge pilings. Pilings were made from Dade County pine. Take railroad ties. The old railroad ties from the Flagler line were mahogany. Jack Kepler could be giving them life even now. Every Key held memories for him, mostly beaches where he found driftwood or landfills where he saved a crabwood limb from the woodchipper at the last instant.

He got lost in Key West. He couldn't remember the street. For that matter, he had trouble with names. "Not the Latin names of trees," he said. Years ago, he spent more than a grand on tropical botany books.

Eventually he found Ken King's house, where he admired the woodpile as King's wife called out the back door: "Jack, if you take our wood, I'll give you a bottle of Dom Perignon champagne." King turned pale. He would rather give away his children than a *Swietenia mahagoni*, which is what he and Kepler call their favorite tree.

But King had no more room for mahogany in his yard. Kepler did. King also had expenses. In the Keys, landfills charge tree-trimmers hundreds of dollars for a ton of branches. A branch from a single, large mahogany can weigh a ton. It was cheaper to invite Kepler down to buy the wood than pay to throw it away.

King led the way to an old Key West house. The roots of mahoganies were caving in its side. The trees had to go. So did the big diseased mahogany yawning over a busy street near the Hemingway House. Kepler wanted them all; he was willing to pay $3,500 for them. "It's a bargain even if I can't use the wood until it ages in a few years."

Kepler was happy. Mahogany pleased him. "Mahogany is so dignified, so solid, so beautiful. At the same time, it has a mammoth ego. Even after death, mahogany wants to contribute. I saw it open, and the mahogany all but screams at me. 'Use me! Use me! Use me!' It wants me to give it a little more life."

Kepler looked healthy enough to me. I figured he should live another quarter of a century if a tree didn't fall on him, if a snake didn't bite him, if he could avoid inhaling the wrong kind of sawdust spore. Seventy-five years is a decent life span for a man. But for a mahogany, seventy-five years is hardly a moment. Some were seedlings when the Seminoles killed Dr. Henry Perrine at Indian Key, saplings when Flagler built his railroad, and young trees when Hemingway put pen to paper for *To Have and Have Not*.

"Mahogany owns my heart," Kepler blurted out on the drive home from Key West. For a moment both of his hands were off the wheel and on his chest. "Mahogany owns my heart and ain't letting go. You know what would make me happy? It's if I can build me a real nice mahogany urn.

"After I'm gone, they can put my ashes in a nice mahogany urn."

SUMMER

35 A Florida Boy Keeps His Cool

I am a Florida boy. When it gets summer hot around here, Florida boys turn it down a notch. We look for shade, breezes, and maybe a porch to lie under. Just kidding about the porch, though if I were a dog that's where I would be. Actually, we like caves and springs. But more about that later.

In June, when things really start heating up, we move around as little as possible. Especially we take to heart the wisdom offered by the late baseball great Satchel Paige: "Avoid running at all times." Better to amble.

We dress sensibly. We never wear ties with our shirts. If we happen to attend a church where other men feel compelled to wear ties, we find another church. Of course, we Florida boys avoid wearing shirts, though if we have to, we wear something in rayon, which feels cool to the skin. Pants? Never long pants, but we will submit to shorts, all the while pretending we are wearing a loincloth or less.

Seldom do we bother with shoes. If we have to, our footwear of choice is a fine leather sandal. Shade? We love shade. We prefer oak trees, which provide a lot of it. We especially like oak trees in parks, where trees grow close together and it's easier to hang a hammock.

In June, hammocks are beloved by Florida boys who need to conserve strength for the barbecue at day's end. From our perch in the hammock, we look through the limbs of the oak trees at clouds that, the more you look at them, begin to resemble spare ribs and drumsticks.

Lying on a hammock is a lost art. Most people don't know how, treating the hammock like a bed. Florida boys know to approach a hammock backside first. Place said backside in middle of hammock while simultaneously pivoting. Head and feet should strike hammock ends at the same time.

Remove harmonica from between teeth and start playing. The harmonica is the official hot-weather musical instrument of Florida boys because it requires so little energy and talent. Blow, man, blow.

After exhausting our three-song repertoire, we read. Florida boys choose reading material carefully. We like stories about people who endure horrendous weather during their adventures, preferably at Mount Everest. We remember the last time we were cold.

Modern Florida boys avoid being outside at dawn or dusk when mosquitoes are most active. It is easier said than done, especially in the evening, barbecue time. We delay going outside until somebody else has to do the cooking. Better to remain inside, drink something cold, and watch old movies.

In air-conditioned comfort we watch movies that make us feel better. We enjoy summer-in-the-South films like *Cat on a Hot Tin Roof*, and not only because Elizabeth Taylor traipses around in a flimsy slip or because Paul Newman seldom wears a shirt. It's the heat and the sweat. We can almost imagine the odor of Big Daddy's cigar and his B.O.

Sometimes, even a Florida boy is forced to leave the comfort of couch and travel. Recently I had to visit the Florida Panhandle, always the hottest place on the whole planet despite all that sweet tea everybody drinks.

When I go, I always look for a good cave to explore. The best caves are at Florida Caverns State Park in Marianna. They feature large formations of stalagmites and stalactites and other structures that look like spare ribs, grits, and fried chicken.

My favorite cavern was discovered in 1938. Workers enlarged the opening and some of the passages, so lazy Florida boys would not have to crawl or stoop very much. Outside the cavern opening it is ninety-eight degrees in the shade. Inside it is sixty-five.

We have a guide, our Dante, a ranger named Frank Strickland, whom we follow into the infernal regions. He has a soft voice and the manner of Mr. Rogers. "Yes, yes, huh-huh, huh-huh—isn't this wonderful?" he asks. And he is right. "Don't crown your heads," he tells us at one point, and it's the only time we have to duck. That's the kind of caving Florida boys enjoy.

Outside, our glasses fog up right away in that unspeakable heat. We immediately drive to Blue Spring at the end of the park road. Tip a toe in. Gosh-a-mighty. It's colder than dry ice. But that's what we want. Two ways to enter a spring. If you're a kid, you jump in, knowing you probably won't suffer a heart attack. If you are an aging Florida boy, creep in. First the feet. Then the calves. Pause as the water laps the thighs and look around. Anyone watching? Yes. Act brave.

A little kid runs right by, splashing and laughing, and of course I am tempted to yell and bare my teeth. But his mama is watching from the shade, so I just wink. I'm hip deep now, a very delicate thing if you are of the gender Florida boy. It is acceptable to gasp.

No turning back at this point. Plunge ahead and do a brisk crawl. Try to warm up while watching for friendly beavers and snapping turtles and thinking about dinner.

On a hot June day, Florida boys think about meals most of their waking hours. A swim in a cold spring, of course, whets the appetite like nothing else. If you have packed a picnic lunch, go at it, but don't say you weren't warned about mosquitoes. A better prospect, at least in Marianna, is a trip to Jim's Grill.

I eat fried chicken, collards, and black-eyed peas at Jim's. Yes, hot food makes me sweat like a pig. But just call me Big Daddy: Good collards are worth a little perspiration.

36 Loincloth Man

"Simplify, simplify," advised Henry David Thoreau, the philosopher who said he'd rather sit on a pumpkin all by himself than have to share a velvet cushion with unwanted companions.

Ed Watts, who enjoyed his own company most of all, valued economy too. When I found him—he lived in the remote woods near North Florida's Santa Fe River—he materialized out of the gloom, gave me the once-over, and uttered a brief "Howdy."

I had no trouble maintaining strict eye contact. Except for his glasses and necklace, he was quite naked. "S'cuse me," he said, vanishing modestly into his palm hut. He emerged clothed in his official Ed Watts uniform: a loincloth. "I'd rather be nekkid," he said, "but I don't like to make folks uncomfortable."

Ed Watts was a throwback to an era mostly gone. Once every corner of our state boasted a genuine eccentric living in the woods or on the water. But like panthers and crocodiles, few were able to survive civilized Florida.

Yet Real Florida, even in the twenty-first century, hung on. There were woods and swamps just big enough to harbor endangered wildlife, and a few hidey holes to shelter an endangered hermit or two.

Ed Watts was fifty. He lived alone, never married or had children. He told me he was born in Lake City, had operated a bar, fished commercially, worked in a grocery, delivered newspapers, and even cut trees.

Like his father and his father's father, he was born with brittle-bone disease. He broke so many legs and arms and hips it became dangerous for him to do manual labor. He got government disability and wondered what he would do with the rest of his life. "Well, I liked the water, especially springs," Ed told me. "And I liked skinny-dipping."

He was canoeing on the Santa Fe River in 1985 when he paddled up a creek and found Lilly Spring. It was more pond than anything; the water clear and cold. It was also full of litter. Ed located the owner and volunteered to clean it up for the privilege of swimming in the buff.

Eventually, he got a no-cost lease. By the time I tracked him down, he was the unofficial caretaker of an unofficial campground that showed up on no maps and in no brochures. Like me, most people stumbled upon him by accident or because a canoe livery on the river issued directions.

Tourists loved to visit him. Ed Watts enjoyed visitors—but tolerated no bacchanalias. "Had to chase away people last week when their four-letter words got real reg'lar," he said. "Told them, 'Just quit now. I don't mean maybe.'"

When he conversed with the sober, he sat on a bench under a stuffed baboon head mounted on the hut he built from palm fronds. His hut had no windows and nothing to stop mosquitoes from flying through the open door. "They don't bother me much," he said. "Now, ticks'll get on ya in the summer, but at least I don't have no problem finding them."

Ed's loincloth, made from synthetic fur, covered only modest sections of his torso. I had been warned: Visitors who make the mistake of voicing their admiration for his wardrobe sometimes regretted it. He would venture into the hut and haul out a plastic box containing twenty assorted loincloths.

"For my guests."

Loincloths wore out. He infrequently purchased material at a fabric store in Gainesville, where he was treated as a celebrity. Folks who had read about him in newspapers learned to recognize him even when he was dressed. He had a prominent bald head and a furry beard like a Dr. Seuss character, leathery skin, and a lower lip usually weighed down by a cigarette.

"I'm ashamed they hooked me on tobacco," he told me. "I don't drink but one or two beers a year, though. Course, if I drank every beer folks offered, I'd be an alcoholic." His beverage of choice, for the record, was cola from Winn-Dixie.

He enjoyed telling visitors he ate grubs and raw animals, but he actually bought provisions at the supermarket and cooked on a hot plate or in a microwave. His other appliances were a lamp, a television for the weather report, a fan for summer, and a telephone for emergencies, like broken bones. His electric bill was $120—for the whole year. He kept medical bills low by avoiding doctors.

Wild man of Lilly Spring. Photo by Carrie Pratt.

Unlike Thoreau, he hardly read, though somebody had given him a Louis L'Amour novel he liked. Mostly he passed his days sitting on his bench and watching the water and the woods for great blue herons, owls, and otters. If he got bored, he dressed and drove to his mother's. Often he spent the night in the little apartment behind her house.

On summer Saturdays, the occasional straggler in a canoe always managed to discover his creek. In winter, paddling season in Florida, he endured hundreds of guests. When he sensed a big visitor day, he often revved up the chain saw—being extra careful to keep his loincloth out of the way—and cut firewood. With his guests, he sat at the fire and warmed more than his hands. Guests over the years included Boy Scout troops and church groups. He had the photos to prove it. Most likely they did too.

When the wind was blowing the wrong way, he sometimes was surprised by approaching paddlers. "S'cuse me," he'd call and grab the nearest loincloth. Nobody, by the way, ever mistook him for Tarzan. He owned a paunch a hibernating black bear would have envied.

"Well, so I'm not Mr. America," he said. "And I ain't a pervert or, what do you call it, an exhibitionist. If every time I heard somebody coming down the river I ran out nekkid and yelled 'Hey, look at me,' then it'd be different. But I try to be quiet about it."

During Florida's hot summer, a loincloth qualified as sensible dress. But even a man in a loincloth suffered from the heat. A dozen times a day Ed Watts jumped into his spring to cool off.

Water from a spring is always seventy-two degrees and as clear as white lightning. On a sweltering summer afternoon, a swim in a spring seemed especially inviting. I asked Ed if I could do a little skinny-dipping.

"Be my guest," he replied.

Stripping away my ridiculous city clothing, I dropped, nekkid, into the refreshing water, being especially careful to avoid the ominous shallows.

"There are snapping turtles in there," Ed called from his hut. "But I still got all my body parts."

⬛ Kiss of the Swamp Angels

Roy Wood pulled on a heavy green jacket and dragged a net over his face. Of course he was wearing long pants, sturdy shoes, and sensibly thick socks. It was his uniform, his armor, so to speak, against the swamp angels.

Other people called them mosquitoes, but old-timers always referred to them as swamp angels. In the summer, in the wet season, swamp angels made the Everglades a living hell. "Ah," Wood said, deep in the hammock, his head engulfed in a black cloud of mosquitoes whose ravenous whines almost drowned him out. "I somehow have a bunch of mosquitoes inside my net. Do I just endure their bites on my face? Or do I open my net and shoo them out?"

Overwhelmed by the mosquitoes myself, I offered no advice. We both decided to endure the bites rather than risk letting more mosquitoes in. It was Wood's job to explain nature to visitors at Everglades National Park.

In the park's tiny community of Flamingo, at the southern tip of the peninsula, mosquitoes dominated nature. In the summer, Wood seldom encountered a tourist who didn't appear shell-shocked. Few had ever experienced such mosquitoes. "Stay off the grass," he warned a welt-covered German couple. "Stay out of the shade. That's where the mosquitoes are."

"*Ja*," said the woman, nodding in the affirmative. "*JA!*"

In most places throughout the South, people were worried, probably too much, about mosquito-borne diseases. Diseases are worth worrying about, though in Everglades National Park, folks historically had been more concerned about being eaten alive by the uncountable hordes. Nobody who had spent any time in the Everglades in summer disagreed with the old folk adage, "Swing a quart jar and catch a gallon of mosquitoes."

The park had forty-three mosquito species, including thirteen that bite people. The worst biter was the salt marsh mosquito. It was the swamp angel that lives in mangroves and the tropical hardwood forests of the Florida coast. Small and brown, salt marsh mosquitoes bit night and day. When they were thick enough, it was possible to breathe them in. Wood had been bitten inside the nostrils and inside his mouth. "I don't have a shirt that doesn't have a blood stain," he said. "And you should see the books in my office. Every page has a mosquito smudge."

Most days Wood toiled indoors, upstairs, in the park's visitor center. To find him, I had to negotiate a passage of doors. The first was a screen door. As I opened it, a blast of air blew the tagalong mosquitoes away from the entrance. It was an old-fashioned Everglades technique made modern. Years ago, any self-respecting Everglades house featured a "losing room," where palm fronds knocked the mosquitoes off the hardy pioneer as he stepped through the doorway.

"Mosquitoes still find a way into the visitor center," Wood told me. "They'll come through a hole in the screen or even a crack in the door." Behind him was a sign that provided the day's mosquito forecast. The forecast can range from "enjoyable" to "hysterical"; the day of my visit it was merely "unpleasant."

It was unpleasant enough in the parking lot. But when we ventured anywhere near the bushes or, worse, the mangroves or the shady hammock forests, we were in for a hysterical experience. Roy Wood was the kind of guy who tempts fate.

He was thirty-seven that summer, a corn-fed Indiana boy who grew up catching birds and snakes and turtles and driving his poor ma wild. Later, he studied archaeology at Indiana State and spent a summer as a park ranger at the Grand Canyon. One summer led to another, and after he graduated, he joined the National Park Service for good.

He remembered his first visit to the Everglades in 1990. It was November, not even mosquito season, when he drove his car to his new apartment in Flamingo at dusk. As he unloaded his luggage, mosquitoes treated him like their private blood bank. "My God!" he thought to himself. "What have I done?" Inside the apartment, he peeked out the window and braced himself for another sprint for the suitcases in the car. His new roommate, a former surfer from California, talked him out of it. "Don't even think of it, dude," the surfer said. "Wait until tomorrow."

It was good advice. "When you live down here," Wood told me, "your whole life revolves around avoiding mosquitoes."

Once a week he drove fifty miles to the nearest town, Homestead, for groceries. In the supermarket parking lot, he was careful to pack the perishables last. Back in hell, bedeviled by swamp angels, he unpacked the perishables first. If mosquitoes were bad, he left in the car the groceries that required no refrigeration. They could wait until the next day, maybe until midday, when the mosquitoes tend to be lazier.

People who worked at Flamingo enjoyed sneering at us city people who panicked the moment a mosquito bit our ankles. Maybe that's why Roy Wood invited me to meet the world's most aggressive mosquitoes.

In the visitor center, he grabbed himself a mosquito jacket—not quite a bulletproof vest against swamp angels—and another for me. We left the safety of indoors and marched briskly through a modest mosquito cloud in the parking lot to Wood's Plymouth van. He drove into a park campground empty except for a squadron of mosquito-eating dragonflies. Only the insane would have been tempted to camp in the Everglades during mosquito season.

At the end of the campground loomed a shady hammock. Wood parked a hundred feet away. Inside the van we donned our armor. The whine in the woods: It was created by millions of voracious mosquitoes beating their wings six hundred times per second. They're females, the biters, and they needed blood to produce their eggs. Even when protected, most humans can't stand it very long.

We ran.

"At Flamingo," Wood said, giggling, "we always give ourselves enough room to run. The idea is to shake off the mosquitoes before you get in the car." That little encounter proved to be a modest one. The worst place in the Everglades, perhaps in the world, was a hammock about six miles away, called Snake Bight Trail. Snakes live at Snake Bight, though you never saw them, probably because they were intimidated by mosquitoes. When U.S. Department of Agriculture scientists tested new repellents, they came to Snake Bight.

Wood suggested a saunter at Snake Bight. "They're going to be more aggressive here," he warned. Inside the hammock, they hovered, they dive bombed, they landed. They found the tiniest crevice, the dime-size spot not covered by netting, and located a patch of bare, succulent skin into which they drove their needles. "I'm not allergic to the bites anymore," Wood said, "unless they get me between the toes or between the fingers. Then I scratch like anybody else."

Bravely, but more likely foolishly, he withdrew his bare right hand from a pocket. In seconds, it was covered, back and front, by mosquitoes. "Now we run for the vehicle," he said. The mosquitoes, perhaps driven mad by Wood's blood, stayed with us stride for stride. No more than a hundred ended up inside the Plymouth with us.

"Now we do the Flamingo Flush," Wood said, hitting the gas. When our speed reached fifty-five miles per hour, he yelled: "Open the doors."

It took three Flamingo Flushes to blow out most of the mosquitoes.

The Calusa people who once ruled the southern Everglades built smoky fires out of black mangroves to thwart mosquitoes. Later, the pioneers erected houses over the water on stilts and cut down the mangroves to remove mosquito habitat. Flamingo's modern dwellers lived in air-conditioned apartments.

They placed mosquito netting over their wall-unit air conditioners. Otherwise, the mosquitoes would find a way in. Not long ago, the mosquitoes had located a hole in the netting of Wood's AC; in the middle of the hellish night, he pitched his tent on the bed. Only then could he and his Border collie, Darwin, catch a few undisturbed winks.

I asked Wood if he loathed mosquitoes. Not at all, he told me. He valued them. Some pollinated plants. But for the most part, they were key to the food chain, nourishing everything from bats to barn swallows. Wood was part of the mosquito food chain too.

Weeks before my visit, the park service had purchased new mosquito equipment for the neighborhood where employees live. Mosquito Magnets, which cost about one thousand dollars, emit heat, carbon dioxide, and a mosquito attractant. When the mosquito lands, it is vacuumed into the machine and dies. Mosquito Magnets have become a popular backyard accessory in Florida suburbs. The park service placed sixteen among the apartment buildings at Flamingo.

Roy Wood told me the new Mosquito Magnets were working overtime. Inside each machine was a bag roughly the size of a coffee can. Each bag could capture a quarter of a million mosquitoes. In normal places, a suburbanite never had to change the bag more than once a year, if that. But not at Flamingo, Everglades National Park. Roy Wood had to change mosquito bags twice a day. Otherwise, the masses of mosquitoes would burn out the machinery. "I guess the machines help a little bit," he said. "But you'll never see me outside barbecuing."

The other park weaponry was chemical. Around dusk, the mosquito control department truck came along, spraying a pesticide in the employee neighborhood. Any mosquito foolish enough to fly into the mist died instantly. The park's other billions and billions of mosquitoes, untouched by the spray, escaped. At the same time, seeing the battle taken to the mosquitoes made some employees feel better. They walked through the spray as if it were holy smoke.

Wood disliked chemicals; he never wore repellent. He preferred heavy clothing, netting, and courage. As the spray truck passed us, spewing poison, we huddled quietly inside the van, accompanied by a few dozen swamp angels, who had found a safe haven from the wicked pesticides outside.

Time for another Flamingo Flush.

38   Cracker Cattle

Joe Joe was in trouble again. He had hopped more than a few fences to look for girls. Joe Joe, who had irresistible brown eyes and a devilish personality, weighed more than half a ton. Joe Joe was fifteen years old, ancient for a bull, but no matter. When a cow went into estrus anywhere nearby, he was ready for business. Viagra be damned.

If a younger, larger bull got in his way, he swatted it aside with imposing horns. If an impetuous bull wanted a tangle, Joe Joe fought until competition lowed for mercy. If ten or more cows were ready to conceive on the same day, or even in the same hour, Joe Joe was unafraid of a challenge.

Sometimes his owner preferred that Joe Joe give another bull a chance to reproduce. On the day of my visit, Joe Joe was locked, pouting, in a sturdy wooden pen topped by barbed wire. It was Stalag 17 for an amorous bull.

"Joe Joe is the bull of the woods," said Joe Sumner, admiration in his voice. "But he's trouble."

Joe Sumner was a cattleman, just like five previous generations of kinfolk. Before Hillsborough became a county, Sumners were ranching cattle on the east side of Tampa Bay.

Not just any cattle. The Sumners raised scrub cattle, which in modern Florida were called Cracker cattle, named after the whip-cracking Florida-born cowmen who tended the ornery critters long ago. Cracker cattle were descended from stock brought to North America by Spaniards five centuries ago. They had all but disappeared, replaced over the decades by tastier and better-behaved breeds. But a few old-timers, as stubborn as their leathery cattle, refused to give up. Sumner, fifty-five, was one of them.

"I'm keepin' their genes alive," he drawled.

When the Spaniards got here, they brought the oranges that gave birth to the citrus industry. And they brought Andalusian cattle. A few cows and bulls got loose and started propagating. As centuries went by, their descendants got wilder and wilder, living not only on prairies but in the woods. Pioneer cowboys had to hunt them down on horseback and chase them through the pines and palmettos, cracking whips. Florida's original cowboys were called cowhunters.

Sumner was part of the tradition. His relatives were chasing cattle near Lake Okeechobee before Florida became a state. Something disagreeable happened—cowhunters often feuded with guns—and the Sumners moved north toward Tampa Bay sometime after the Civil War. When Joe was born near the end of World War II, the Sumner clan was an established name in Florida's scrub cattle business.

In some ways, scrub cattle were the perfect breed for the state. Over the centuries they had evolved to endure heat and flood, fire and humidity, ticks and mosquitoes, alligators and rattlesnakes. They didn't need special grass. What grew in Florida was fine with them. They didn't need a specialist to manage their breeding. Unlike other cattle, they grew up early and randy. A cow might have a calf like clockwork for a dozen years without the help of science.

But they were a heap of trouble too. Wary, they hid from cowhunters who typically had to drive the cattle from the Florida interior to a coastal city such as Tampa for shipping. They reacted to a rope or whip by going mad with horns and hooves. Many a horse and rider ended up scarred and crippled. Scrub cattle's meat was tough and stringy, though good enough for Floridians and for the Confederacy.

What almost led to the breed's extinction was big business. Ranchers, looking for better-tasting beef and less danger, began introducing other breeds into Florida pastures in the 1950s. Some of the new breeds mated with Cracker cattle, diluting genes and behavior. Like a lot of ranchers, Sumner made his living from the Braford and Brangus he bred on his two thousand acres. He never got rich, but few cattlefolk did, and he accepted it.

His passion was his little herd of scrub cattle. He was among the dozens of ranchers around Florida who kept at least a few of the cattle around for posterity, genes, and excitement. Even the state was involved and maintained a herd at Lake Kissimmee State Park near Lake Wales and

Paynes Prairie State Preserve near Micanopy. Rangers, who often had to catch them for veterinary care, dreaded the job because of the danger to them and their horses.

Sumner had grown up on horseback, though when I met him he was doing his cowhunting from the seat of his 1996 Ford F-150 while listening to Merle Haggard tapes. Scrub cattle, I learned, were tougher on trucks than a mall parking lot. His vehicle was dinged from bumper to bumper by cattle horns.

"My granddaddy, Jule Sumner, loved his scrub cattle," Sumner said as we bounced across a pasture. "And he always liked to keep a few mean ones around. He thought it kept the boys on their toes."

Julius Sumner was very much like his scrub cattle. He was wily and tough. He could shoot straight and look a bull in the eye. He read his Bible but also kept up with current events in the newspaper. He died in 1969, but even at the end, he did his best reading in an outhouse.

"He just didn't believe in using indoor plumbing," his grandson told me. "Just thought it was wrong to do that business in the house." The old man hated waste and preferred the *Tampa Tribune* to store-boughten toilet paper.

When he got a spare dollar, he'd buy land. One time somebody asked if he wanted to buy up the whole state: "Nope," he said, "just whatever land that joins mine." His grandson had the run of seventeen thousand acres of Jule Sumner's spread. "I can't tell you what it was like to grow up in that kind of Florida," Sumner said. During the school year, his daddy and uncle would pick him up at Ruskin Elementary with a horse trailer and a list of chores. "This was the 1950s. Cowboys was somethin' back then. My friends, they knew I had my own horse, and they figured I must know Roy Rogers, too."

He'd help any way he could, even if it meant being chased by a bull or two. But it was the summers that he lived for. "I'd go out in the morning with my shotgun and rifle and fishin' pole, with camping gear, and get on my horse." He'd be gone for a week. He'd shoot rabbits, quail, and turkey in the woods, catch bass in the Alafia, and gig frogs in Big Bullfrog Creek. Relatives throughout the acreage greeted him warmly. Among other things, he gave them fish and game.

After high school, he joined the navy and did three tours in Vietnam. He worked for the electric company, grew watermelons, got married, had children, and owned a tree farm. He sold some of his land. Finally, he was settled enough to join the family business.

"I'm home for good," he told me. He showed me the Cracker cow-hunter house he had built in the woods with his own hands. It was cypress and cedar and had big windows, wide porches, and a huge tin roof. The best thing about it, in his opinion, was the location: the woods, a far piece from everything else, including paved roads.

"I'd rather live here in a hollow log," he said, "than in the finest house in Hyde Park."

Sumner never ate his Cracker cattle. In fact, he spoiled them by bringing them treats. The day I was there they came running when they saw his truck approaching. He drove a mile and they followed a mile, lowing all the way and whacking the truck with their horns to get his attention. When Sumner finally stopped, he fed them by hand, all the while watching the horns from the corner of his eye.

"I'm a fat man now," he said. "I got to be careful." He had the girth of a man who had enjoyed life, it was true, but he still was confident enough to climb a fence or two. Tanned and leathery, his skin was covered with scars from encounters with barbed wire and Joe Joe's horns.

"He's over here a ways," Sumner said, driving to a wooden pen, to Joe Joe and his cellmate, Joe Joe's son.

Junior, four, had a bad reputation like his pa. He had taken to jumping fences too. He was young but liked his ladies. Trouble was, he had to beat his dad to them, and his dad didn't care for it. Junior was covered by scars from dad's horns.

As I watched, Joe Sumner climbed into the pen with his bulls. Feckless Junior, of course, trotted over and ate out of his hand. Enough was enough: Competitive Joe Joe lumbered over and swatted his boy out of the way. Now he ate from Sumner's hands. Junior tried to sneak back, and Joe Joe whirled, leathery horns flashing. I shut my eyes.

I was relieved when Sumner escaped the pen. He was bleeding, not from horns but from barbed wire. Florida elsewhere was rapidly gentrifying, but not within the Sumner clan.

A widower, Sumner had two grown daughters and a son. The son, twelve-year-old Joe III, lived with him. Like a lot of modern kids, he enjoyed playing video games and Little League baseball. But he also was being groomed to be a scrub cattle cowhunter like all the Sumners before. One day he would have to match wits with the likes of Joe Joe.

"I'm going to let you out soon, pretty boy," Joe Sumner cooed as flies swarmed his favorite bull's twitching ears. "But you like the girls a little too much sometimes."

Granny would have admired Joe Joe's grit. Granny was Emma Sumner, wife of outhouse-loving Jule. She died in 1992 at the age of ninety-six. An original woman's libber, she could ride better than a man and shoot better too. "Everybody in the county was scared to death of her," her grandson said. She liked to ride the range at night and surprise poachers with her whip.

She distrusted government. Several decades ago, a government bureaucrat came to her house, wanting to buy land where I-75 was proposed in southern Hillsborough. Emma told him he needed to disappear if he wanted to live until morning. A few days later, surveyors arrived anyway. She waved her shotgun. Eventually, the sheriff was summoned, and he convinced Granny that progress was inevitable.

But not without a fight.

"She called me over and said, 'Now, Joe, why don't you go over where they're buildin' that interstate and pull the stakes up?' I always obeyed my grandma. I pulled up the stakes. Course, next day they put the construction stakes back in. So I pulled them again that night.

"Soon they had lights and guards out there. I told my grandma, 'they're going to arrest me. I expect I have to quit.'

"She let me quit then. Now you drive through our old land when you're on the interstate."

39 Florida's Deepest Roots

The mayor reported to city hall wearing short pants. In Florida's Panhandle, only a few steamy miles from the Alabama border, the merciless sun beat down hard enough to leave bruises.

Nobody was shocked by Riley Henderson's summer wardrobe. In the little town of Jacob, where strangers stood out like scarecrows in a cornfield, everybody knew everybody else down to their favorite Bible verse. Folks born in Jacob usually died in Jacob. They were buried in Jacob next to their fathers and mothers and grandparents and great-grandparents in Jacob's ancient cemetery.

Although the rest of the world had paid Jacob scant notice for two centuries, the U.S. Census Bureau had finally called attention to its specialness in 2002. Tiny Jacob, whose 281 forlorn souls failed to rate a dot on most road maps, boasted the highest percentage of Florida-born residents in the state. Nearly 91 percent were down-home Florida natives. Contrast that to Tampa, where about 45 percent were true Floridians, and with St. Petersburg, where only 36 percent were born here.

I wanted to know more about Florida's most Florida city. So I drove up and found out.

Generations passed in Jacob, but few names changed. It all left Jacob stranded somewhere between antebellum Florida and the Florida most of us knew, the Florida of Disney, tabloid fodder, and international intrigue. In Jacob, where an hour seemed longer, there was no such thing as small talk. Folks graced supper tables with home-grown collards, yams, and fried chicken. Grown-ups relaxed on front porches in the summer evening and talked about the old days while their children played basketball in bare feet. After dark, the Milky Way—illuminating every backyard—served as a reminder to the religious-minded townfolk of the presence of the Almighty.

Here was something else I learned about Jacob: It was virtually an all-black town. Mostly poor, 25 percent of its families lived below poverty level. Jacob had no doctor or library or school, or even a store to buy a Band-Aid. A thirsty resident had to drive two country miles to the big highway to find a Dr Pepper.

Isolation, I learned, wasn't always considered a bad thing. In Jacob, it had blunted the harsh decades of southern segregation, and because everyone was poor, no one felt poor. When desegregation arrived in Jackson County, it carried a price.

"When things opened up for us after integration, and people felt better about going out of town, they could buy stuff cheaper than they could ever here," Mayor Henderson told me. "Our businesses died."

Like many in Jacob, Mayor Henderson welcomed prosperity—he hoped prosperity would encourage young folks to stay—but he didn't trust prosperity either. He wondered if it would ruin Jacob's small-town ways.

At forty-five, the mayor had lived in Jacob all his life except for the four years at Florida State University getting his degree in social work. His parents were born and raised in Jacob, as were his grandparents and several generations before. Manning his unpaid post at city hall, Henderson tried to define his little town.

"We're a fragile place," he finally said.

The mayor could walk around Jacob in about half an hour. He could drive through town in five minutes. Jacob had two paved roads and about half a dozen unpaved ones. It had stop signs but not even a blinking light. When the mayor drove his old Nissan pickup through town, he usually had the dusty roads to himself, at least during the day. Most Jacobites worked in nearby cities. "We're a bedroom community for other towns now," he said. "There's no work here. It's just a place to live."

Jacob had about a hundred modest houses and mobile homes. A few residents still lived in shotgun shacks, so called because a buckshot load fired through the open front door would pass down the hall and exit through the open back door. Those old-timey houses had tin roofs and crawl spaces just right for sleeping dogs.

By 2002, everybody was wired for electricity, and many homes boasted air-conditioning. Few people owned computers, but almost everyone watched television, though cable had yet to arrive. Eleven percent of Jacob did without telephones.

Years before, everybody had depended on wells or rain for their water, but today's Jacob had a water system, though it was failing and many residents used bottled water. Most homes were neatly kept and had vegetable gardens in the backyard or flower gardens in the front yard. Some residents posted religious scripture on their mailboxes or fences. "Gone to church," said a sign on the screen door of a house a few doors from city hall.

People counted their blessings.

"Praise the Lord!" declared Ardelia Blount, at seventy-eight a Jacob matriarch. "We were poor, but we never went hungry. And now we've got water, honey. We've got electricity. The Lord is with Jacob!"

What Jacob lacked in commerce, I discovered, it made up in religion. It had two churches, including the community's oldest institution, St. Mary Missionary Baptist Church, with another in the offing. The old city hall, which over the years had served as a hellsapopping juke joint, was now the New Beginning Outreach Ministry.

Practically everybody on the city council was a church deacon somewhere and sprinkled conversation with Bible verses. When Mayor Henderson was not attending city business he was a pastor at St. Luke Missionary Baptist Church in Marianna, the nearest big town ten miles away.

Jacob was a shady place with lots of pines, tall grass, and overgrown lots. Surrounding the town were peanut and cotton fields, usually owned by outsiders. Arthur Lee Rhynes, fifty-eight, was the exception. The last black farmer in Jacob, he devoted twenty acres to peanuts, forty to corn, and twenty to his cattle. He sold enough to break even, but it long had been a struggle. Outside Jacob, he worked nights as a prison guard.

He also liked to argue with city hall about his tax bill. "I don't mind paying city taxes," he complained to me. "But just tax my house. Don't tax my farm. I can't afford it."

"I don't blame him," said Mayor Henderson. "We hardly have a tax base. We're poor. We're always looking for money so we don't have to rely completely on state and federal funds."

Jacob got its name from Jake Jones, who lived down by the present railroad tracks about 250 years ago. Not much is known about Jones, except he was a white man. Only 5 percent of the population was white in 2002, and when I drove through town, folks took notice. Even before I arrived at city hall, Mayor Henderson knew I was on my way.

The mayor, when I met him, was stocky and tall and wore metal-rimmed glasses, a White Sox T-shirt, and sneakers. He was the third mayor since Jacob became an official city in 1984. He was proud of what was happening. "We've come a long way," he said. A few years ago, Jacob had purchased land for a city park. Recently, at a city council meeting, he accepted bids from contractors from outside of town who want to build a picnic shelter and a restroom and finish the basketball court at the park. "We've got fifty thousand dollars to do that work, and that isn't much," Henderson said. He'd put on hold his desire to bring Little League to Jacob.

Henderson drew no salary as mayor. One salaried city employee was Saundrette Taylor—clerk, manager, receptionist, and almost everything except handyman. Handyman was "Mister Buddy"—his real name was Alfonso White—who had spent virtually every day of his eighty-four years in Jacob.

"Mister Buddy" was a farmer until he got too old to handle a mule-hauled plow. He still wore a farmer's bib overalls to work and told me the big-city lights of Marianna, population 6,230, held no attraction for him.

Marianna is the seat of Jackson County, named after Florida's first governor, Andrew Jackson, who made war against Seminole Indians partly because they harbored escaped slaves. Mayor Henderson told me he remembered visiting Marianna as a boy and automatically going through back doors so as not to upset white residents.

Integration in the Panhandle came late, long after it arrived elsewhere in Florida. In the 1970s, when Henderson was a teen, the municipal pool in Marianna closed for the summer rather than admit black children. "But that was the beauty of living in Jacob," the mayor said. "In Jacob we weren't outsiders. It was our community. We had everything we needed."

The mayor graduated from an integrated high school, attended community college, and finished at FSU. He worked as a mental health counselor for years until he heard God calling him into the ministry. He has never thought about living anywhere but Jacob. "I travel, but I'm always glad to get home," he said. "I'm a small-town boy."

He pointed his truck down a red-clay road next to a forest. "Hey, look back there. See, back there in the bushes? We had a hole. Our swimming hole. It's dried up now, but every day in the summer, that's where we kids went."

They caught catfish and bream in the swimming hole and toted them home in time for dinner. Everybody had gardens and grew greens and field peas. Riley Henderson was probably the only mayor in Florida whose resume could include the ability to shell peas and slaughter a hog.

The hog work always happened on a cold Saturday in winter. The young men would do the killing, their wives the butchering, and their kids the removal of the hog's hair. Nothing went to waste. Lard was used to make lye soap, and bones were saved for soup or for dogs. All the while the old men sat under the biggest oak tree in the community and played checkers on a homemade board using bottle caps for pieces.

The Jacob community had a grocery and a gas station. No more. It had a mill where farmers brought their corn to be ground into meal and grits. No more. One family had a sawmill. Gone. Others had mills to grind cane stalks into syrup. R.I.P. Jacob had its own school. In 2002, kids went for schooling to Graceville or Cottondale, bus rides that lasted forty-five minutes.

Jacob in the old days wasn't heaven, of course. In segregated Florida, black communities often had to rely on folk medicine. Chicken pox was warded off by waving a hen over the fevered brow of the sick child. Mumps? "I still can't eat sardines," the mayor said. "The cure was rubbing sardine juice all over your body."

If somebody got really sick, if someone was badly injured, usually the white doctor in Marianna or Graceville might treat the black patient at the end of the day. Now modern medicine is accessible even to the poor.

"I grew up poor," Henderson said. In 2002, residents were better off, but only slightly, with median family income in Jacob $22,292. "But at least when I was a kid, you didn't know you were poor. Now it's different. Everybody has TV. It doesn't take long for a kid to know he can't have those hundred-dollar Michael Jordan sneakers."

He drove past his old house, today a storage shed. His father, Mingo, now dead, worked four decades for the railroad. The mayor's mother, Lottie Mae, ruled her family with an iron hand.

"What was that book Mrs. Clinton wrote? Oh. *It Takes a Village*," said the mayor. "That's how it was in Jacob when I was coming up. You go down the street and throw a rock and Aunt Susie on her porch sees you and says 'Stop it!' And that night, when you come home, your momma knows about it. We didn't need no crime watch in Jacob."

Kid hurled a stick across the dirt road.

"See that?" asked the mayor, slowing down. "That's me. That's me as a boy. See, we could amuse ourselves. What bothers me today is kids don't have imagination. Don't have to. They have toys, they have computer games, that provide the imagination for them. I like a kid who throws a stick."

Jacob never lacked ministers who kept a stern but loving eye on its youth. The Reverend George Bowers, forty-nine, started preaching in high school. When I talked to him, he'd been pastor for a dozen years at Jacob's largest institution, the red-brick, century-old St. Mary Missionary Baptist Church. Almost everyone in town was a member. He baptized them, married them, and buried them across the road in the cemetery among graves dug during slave times.

"We're important," Bowers said, taking a break from preparing his next sermon, which he planned to base on Genesis, chapter 37, about Jacob's family and the teenager Joseph, the one who had such a fine, colorful coat and many jealous brothers. "We devote a lot of time to working with the young people," said the Reverend Bowers. "We need to keep them on track."

His church had youth programs three nights a week. Basketball games went on way past dark. As boys worked on their layups, girls practiced dance steps nearby. "I want to be a singer like Brandy when I grow up," Shantae Hall, a sophomore at Cottondale High School, told me. A pop-music career might be difficult for a kid who stays in Jacob. "I like it here, but there's not a lot to do," she said. A perfect night for teens was a shopping trip to Wal-Mart in Marianna.

Many adults, including the mayor, worried about their restless children. They worried about the shack at the edge of town, rumored to be a drug house. But they wanted to believe Jacob kids stayed away. With no police department, Jacob had to rely on county law enforcement dispatched from miles away.

"We don't have a lot of crime to speak of," said the mayor. "At least nothing really violent. It's not like in the big cities where everybody is anonymous. Here, a kid who snatches a purse, why he's messing with somebody's mamma or grandmother."

The mayor and his wife, Wanda, had four children. The youngest, JJ, was poised to be a freshman at Graceville High School when we spoke. He hoped to become either a professional athlete or a lawyer when he grows up, even if it meant leaving Jacob.

His sister, Leticia, twenty-six, left Jacob to go to college. "It was hard," she told me. She remembered when she arrived at the University of Florida to claim her scholarship. "It was so big," she said. "But after a while I loved it. It was the idea you could find anything you needed right there, like a hamburger."

She graduated with a psychology degree, then got her master's degree at Troy State University, just over the state line, in Alabama. She counseled the mentally ill in Marianna and lived there too. "My idea was not to stay around here," she said. "My idea was to get on my feet and then move on. That's what most people my age who grow up in Jacob do. They just come back for Mother's Day and Father's Day. But then being close to home grew on me again.

"I still go back to Jacob all the time. That's where my family is, and my church. I keep praying that something is going to happen, that maybe somebody will open a store or something, right there in Jacob.

"Sometimes I really believe that will happen."

Over the years, a lot of government money was invested in building forty new houses for Jacob residents. At one time, many folks lived in shacks that lacked running water, bathrooms, and even electricity. Most people stood in line to get a modern home.

"Not everybody wanted to be modern," Mayor Riley Henderson told me during our last drive around town. Change, even change that promised a better life, was greeted warily in Jacob.

One elderly couple refused to give up their old shack. "They just didn't trust government," the mayor said. "They didn't even trust me, somebody they knew. See, a lot of the old people, years ago, they might leave town and go to the city and buy something, and sign their names on a contract, without really understanding what they were signing. What they were signing was an agreement to forfeit their property if they couldn't, say, pay off a piece of furniture. Some people actually lost their land because they signed the wrong piece of paper.

"Anyway, I couldn't get that couple to sign the piece of paper that would have gotten them a new home. Sure enough. We had a cold winter, a real cold night, and they stacked newspaper along their walls for insulation. They went to bed under their quilt, and somehow it caught fire. He was burned to death, and she was horribly burned.

"We don't have a fire department."

40 Shell Woman

At dawn the sand road was dim and foreboding. Dead limbs cracked under the assault of a wild hog—or was the morning's soundtrack courtesy of a bull alligator on the prowl?

Carol Sellars, the eighty-five-year-old shell woman of this remote island, headed for her appointed rounds. Walking briskly, she switched the humid air with a spindly branch from a wax myrtle. A twig was a poor weapon against hogs and gators, but it was perfect for knocking salt marsh mosquitoes out of her path.

As tough as a coconut, she lived in a modest house that lacked most conveniences. Rain provided drinking water; candles for the most part kept things bright enough at night. One of four full-time residents on the ten-mile-long island near Sanibel, she sometimes missed human company. Mostly she was happy in her solitude.

"What I love is the beach and the shells and the lack of people," she told me after I took a boat trip to see her.

For many modern Floridians, the idea of living on a remote island probably sounded romantic. They imagined icy drinks, bare feet, and Jimmy Buffett on the stereo. The reality, I discovered, was somewhat different. The drinks usually turned out to be warm; ravenous insects attacked bare skin; and batteries in the boom box lost steam in the tropical heat. The sun was so hot the landscape wanted to melt like a Dali clock, and when the afternoon squalls finally ended, one was tempted to cut through the Venusian humidity with a machete, already necessary for battling tropical vegetation that seemed to grow inches by the hour.

Like her writing hero Thoreau, Carol Sellars, known for wearing the occasional pith helmet and mosquito netting, marched to a different drummer.

"I guess some people consider me a little far out," she allowed. "But I don't think I'm that far out."

Afternoon. As thunder rumbled in the distance, Carol took notice. She respected lightning. Caught on the beach by weather one summer afternoon, she crawled home bush to bush, keeping her head low.

"You get used to the elements here," she said. June was horsefly season. Then would come the July and August rains and the inevitable mosquitoes. Hurricanes were most likely in the gulf in late summer or early fall.

Her house lay on a small hill. She never had been forced to evacuate. "When we have tropical weather, water comes right to my steps," she said. After storms, alligators swam into her yard and eyed her cat, Maggie, named after a character in a Tennessee Williams play.

Carol Sellars once had been a city person. She was born in coastal Maine and lived in New York City, Pompano Beach, Key West, Winter Park, and Sanibel. She enjoyed her years in Hawaii too. But like a cat on a hot tin roof, she jumped. She had been a teacher, a principal, a librarian, but her destiny was to be a beachcomber.

She also had been a wife—six times a wife. Max, her last spouse, was the best of the lot. "He broke my record for marriages," she said with a grin. "I had a cat, Murf, who lived to be nineteen. Of all my husbands only Max was with me longer than my cat." They were married twenty-three years and spent most of them on Cayo Costa.

Cayo Costa lay between two of Florida's most developed island escapes. Sanibel-Captiva was immediately south and Gasparilla Island, home of Boca Grande, was just north. Both were attached to the mainland by bridges. A true island, Cayo Costa could have been a million miles away from modern Florida. The state owned 90 percent of Cayo Costa and managed it as a wilderness. The state would acquire Carol's land after her passing.

The Florida park service allowed camping on the island and had a dozen primitive cabins that lacked water and electricity. There was no place to buy a hot dog or mosquito repellent. Overnight visitors had to like their nature untamed. Even thick-skinned campers, when they were honest, probably were relieved to return to the electrified mainland after a sticky, buggy night.

Carol, a passionate sheller and birdwatcher since her youth, loved Cayo Costa from the beginning. Her husband liked it too, but not enough to want to stay. "I'm not living anywhere that doesn't have electricity," he declared. But he softened, and they bought a prefabricated house that arrived, piece by piece, by boat. Max, a mechanic before retirement, added a workshop and a gasoline-powered generator that could produce a little electricity.

They both came to love their island, the birds, the sand, the wind, the rain, the gopher tortoises, the snakes, the scorpions, the lizards, the hostile flora that included prickly pear cacti almost everywhere they put their feet. "Max was a perfect husband," Carol told people years later. "He loved to cook and clean. His only vice was smoking."

When Max died of emphysema in 1994, Carol placed his ashes in a nearby canal. She decided she'd stay on the island until it was her time to go too. "I'm pretty healthy," she told me, knocking on her head as if it were driftwood. "Never have to go to the doctor. I've got my own teeth."

She had a small pension and Social Security and lived below what the federal government called the poverty level. Her expenses amounted to only a hundred dollars a week. The roof kept her dry, and the shower dripped enough for her to stay clean. Her bed was soft, and hummingbirds showed up at her kitchen window every morning.

"I never get bored." I believed her. She had her beach and her shells and her Emily Dickinson poetry. She also had—and let's be candid—a pretty serious vice. At noon, she fired up her gasoline generator that powered a dilapidated Philco television and watched the soap opera *The Young and the Restless*. "I'm slightly addicted," she said.

Like Thoreau, who escaped cabin fever at Walden Pond by sauntering from time to time to Concord, Carol enjoyed her civilization in small doses. She gave her boat to old friend Phil Capper, who weekly cruised over from the mainland to deliver groceries and maybe a little gossip. "She's as tough as Totch Brown," said Capper, talking about the late alligator poacher who was a legend in Southwest Florida. "But without Totch's bull."

Capper sometimes transported Carol to the civilization of Pine Island for groceries from the new Winn-Dixie and a visit to the beauty parlor. She always tried to look nice for guests. Charter-boat captains from the mainland brought shelling clients to Cayo Costa to meet her. She gave them shelling lessons. Some visited regularly and sent gifts.

She once shared her knowledge of island history with a University of Florida archaeologist; he returned later and tuned her piano. She liked to play Beethoven and Mozart, for the record, but probably her favorite gift of all time was a box of Girl Scout cookies, Thin Mints.

By radio she spoke daily to park rangers to let them know how she was doing. She had a cellular phone for emergencies, but couldn't remember any emergency to speak of. She was comfortable with people, even strangers.

"One man showed up and hung around the island. He drank beer all day out of this, like, German stein. He had a nice, firm handshake and I figured he was all right." He turned out to be an escaped convict who was eventually captured.

"You hungry?" Carol asked me. She fixed us hot dogs, lettuce, and tomatoes and poured us bourbon, chilled by tiny ice cubes eked out by an ancient propane refrigerator. Suddenly came a knock on the door, always a rare event. She jumped—in her eighties Carol was wiry enough to jump—as if she'd been shot.

"Oh," she said, looking out. "It's Walt." The old gentleman from a nearby island looked into her clear blues eyes and seemed smitten as a schoolboy.

"I thought you might be able to use a mess o' fish," he said.

"What did you catch?"

"Trout."

"I love trout. Thanks."

Walt, who wore overalls and a ball cap, stood quietly on the porch.

"Well, Walt. Thanks again," Carol said politely. Walt waited expectantly.

"Thanks for dropping by, Walt."

Bewildered by his dismissal, Walt departed, looking back all the way to his boat, just in case Carol was teasing.

The bourbon went down smooth and easy.

After supper, Carol watched the television news for the weather. At dark she shut the doors and windows against the night. She said she was afraid of the raccoons, which invaded her porch and messed with her things and hissed at her cat.

She was used to her sweltering home and said she always slept like a baby. I was less optimistic about my sleep prospects. In the dark I stumbled through the woods to a primitive state park cabin and passed the night watching palmetto bugs and swatting mosquitoes. At dawn, I returned to her cabin.

She was already awake and waiting, dressed in a bathing suit, flower-decorated pants and a mesh blouse. She already had eaten her regular breakfast: Total cereal with milk and eight strawberries, half a grapefruit, four prunes, and coffee.

Putting on her straw hat, she headed for the beach, about a mile away, in the dark. When we arrived, day had broken, and the yellow coreopsis flowers at the dunes were lit like neon. The wind rustled the sea oats and the waves crashed and she was filled with a transcendentalist's joy.

"Every day on the beach is different," she announced to the sky.

What shells had the gulf brought her during the night? Over the years she had collected thousands. Years ago she even sold some, a fact that embarrassed her now because she didn't believe conservationists should sell shells. She collected only for museums, herself, and visitors. She never took a live animal.

Walking, she picked up empty shells and dropped them into her bag. A kitten's paw. A sand dollar. A rough scallop. A Van Hyning's cockle. She planned to give them to a new friend.

A woman with purpose, she walked with head down, eyes glued to the sand, and hummed Beethoven's third symphony. "Only had back trouble once," she declared. "Fell off a horse when I was twenty-seven. I'm fine now."

Spiny jewel box. Sun ray Venus. Ivory tusk.

"This is a purple semele, *orange* form."

She had no scientific training. She had taught herself by reading books and talking to experts and collecting shells for more than half a century. "What do you think this is?" I didn't know. The correct answer turned out to be purple semele, *purple* form.

Lightning whelk. Cross-barred Venus. Florida fighting conch.

Thoreau, who valued self-reliance, simplicity, and nature's beauty, remained her role model. Her favorite quote from Walden was "Heaven is under our feet as well as over our heads."

Apple murex! Gaudy natica! Angel wing!

41 Wakulla Springs

The poet Walt Whitman wrote that a common field mouse was miracle enough to stagger sextillions of infidels. I feel the same way about mullet and springs. I was snorkeling at Wakulla Springs, a state park south of Tallahassee. The water was seventy-two degrees, which felt cold on ninety-eight-degree skin overheated by summer. Gooseflesh growing, I swam behind the mullet to stay warm.

Mullet are long, silver saltwater fish that do fine in fresh. They journey miles from the Gulf of Mexico to the springs. Cruising over eel grass in a school, they open and close their mouths as if chewing cud. When the fish at the front turns left, all the others turn left, cowlike, too. What goes through the mind of a mullet? Emerson once wrote that if we could understand a blade of grass we could understand the universe.

A mullet, I knew, was better at being a mullet than a person was at being a person. We are a bundle of anxieties about the future and regrets about the past. A mullet, fashioning life out of the present moment, is unlikely to worry about getting old and sick or ending up in the smoker at Ted Peters's restaurant in Pinellas County. A mullet exists to swim, eat, mate, rest, defecate, and to jump out of the water for reasons only mullet understand.

Springs are to Florida what the Grand Canyon is to Arizona—they're the natural phenomenon most likely to provoke the word "Wow!" Wakulla is most dramatic. The deepest freshwater springs in the world, it is two hundred feet from the water's surface to the floor of a cave from which four hundred thousand gallons of martini-clear water gushes forth by the minute.

If Florida had monsters, they would live down in the dark-blue void. In fact, one of my favorite childhood movies was filmed at Wakulla. In *The Creature from the Black Lagoon*, venal explorers try to capture the strange, air-breathing mutant lizard that, alas, falls in love with a beautiful scientist.

When dinosaurs ruled the Earth, Florida was under the sea. After the emergence, we had wonderful animals that included weird horses and wolves and elephants. At Wakulla, a glass-bottomed boat takes you over the springs and the bones of a mastodon, one of those ancient elephants. What other wonders are contained within that mystery?

There's something prehistoric about even today's Wakulla, from the primeval cypress trees to the abundant reptile life. Water moccasins sun themselves on lily pads. Turtles of every size and description swim along the bottom and crawl up onto logs for R&R. All the while, alligators glide in the distance, keeping their cool.

Gators grow large on this wide river; twelve-footers are common. In 1987, a college student snorkeled away from a roped-off "swimming area" down the uncivilized part of the river and was never seen alive again. During a boat tour later in the day, his corpse was discovered in the jaws of a mighty alligator.

The gator was destroyed—standard operating procedure after an alligator attack. Once a gator has sampled human flesh, the thinking goes, it will come back for more. That may be true, though a better strategy—for people and hungry reptiles—would be to discourage swimmers from invading the lair of the largest alligators. On the other hand, a lot of us are willing to take a chance for the pleasure of swimming in a spring. Of course, we're more likely to be struck by lightning while playing golf.

At Wakulla Springs, as I snorkeled through the eel grass, "secure" within the roped area and watched by lifeguards, my mantra was "safer than golf." Anything toothy coming up the fairway?

William Bartram, the eighteenth-century botanist who toured the South at the dawn of the Revolutionary War, was enamored by Florida's clear-water springs, "where the trout swims by the very nose of the alligator and laughs in his face, and the bream swims by the trout." Bartram was a Quaker who did not believe in violence, but he was a patriot too. It's no wonder he described the natural history of springs in democratic terms.

At Wakulla, bream do swim inches away from the noses of bass. Minnows swim uncomfortably close to the beaks of anhingas. Gators, of course, wait for the anhingas to make a mistake. Edging toward the spring, I dogpaddled in deep water and tried not to think.

"Look out, below!"

That was not me screaming about an attacking alligator. That was some skinny kid at the top of the twenty-five-foot tower at Wakulla. A potential jumper typically inches up to the platform's edge, retreats, takes a careful look, backs off, works up nerve, gets shamed by older kids, runs, and finally jumps, kicking legs and screaming all the way down.

"You call that a jump?" I mumbled to myself. Even with gray hair, I'm competitive. I climbed the tower and decided to give the whippersnappers a jumping lesson. In fact, I thought I'd show them how to do a cannonball. Standing on the platform, suffering vertigo, I decided to forsake anything fancy. Heart in my throat, I plummeted into the depths, feet first, feeling years younger than my age.

42 A Fisherman Named Hemingway

You sit in the fighting chair as the line buzzes off the reel, and you hold on to the rod that bows to the fish, a big marlin greyhounding away from your boat, then sounding, then coming up to jump again, and your back muscles ache even while you are thinking about Ernest Hemingway.

His memory was honored in 1999, the one-hundredth anniversary of his birth, on the day I visited South Florida's International Game Fish Association Museum. Museum displays included everything you would want to see and experience on the water—even virtual reality fishing. You could fight a pretend marlin on computer video and experience the power and brag and even write about what happened. It wouldn't come out sounding like Hemingway though.

Hemingway once was asked how a writer should train himself for literature. At the time, he and his interrogator were afloat far offshore and hoping for marlin.

"Watch what happens today," Hemingway answered. "If we get into a fish see exactly what it is that everyone does. If you get a kick out of it while he is jumping, remember back until you see exactly what the action was that gave you the emotion.

"Whether it was the rising of the line from the water and the way it tightened like a fiddle string until drops started from it, or the way he smashed and threw water when he jumped. Remember what the noises were and what was said.

"Find out what gave you the emotion, what the action was that gave you the excitement. Then write it down, making it clear so the reader will see it too and have the same feeling that you had."

When you live in Florida near water blessed with fish you become curious about them. What do they feel like in your hand? Are they slimy and do they stink? Are they strong? You pick up a rod, bait a hook, and try to find out.

Maybe you hope to bring home the fish, dress it out, and eat it for supper. Nothing wrong with eating your kill. But mostly fishing is for another reason. It is about connecting with something wild and primitive and stronger, pound for pound, than any human. It is about celebrating life and considering the possibility of death.

Hemingway knew it and knew how to write about it. In 1953, *The Old Man and the Sea* won a Pulitzer, and it led to a Nobel Prize in literature for lifetime achievement. Some critics consider *The Old Man and the Sea* inferior Hemingway. Perhaps those critics never felt the power of a big fish, never suffered the muscle cramps or the dry mouth, the triumph or the humility.

Even before *Old Man* were the Nick Adams stories. Nick Adams was Hemingway's alter ego. You read about Nick as a boy and as a young man trying to reclaim his innocence after returning from World War I. Read the "Big Two-Hearted River." It is a war story hidden in a trout stream.

"There was a long tug. Nick struck and the rod came alive and dangerous, bent double, the line tightening, coming out of water, tightening, all in a heavy, dangerous, steady pull. Nick felt the moment when the leader would break if the strain increased and let the line go."

He lost the fish anyway.

"Nick knew the trout's teeth would cut through the snell of the hook. The hook would imbed itself in his jaw. He'd bet the trout was angry. Anything that size would be angry. That was a trout. He had been solidly hooked. Solid as a rock. He felt like a rock, too, before he started off. By God, he was a big one. By God, he was the biggest one I ever heard of."

Hemingway grew up in Michigan but spent a dozen years in Florida and two decades in Cuba. In 1939, when he was living in Key West, he helped establish the International Game Fish Association, an organization devoted to sport fishing and conservation.

The IGFA opened a new museum in 1998 and its Hemingway exhibit on July 21, Hemingway's birthday. The museum, which cost $32 million, has a great hall with hundreds of mounted fish, all world records. There is the largest fish ever taken on rod and reel, a sixteen-foot, six-inch great white shark that weighed 2,664 pounds, caught by an Australian, Alf Dean.

Hemingway never had a world record. But he liked engaging big fish. He developed a way of catching marlin and bluefin tuna that thwarted shark attacks. Hemingway fought his marlin aggressively, putting all the pressure he could on them at the risk of a broken line. He knew if he let the fight go on long, the sharks would come up the current and smell the fear and weakness in the marlin and eat it.

Hemingway's fishing story was told through museum exhibits. There were pictures of him as a boy wearing a straw hat, fishing for trout in Michigan, and as a barrel-chested man posing with marlin or tuna. There were his manuscripts, written in pencil, and his old Royal typewriter, on which he tapped out journalism. There were paintings and tackle and letters and pieces from his old boat, built from black mahogany, the *Pilar*.

The memorabilia is property of a Hemingway museum near his former home in Cuba. The Cuban museum lent it to the IGFA at the prompting of Hemingway's family. The IGFA will keep the display for a while.

Hemingway helped establish Florida as a sports fishing mecca. He moved to tattered old Key West in 1928 because of the fishing and the quiet it provided a writer. He wrote in a studio next to his house. He stood and wrote in pencil in longhand. He finished *A Farewell to Arms* and wrote *To Have and Have Not* while a Key West resident.

He was disciplined in his writing, starting early, even when he had a hangover. He wrote for about five hours a day and liked to quit when the writing was going good and had momentum. Then he would put it out of his mind and go fishing.

Sloppy Joe Russell was his captain. They'd fish until nightfall and drink until drunk. Hemingway was an angry drunk. One time he broke the jaw of the famous poet Wallace Stevens because Stevens insulted his work in front of Hemingway's daughter. Another time he was discovered, in the morning's wee hours, using a dead tuna for a punching bag.

Hemingway got famous for his writing but also for his feuds and his marriages and his affairs and his hunting trips and fishing trips and plane crashes and the injuries he suffered. He became a larger-than-life celebrity. He became Papa, forever Papa, trapped as Papa.

He divorced his second wife and married a war correspondent. He divorced her and married again. He wrote less, fished more, battled his demons always. Critics delighted in claiming he was a drunken washout.

He still had a book in him. The public loved the novella *The Old Man and the Sea*. Critics said it wasn't his best work. The critics said the novel couldn't really be about an old man, Santiago, who had fished eighty-four days without catching a marlin, who finally catches a giant marlin only to lose it to sharks, and sails home defeated with the marlin skeleton to be met only by a neighborhood boy, his only admirer.

The critics said Poor Hemingway's novel could only be about Hemingway and his own sharks, the literary critics who enjoyed ripping him to shreds. Hemingway said no. He wrote a friend: "The sea is the sea. The old man is an old man. The boy is a boy and the fish is a fish. The shark are all sharks no better and no worse. All the symbolism that people say is shit."

No American writer has been psychoanalyzed more. No modern writer has been so imitated, praised, or criticized. Some people will tell you he is the greatest American writer of the century. Others will say don't be ridiculous. He was a man-boy who was overly fascinated by war and bullfighting and fishing and hunting. Macho died, thank heavens, with Hemingway.

Most agree he was the most influential writer of the twentieth century. He hated mush, hated the complex, valued economy. He wrote in short declarative sentences that packed an emotional wallop. He made writing look easy, but it never was, not for him or anyone else who yearns to be a writer. Yet he made people want to be writers.

People are fascinated still. There are thirty-seven books about him in print, and since his death editors and family have released five works of fiction, including the recently discovered *True at First Light*, which was published to catcalls. Hemingway had struggled with the book and knew enough to give it up as a bad job. It will no doubt make the publisher a lot of money.

After *Old Man*, he wrote for publication sporadically while drinking heavily. In 1960, he checked himself into Mayo Clinic to be treated, in secret, for depression. Shock treatments failed to help. He wrote a note to be posted on his hospital door. "Former Writer," the note said.

He was discharged and headed for his house in Idaho. His old tonics, hunting and fishing, didn't pull him out of his gloom this time. On the morning of July 2, 1961, his wife came downstairs and found him lying in his pajamas on the floor.

His favorite shotgun, a double-barreled 12-gauge, lay beside him. His wife told the press it must have been a gun-cleaning accident. Hemingway had had the last, memorable word. He blew his brains out.

"All stories, if continued far enough, end in death," Hemingway once wrote, "and he is no true-story teller who would keep that from you."

43 Man out of Time

Clifton Huston lived close to a Publix. A Kash 'N Karry and an Albertsons were in the neighborhood too. A good hospital was a five-minute car ride. Civilization had it all.

Sometimes he was sure he would trade the conveniences of modern life for the sweaty, gritty, primitive St. Petersburg of his youth, when acres upon acres of piney woods were thick with deer and vast palmetto prairies hid countless quail. Tampa Bay, as clear as moonshine, was home to ducks by the thousands.

If a man wanted to shoot his own food, or catch it on rod and reel, he had no problem finding critters, and no problem with the politically correct crowd who thought that hunting and fishing were horrors committed by barbarians.

Clifton Huston was eighty-one when I talked to him, and he felt like a man out of time.

"Why the hell does a newspaper want to do a story about me?" he roared when I tracked him down. A man out of time was no fan of modern media. He was sure that a pointy-headed reporter was looking to blame America's violence on God-fearing, gun-owning folks like himself. Why should he cooperate? Okay, he'd talk. But first he had to do something about his itchy trigger finger.

"Don't know if I can still shoot worth a damn," he growled. Joints aching, he sprawled belly-down on the hard ground, took careful aim, and fired his trusty Winchester. The smoke cleared; he used a scope to check out the results. He hadn't slain a deer, but at least he had hit the target an inch or so from the bull's-eye.

Of course, he couldn't fire at tin cans in his backyard like he once did, when the woods began blocks from his door and everybody seemed comfortable with firearms. Now he did most of his gunning at the last big-time range in Pinellas County, the Wyoming Antelope Club, and toted a fourteen-pound rifle that featured a veritable telescope for a sight.

Once he had been among the best shots in North America, finishing near the top of the national shooting championships held in Ohio and in Canada. Now he had an old man's weak eyes and arthritis. "I damn sure haven't quit," he said. "When I compete I hope to win, even if I don't have a chance."

He looked forward to fall. When the air cooled in November, when the deer were in rut and a trifle careless, he hoped he might get lucky. He might go hunting in North Florida or in South Georgia, but he intended to get his deer, perhaps an eight-point buck that would provide a year's worth of meat.

"I've got me some venison in the freezer right now from last fall," he said. "I know that offends some people, but I don't give a damn. Hell, modern folks don't know even where food comes from. Publix, they guess. Hell, they don't even know hamburger is meat."

The man out of time was born in Ohio. His dad, a bricklayer, found temporary work in Florida. Driving across the state from job to job, Jessie Huston noticed alligators, deer, and panthers roaming dirt-road highways and decided to stay. An outdoorsman, he moved his family to Pinellas in 1925.

"We lived in a place that's gone," Huston said. "It was called Pine City back then. It was the north end of St. Pete. Poor people from all over the country lived there. We had neighbors who walked to Florida from Iowa carrying everything they owned in a wheelbarrow."

Nobody had to go hungry.

"My granddad had a big garden. Over at the bayou—it's close to where the VA hospital is now—you could catch trout and redfish on every cast. Take a boat into the gulf, and you got all the grouper and kings you wanted.

"My dad gave me my first gun when I was twelve. He said, 'Don't hurt yourself.' It was a Model 12 Remington Pump, a .22, and I still have it. Game was everywhere. Rabbits, squirrel, ducks, quail, dove. And I got me my first deer about then.

"Now let me tell you something about my dad. He didn't let work get in the way of his hunting. November rolled around, and he'd tell the boss, 'See you in two months.' Boss would say, 'You can't leave!' Dad would leave anyway.

"My dad died a poor man. But he was happy. Ain't nothing wrong with that."

Shooting his rifle, talking about the old days, he worked up an appetite. He suggested we eat lunch at the Family Place Restaurant in his St. Petersburg neighborhood. It was one of those old-fashioned eateries where a man can find meatloaf, soup, and a vegetable for less than five dollars. The old carnivore ordered heart-friendly bean soup and salad. Even a man out of time couldn't live by meat alone.

"Don't mind me shaking the table," he bellowed, threatening his greens with a knife. "I've got to cut up this grass here." His wife, Kitty, leaned over and made a "quiet down" motion with her fingers.

"I've shot so many guns I'm hard of hearing," Huston said in a more civilized tone.

"I'm not deaf," said Kitty, still an expert hunter and markswoman herself. "And I shot."

Her husband grinned. They met at St. Petersburg High School on the first day of school in 1936. She was a sophomore, and he was a year older. He approached her in the courtyard and asked her name. She thought to herself, "Who's this bold guy?" Then she told him: "Puddin' tame. Ask me again and I'll tell you the same." In depression-era America, her sassy reply qualified as a put-down.

But in homeroom, her name was called, and he grinned with satisfaction. They began dating and married after graduation. When I talked to them, they were looking forward to their sixty-third anniversary, still held hands, and laughed when they exchanged old hunting stories.

"Remember that guy in Ocala National Forest who chased the bear . . . ?" Kitty began.

"He forgot his gun," Clifton roared. "Suddenly the bear rears back and smacks his dog and chases him."

Clifton and Kitty heard a piercing cry from the deep woods. The hunter had no gun, but at least he was carrying a police whistle. Nobody knows if the bear laughed at a hunter armed with only a whistle, but at least it gave up the chase.

"Florida has some big-ass bears," Clifton roared. All over the restaurant heads turned our way. Kitty put her fingers to her lips. Her husband hushed up.

If Huston could have hunted for a living, he would have. But like his dad, he was a bricklayer and later the owner of a construction company that helped transform the county from a rural paradise to an asphalt jungle that eventually ruined the hunting. The change took a while, and for years he still found places to fish and hunt and hobnob with like-minded folk.

The fishing wasn't as good in modern Florida. There was no place to hunt anywhere near. At least he had his guns. He liked working on his guns. In his sprawling old house—over the decades the Hustons had added rooms and nooks—he was most proud of his grand workshop. He enjoyed building his own rifles and repairing rifles and shotguns belonging to friends.

He had every tool, every machine, known to a gunsmith. Even in old age, he was a 12-gauge shotgun of a man, robust and with a kick. When he bumped into me by accident while moving around his workshop, I was swatted aside like a sand fly. He had huge hands and gun grease under every fingernail.

"Modern people hate guns," he said. To him, Charlton Heston was not the Moses of the film *Ten Commandments* but the NRA mouthpiece who would give up his gun when liberals pried it away from his cold dead fingers.

"Most of what I do is shoot at targets and do hunting," Huston went on. "I never hurt anybody. If I don't eat it, I don't kill it."

It had been years since hunting was permitted in Huston's home county, which had very little wilderness remaining and nearly a million people, shopping centers galore, and traffic-clogged highways. He preferred remembering a simpler time, when ducks swam in mile-long rafts along mangroves in Tampa Bay and a good man with a shotgun could get enough to feed his family. Now most of the mangroves were gone and with them, the ducks.

In his time, he knew how to hit a target, even if it was more than a half mile away. He'd adjust his sight to fire well above the bull's-eye, figure out wind velocity, and even account for the rotation of the Earth.

"It's complicated, and I won't bore you. The only thing I'll tell you is when you hit a son-of-a-bitch target, there's no finer feeling in the world."

A man out of time wasn't sure he could hit targets with the same success.

"I can't hear, my eyes are funny, I've got bursitis in both knees, and my back is about gone. But I ain't complaining. My life has been damn good."

44 For a Song

"Old people get lonely, and we like to talk," Charles J. Milazzo told me. "I hope you don't mind."

I didn't.

"Thank you for coming over. I wanted to talk to somebody. I wanted to talk about my music. I have written over two hundred songs. I'll bet you didn't know that. I have songs that would knock Irving Berlin for a loop."

That was saying something. Berlin wrote "God Bless America," not to mention other standards.

"I'm the Italian Irving Berlin," Milazzo continued in a Brooklyn accent. "Here, let me show you some of my songs."

He almost lost his balance as he shuffled to a cabinet filled with notebooks containing words and music to his songs.

"I wrote this one when I was in the service and stationed in Japan. It's called 'Have a Good Time When You're in Your Prime.' I liked this one: 'Sayonara Boogie.' How about 'So Ripe for Love?' 'Stolen Sweets?' I wrote them all, and no dirty stuff."

None were hits. He never made a dime. He wrote them for fun. He had been many things in his life—writer, editor, soldier—but he preferred thinking of himself as a songwriter.

He was ninety-two and living alone when I visited. He'd been calling for weeks and asking me to come. To tell the truth, people call newspaper reporters all the time. Sometimes the callers have a story, sometimes they just want someone to talk to. But that's okay. We all need somebody to talk to.

Charles J. Milazzo told me he'd served in the army for more than three decades. He told me he was in the infantry when it stormed Omaha Beach during World War II, but most of his military career was spent keeping morale high, writing plays, making music, and putting on shows for other soldiers. He wanted to think he had one more good song left in him.

"Let me tell you what makes a good song. Good melody. Naturally, you say. I like to write in minor keys. A minor key song stays with you. And of course you want to have universal lyrics. A universal lyric is usually happy."

The telephone rang in his den. It took him so long to hobble to the phone I was sure he'd miss it. But he didn't. It was a neighbor thanking him for putting a bag of grapefruit next to her fence.

"You're welcome," he said and hung up.

"I've got a good grapefruit tree," he told me. "Do you like grapefruit? Be sure and take some! Well, where was I?"

I asked what goes into writing a good song.

"I like topical songs. I like songs with a moral. That's why I wrote 'Very Soon.'"

Charles J. Milazzo had retired from the military a quarter of a century ago. Like so many northerners, he and his wife, Jeanne, settled in Florida. They liked the climate and the birds and the wonderful water.

"'Very Soon' is about the environment. You can't help noticing the environment is not what it used to be. Am I right? Did I show you my environmental folder?"

He hadn't.

"I clip out stories from the newspaper about the environment and put them in my folder. I try to stay on top of things. I'm pretty organized that way. I'm always looking for an idea."

Pencils and papers lay neatly on every table in the house waiting for inspiration.

"You remember that song a while back? I think a Negro singer wrote it as a benefit for people who were starving."

Michael Jackson and Lionel Richie had written "We Are the World."

"I want 'Very Soon' to be like that one. I want it to do some good. I had that idea for a song and wrote it all down. Then I sat at my keyboard. Did you know I also play the ukulele? Did you notice the ukulele when you came in?"

As a matter of fact, I had.

"When I was in the army in Hawaii, I picked up a ukulele and learned it pretty fast. Once you can play three or four chords, you're an expert.

But I usually write my music on the organ. I have a drum machine and a tape recorder. I try to get it all down on the tape recorder. Where am I going with this? Old people, their memories aren't as good."

I reminded him he'd been talking about "Very Soon."

"I wrote this song for the environment. I didn't want it to be gloomy. But the first two choruses are gloomy. Still a negative angle going. Then I turn the song upside down. I make it positive. We're going to be okay, because we're going to do something very soon."

In a wobbly voice, he sang the happy part of "Very Soon."

But if we do things the right way
We'll sing loud a joyful song
It will convey we're here to stay
Very long!

"I thought of calling it 'All Too Soon.' But I think this is a good song the way it is. I think it'll hit people right between the eyes."

I told him I hoped so.

"I wish somebody would promote the song and sing the song. I wanted George Bush to have it for his campaign, but my friend Tom said no, that Al Gore would be the one because he cares more about the environment. But one thing led to another, and we never got it to either of them. I hope the president gets to hear my song someday."

I told him stranger things had happened.

"I've had my ups and downs, you know. My wife passed away last year. A lovely woman. So, so sick. Everything just went wrong at once. She was only eighty-four. Now I'm alone. Somebody cleans my house, and my daughter stays with me on the weekends, but I'm lonely. That's the worst thing about getting old. You're lonely. You want somebody to talk to."

It had to be difficult.

"Well, that's the way it goes. Me, I've had two heart operations. My days are at an end. I could drop dead any minute. I come from a family of twelve kids, and I'm the last one left. I try to eat well, I try to sleep, I try to pray."

Prayer can be important.

"Yes, it is. Listen, thanks so much for coming over. I know I talk too much. I've been talking your darn ear off. Thanks for listening to an old man talk."

"Very Soon"

Very soon! All too soon!
We may fight to stay alive.
Weak or strong! Just how long
Can we manage to survive?
When the air and soil and waters
Are polluted everywhere
Then our future sons and daughters
Will have nothing left to share.

45 Soul Food

He gives food in abundance.
—Job 36:31.

Gloom. Doom. Death. I had been reading the newspapers. I had been watching television. Everything I read and heard was about gloom, doom, and death. Elzo Atwater Jr. told me to banish dark thoughts. They make a man feel old and defeated.

"How old do you think I am?" he asked. "I'm forty-five. I am forty-five years old! I'll be forty-six in the fall. Nobody ever believes it. Ha! I fool 'em every time."

He seemed younger. His eyes blazed with youth—they appeared alert and happy. "God is good," he said. "God is great."

In church he had learned forgiveness—even for the man who left him for dead. Then again, someone at peace can find joy in a cold glass of lemonade. Elzo Atwater Jr. made a great glass of lemonade. His siblings and his nieces and his nephews were good at lemonade too. They made it and sold it at the family cafeteria at 895 22nd Ave. S, a few blocks from where I work. During the summer, when I develop a craving for their lemonade, I tried to visit often.

Lemonade cost a dollar a glass, though some folks inevitably offered to pay double. Of course, Atwater customers visited for more than the lemonade. In the morning, Atwater's Cafeteria was well stocked with eggs, grits, bacon, and sausage. The dinner and supper menu usually featured fried chicken, pig's feet, collard greens, and butter beans. For some people, Atwater's meant country comfort cuisine. For others, what was on the plate could only be classic soul food. Smart ones washed it down with lemonade.

Elzo Jr. helped his parents, Elzo and Mattie Atwater, start the cafeteria in 1977. Before that his father and mother owned the Harlem Cafeteria near Jordan Park.

Soul food. Photo by Jamie Francis.

The Atwaters had seven sons and a daughter. They all learned the restaurant business from their parents and from Annie Wright, a well-known southern cook who ruled the kitchen with discipline and love. Any Atwater could fire a stove, cook chitterlings, and scrub a pot. It was in the blood. Mike Atwater, thirty-five, was manager when I visited, but he counted on kin to help.

In the afternoon, Elzo Jr. showed up to cook meatloaf, corn bread, and black-eyed peas for sale that evening at the cafeteria, at his concession booth at the baseball stadium, or for a catering job. While he cooked he helped himself to a cold glass of lemonade.

"It's the real thing," Elzo Jr. told me in the steamy kitchen while we watched his eighteen-year-old nephew, Deonta Atwater, make lemonade the Atwater way.

"I'll show you the Atwater way," Deonta said. "Please follow me."

He led me to a walk-in refrigerator and grabbed a box of lemons. "Most places, they use concentrate," he said. "Not Atwater's. Here we always start with fresh lemons even if it's more work."

As his uncle watched critically, Deonta sliced his lemons, flipped them into a five-gallon bucket, and crushed them with a huge potato masher. He added water and a big spoonful of sugar. He threw in ice and ladled himself a cup. He made a face, shook his head "no." He squeezed another lemon and tossed in an extra handful of sugar. That, Mister, was Atwater lemonade.

"Family recipe," Elzo Atwater said. "We got family recipes, yes we do, isn't that right?"

"That's right," said his nephew. "We won't tell the recipe. That's the family rule."

Elzo stopped laughing. "I was just thinking. I was just thinking we're coming up on my anniversary."

I asked how long he had been married.

"Not that kind of anniversary." He lifted his shirt and showed me the scar on his right side.

"In August it'll be nineteen years ago that they found me right on the floor, exactly where I'm standing right now. If it wasn't for the glory of God I would have bled to death."

> For I was hungry and you gave me food.
> I was thirsty and you gave me drink.
> —Matthew 25:35

Atwater's was not one of those cookie-cutter eateries that seem to be springing up all over. Inside it was dark and a little dusty and felt twenty degrees too warm. The air conditioner worked, but barely. Decoration was spartan, aside from a few family photographs and simple paintings. It lacked the ferns, clever signs, and oak tables often found in suburban restaurants.

The tables had plastic coverings and legs that didn't take the trouble to reach the floor at the same time. If you were too aggressive while slicing your pork chops, the table rocked dramatically and spilled your lemonade. Regular customers learned the art of folding a napkin for strategic installation beneath the short table leg.

Atwater's once had more customers. In 1996, a neighborhood civil disturbance cost the cafeteria the most nervous white clients. Some trickled back, but not enough for anyone to celebrate. Still, Atwater's remained a democratic place. Customers included local preachers, church ladies wearing flowered hats, a sweaty lawn-maintenance guy, a bail bondsman, the police chief, and even the mayor. Jeb Bush, the governor, stopped for beef brisket, collard greens, macaroni and cheese, and the lemonade Deonta Atwater had squeezed moments earlier.

Sundays were the busiest. When church let out, folks by the dozens showed up in their best clothes. They took up every table and even lined up on Martin Luther King Jr. Street for a chance to come in. Preachers took possession of tables in back and discussed their respective sermons. The neighborhood drunk sometimes staggered in—he had saved three bucks in nickels and dimes—and bought breakfast. The grits stuck to his bony ribs better than a good homily.

Elzo Atwater Jr. was born when Ike was president and civil rights were a new concept. He learned to work and cook and study. After high school he got married—he and Janet have been together going on three decades—and headed for college.

He cooked during the day, studied at night, read his Bible every Sunday at Macedonia Free Will Baptist Church. Most of all he wanted to make Atwater's Cafeteria famous. Filled with ambition, he started a catering company and was able to expose Atwater food to people who otherwise might be timid about frequenting a restaurant in the black community.

It was a little after midnight on August 22, 1982. Elzo, then twenty-six, and his brother Michael, then fifteen, had just catered a supper. They parked outside their cafeteria to unload pots and pans. Two men materialized from the dark. One had a gun. He forced them into the back door of the empty restaurant and demanded money.

Michael turned over a twenty-dollar bill. Elzo had nothing but the check he'd gotten for the catering job. The guy with the gun said to open the cash register. Not even a dollar. He told the brothers to lie down.

Michael moved quickly. Elzo was a little slow. He wanted to pray first. "Lie down!" Michael shouted at him. "He's got a gun to your head!"

The gun went off. Twice. Michael was hit in the arm. A bullet entered Elzo's chest and lodged in the left ventricle of his heart.

And whenever you stand praying, if you have anything against anyone, forgive him, that your Father in heaven may also forgive you your trespasses.
—Mark 11:25

"I'm fine now," Elzo Atwater Jr. was saying. "I was weak a long time, but now I got more energy than I know what to do with, praise God."

The police arrived after the shooting. Then the ambulances. Michael suffered a flesh wound—after treatment he went home. But Elzo was close to death. Six weeks in the hospital, he endured four heart operations. He needed more blood than was available at the hospital.

Outraged by the crime, people from all over the community donated blood. They included white people who had never met Elzo Atwater Jr. and white people who had enjoyed eating his food and drinking his lemonade. But most donors were black folks from the community, mostly people who had never donated blood before. A record 113 gave their blood.

The robbers were arrested after another crime. One became a witness against the shooter, Larry Martin, who was convicted. Elzo Atwater Jr. felt well enough to attend the sentencing. He didn't mean to, but he wept when he spoke to the judge while looking at Martin. He asked the judge to put Martin away.

Martin, who was twenty-three at the time of the crime, received a long sentence. Department of Corrections prisoner No. 090099, Martin now resides in a Sumter County prison scheduled to be his home until the year 2033.

"I'm glad," Elzo Atwater Jr. said quietly. "He is probably the kind of person who might hurt somebody else. He didn't have to shoot me. If he'd asked me to cook for him, I would have been happy to feed him. But he shot me."

He stirred ketchup into his meatloaf.

"I have forgiven him. What's more important is God has forgiven him. I hope he thinks about that. I hope he prays."

Elzo Atwater Jr. believed in prayer.

"People say to me, 'How can you be so nice?' but it's not a matter of being nice. If you know your Bible, you know it's not your place to judge. God is the judge. You can't hold the world hostage for what happened to you in the past. It will just make you sick. Better to live in the present, thanks be to God."

That was his recipe for life. It was a little like his recipe for lemonade. Add sweet to the bitter. Suddenly an otherwise sour concoction becomes more than palatable. It's grace.

"Well, listen. You'll have to excuse me. I have some cooking to do. I have a catering job this evening, and I've really got to finish this meatloaf. You ever taste my meatloaf? It's the best. And did you ever hear about my peach cobbler? You've never tasted anything as good as my peach cobbler."

46 Dark Night of the Soul

No Light, but rather darkness visible.
—John Milton, *Paradise Lost*

Try an experiment sometime. Wander outside and aim your nose at the heavens. If you like stars, if you grew up in a dark place where the night sky inspired wonder, crowded coastal Florida will seem to you something like a paradise lost.

Maybe a street lamp blocks your view of the constellation Leo, or your neighbor's porch light blinds you to the Milky Way. Comets? Maybe the Space Telescope will post cool photos on the Internet.

Away from coastal Florida, away from big cities and light pollution, the sky puts on a grand show.

"Looky here," Melissa Sue Brewer was saying as she stabbed the air with a glowing cigarette on a summer evening, "when it's dark here it's really dark. We like the dark in Myakka City."

Blond and tan at fifty, Brewer had invited me out for a visit to her rural Manatee County home. Right off she told me her story. She had been a conscientious cop, a compassionate nurse, a tireless tree planter, an ardent bird watcher, and a burr under bureaucratic saddles.

Now, in what seemed like a hopelessly quixotic gesture, she was rallying neighbors and arranging meetings with bureaucratic big shots she hoped would help her ward off the lights that come with the progress that at the turn of the century marched inexorably toward Myakka City.

Brewer wanted dark skies for reasons beyond just enjoying the stars, which, by the way, were spectacular in eastern Manatee County. She was convinced that for quality rest, her precious birds and foxes and snakes needed a black night.

There also was the innocence factor. She wanted her community to stay a community, a town with old-fashioned front porches where lovers

Saving the sacred night. Photo by Kevin Sullivan.

could rock together on the swing, gaze into each other's eyes, and admire a starlit black sky.

"We're not against progress in Myakka City," Brewer said in her fried catfish accent. "But goldang, why can't you have stars and have progress?"

There was one more reason Melissa Sue Brewer wanted to keep the skies dark. For more than a decade she grew sad and afraid after dusk, a natural consequence of what happened a long time ago, in the deep woods, on a dark night.

"A bad man took the dark away from me," Brewer told me. "Myakka City gave it back."

Myakka City had no traffic light, unless I wanted to count the blinking beacon where State Road 70 met Wauchula Road. It had a convenience store and a restaurant and a place to buy feed. It had a medical clinic but no hospital. It had a fire station and a school but no library. It had churches and tomato fields and sod farms.

Mostly Myakka City had pastures and orange trees and maybe a thousand or so folks spread far and wide, in fine ranch homes, tin-roofed

Cracker houses, and dilapidated trailers. Brewer moved from Pinellas County in 1996. Her cute white house lay among the palmettos and pines in woods filled with the music of twittering birds. Even with detailed directions, her property was a challenge to find.

Parking by her back door around dusk, I was careful exiting my truck in case rattlesnakes were warming themselves on the driveway. When I rang her bell, I braced myself for what sounded like the Hound of the Baskervilles. The mighty roar alerted the household that a stranger was about.

Melissa Sue's husband, Phil, creaked open the door. Blackie, their ferocious Lab, tried to lunge past. Phil harvested cheese from the fridge and handed it through the door to me. I handed the cheese to Blackie— with care. The big dog accepted my bribe but never stopped watching.

Phil, a police sergeant in St. Petersburg, commuted a hundred miles a day. Many folks from Bradenton, Sarasota, and St. Petersburg had discovered Myakka City in the 1990s. If Paul Revere had been alive, he'd have been yelling, "The people are coming."

Melissa Sue and Phil told their neighbors: "That's right. People are moving in. But looky here. Maybe we can get them to turn off the lights and hang on to the dark and our country life."

After sundown, looking west, folks in Myakka City saw progress headed their way. They saw the bright lights of I-75 fifteen miles away, and beyond it they saw the glow of Bradenton. Closer to home, the Amoco under construction on the corner was sure to feature wonderful gas station lighting. The Brewers had a growing galaxy of neighbors who loved porch lights and had installed pole lights next to their garages.

Brewer and her husband knew an astronomer in Bradenton who once was arrested for shooting at the street lamp that ruined his view of Mars. Melissa and Phil intended to keep their pistols holstered at least for the time being. "I'm asking folks to turn their lights out," Melissa Sue said. "I'm asking real nice. I'm hoping it'll be easy peasy."

Imagine how your neighbors would respond to such a request. As the Bible said about those unfortunate wretches who were cast into darkness, there would be wailing and gnashing of teeth. "Are you nuts?" somebody would ask. Someone else would tell you about the great-aunt who got mugged on a dark night. Someone else would wonder what's special about stars.

Maybe it was luck, maybe it was Melissa Sue Brewer's steel magnolia personality, but things had gone easier peasier than she expected.

Like a cactus rose, she was prickly yet sweet. She was a sophisticate who enjoyed visiting Manhattan for the theater and an Earth Mother who liked nothing more than planting an oak. She was an intellectual who liked philosophical discussion about new ideas and a conservative who lived by old-fashioned values. She acted soft as a summer dress—"oh, lamby," she called people she barely knew—but could cuss like a saddle-sore cowboy who got caught in the rain.

She avoided alcohol but smoked Carltons as if they were candy cigarettes. She almost never answered the phone—the news of the murder had reached her by phone—but enjoyed chatting with strangers and friends over the Internet. Or she accosted them in their driveways.

"You know, I never even thought about it," said Daniel Bryan Beachler, who lived on the other side of the woods. After a talk with Brewer, he extinguished his porch light. Neighbors Polmerine Hamilton, Jack Routsong, Bernard Borgeron, Scott Runge, Pedro Martinez, and Carl Blue were persuaded, too. "Good idea," agreed Ginki Miller, editor of the *Myakka City News*, which published an item about the splendid advantages of the dark. In the next week, more porch lights switched off.

An air force brat, Brewer grew up all over the place and was interested in everything, especially literature, especially William Faulkner, he of the stream-of-consciousness prose and southern Gothic sensibilities. After she and Phil moved to Myakka City, a pair of rare scrub jays built nests in their palmettos; Brewer named them Sartoris and Snopes after Faulkner characters.

But that's getting ahead of the story. As a kid, Brewer considered becoming a nun but discovered rebellion. In college, she studied chemistry and ended up in St. Petersburg inspecting sewers, "where I knew every albino cockroach by name." She tried police work. It was noble toil, though she hated the domestic squabbles and calling for a backup only to learn that other cops were busy and she'd have to go it alone with some drunken lout who had just beaten his wife.

Eventually she joined the state conservation commission. An animal lover, she became an expert at gutting hunter-slain hogs so scientists could study the remains. She didn't join the wildlife agency for that: What she wanted was to be a game warden, like Peggy Park.

She and Peggy would shoot target practice at Lower Hillsborough

Wildlife Management Area and swap tips about strengthening their trigger fingers. Afterward, they would wolf down boiled peanuts and roll their eyes about the good old boys they worked for and policed.

Peggy Park became a regular officer; Melissa Sue Brewer joined the reserves. Peggy's territory was the last real wilderness in Pinellas, a ten-thousand-acre preserve near the Pasco-Hillsborough line known as Brooker Creek. But Pinellas is so urban she spent most of her time writing traffic tickets on U.S. 19.

Patrolling the woods one night in December 1984, Peggy Park came across two men in a van. Hunting is illegal after dark in Florida. They told her they had no guns, but she found a Luger under the front seat. Peggy asked for the big man's driver's license. Walking to her patrol car, he smashed a flashlight over her head. She squeezed off a shot but missed. Martin Grossman was six feet four and weighed 225 pounds. Peggy Park was barely five feet four and 115. He wrenched her gun away, breaking her fingers.

About an hour later, the phone rang at the Brewer house in St. Petersburg. Phil answered. A colleague told him a wildlife officer was dead at Brooker Creek. Even now, people ask Melissa Sue Brewer why she moved to Myakka City. She tells them:

"On account of I was tired of having eyes that saw bad boys wherever I looked."

And the light shineth in darkness;
and the darkness comprehended it not.
—Gospel according to St. John.

She quit law enforcement, returned to school, and got a new degree in nursing. She went to work on the AIDS ward at Bayfront Medical Center, at the Veteran's Administration Hospital, and at private homes. Her husband stayed in police work. They scrimped and saved to buy their land in Myakka City, where the night soundtrack was not provided by sirens, but by hooting owls. She woke early and put feed out for the birds, mowed six acres, and planted her oak trees.

Her trees introduced her to crime, Myakka City style. One morning she heard the roar of a helicopter. It was hovering over the pots in which she grows her oaks. The police wondered if she were growing pot in those pots. Marijuana long has been a lucrative sideline for some people in the most rural areas.

Any crime made Brewer nervous. That's why she learned to value snakes. A big one, coiled fearlessly, sometimes waited in the dark of her driveway. It was the rubber serpent she put out to discourage burglars. "Looky here," she told me once, "folks round these parts are more scared of snakes than the dark." Her neighbors had a healthy fear of the rattlers that lurked in the ocean of palmettos. Pickup trucks still went out of their way to run them over. Others shot them on sight. "I like snakes," Brewer said. "People tell me they kill snakes and I want to slap them bald-headed."

Even after a rattler bit her on the right shin she continued liking them. In her opinion, snakes had the same right to happiness as she did. She was also sure they preferred sleeping in the dark. Looking for an ally, Brewer contacted a notoriously cranky ornithologist to chat about the needs of scrub jays. Hers, the ones she named after Faulkner characters, visited for years. Then they up and disappeared. Could it have been the outside lights of her new neighbors? The scientist pooh-poohed her dark theory. But he also admitted that nobody had studied the impact of light on birds.

Brewer, happy that she planted a bug in at least one scientist's ear, started planting others. She invited federal wildlife biologists to her home to discuss not only scrub jays but panthers. She and her husband saw one. Panthers, the Brewers told people, probably like the dark too.

In some parts of the world, especially near major astronomical observatories, light pollution had become an expensive problem. Cities spent millions of dollars to reduce the glow. But even nonastronomers resented that they couldn't show their kids Betelgeuse, Vega, and Rigel. No city kids could admire the neat globular star cluster in Hercules or a good comet.

If star-hungry people were to ever mount a national campaign, I felt sure that Melissa Sue Brewer would be on the board. She would nominate others too. They would speak in soft southern accents, eat grits for dinner and fried chicken for supper. The cook would be Juel Gill.

Juel Gill, Brewer's hero and the matriarch of Myakka City, was eighty when I looked her up. Juel Gill had been a farmer and a cowgirl, a waitress and a real estate agent. She was the postmaster and a schoolteacher, wrote a column for the *Myakka City News*, and proclaimed herself the best fried-chicken cook in Myakka City—even if she wasn't eating chicken at the time.

"I'm on the hallelujah diet," she said. "I'm eating fruits and vegetables like they did in the Garden of Eden." A road was named after her, though she put on no airs about it. After all, Knucklehead Boulevard was only a country mile away. What was Florida like before all the bright lights? Juel Gill told Melissa Sue Brewer all about it.

Her mama, a schoolteacher, rode a horse. Her daddy, a Baptist preacher, got a Model-T. Juel learned to drive when she was thirteen. Sometimes she rode the range on a horse and carried a rifle. She remembered when people first put screens on windows. She remembered being invited to a potluck supper where manatee was in the pot. She spent a teenage winter working as a South Florida waitress and bought the first electrified iron she laid eyes on. Alas, there was no place to plug it in at Myakka City, which finally got that modern convenience just before World War II.

On the morning I looked her up, Juel Gill threw her little three-legged mutt, Buttons, into the back of an ancient Chevy with 180,000 miles on the odometer. It was her day to deliver Meals on Wheels. Maybe she'd get a chance to promote dark skies too. People listened to her; she had known some folks since they were in diapers. "People who have just moved here from the city, they're scared of the dark," Juel told me. "It takes 'em a while to get comfortable with it."

Juel squinted; something was wrong with an eye. But she saw better with one than most people with two. At night she could see the stars just fine. Even in the rain she kept the car mostly on the road. "When I get to the age when I can't drive, they might as well dig a hole and put me in," she declared. "I'll make a lot of lives miserable."

She had outlived one husband and divorced another. Her kin grew up fine: They went away, saw the world, returned to Myakka City. Now they were fighting for the dark too. Her son-in-law, retired engineer John J. Miller, told me he thought keeping out the lights was a fine idea. He was at the big meeting Melissa Sue Brewer called in her community.

Brewer invited big shots from Manatee County, from the sheriff's office, and from the Peace River Electric Cooperative. "They think we're all hayseeds out here, with straw between our teeth," Brewer said. "I am sure they thought I am the lady of the corn." They learned different; she was as serious as a bad case of ringworm. A sheriff's deputy told the group that when it comes to crime, bright lights aren't all they're cracked up to be. In fact, in a dark place, lights often show burglars where to go. Nervous folks are better off with motion-detection lights; at least they go off after a while.

A county commissioner, Jonathan Bruce—"He's my lamby,"—said he was all for dark places. He tried in vain to stop the new Hess gas station near the interstate from installing stadium caliber lighting, now visible for miles.

William Mulcay of the power company was cooperative too. A missionary's son, he grew up in Africa and in rural Florida and remembered what the skies had been like. He told Brewer he would make shielded lights available to anyone in Myakka City who asked. "We haven't gotten that many requests in the past, but maybe we will now," he said when I called.

Brewer told him the shielded lights he was offering were no good at all. One neighbor, Arvind Rawana, got a shield, but it didn't do the trick. His light still intruded on Brewer's dark. Brewer told Mulcay that she had researched the subject of shielded lights on the Internet and found out where he could buy better shield lights, in bulk, for a good price. "That's the carrot on the string," she told me. "If the power company doesn't provide better shielded lights, some people will request the power company to disconnect the light poles they have. That would be expensive."

She paused a spell.

"Myakka City isn't going to roll over and play dead."

At night, if you desired society, the Myakka City Grocery on State Road 70 was the place to go. Teenagers in cowboy hats parked their pickup trucks and played hip-hop over radios; their barefoot girlfriends sashayed in for Pepsi and pork rinds.

The only place within twenty-five miles to buy serious vittles, the store was always busy; residents called it Downtown Myakka City. Some folks just hung out, some visited to admire the stuffed animal heads on the wall, and some to read the notices taped to the window. While I ate pork rinds, I read notices about a lost puppy and a gospel show. But nothing about keeping Myakka City in the dark.

Linda Werlein, wearing a cowboy hat and a scowl, stood next to me outside the store. "Who needs lights?" she growled. "People here are armed to the teeth."

Cleaning closets one afternoon, Melissa Sue Brewer found the old photo that reminded her that the world had become a violent place, a photo of her old friend. It flooded her with memories: Peggy's little hands, her broken fingers, the bloody handprints inside the patrol vehicle, her shattered skull.

"Her cute little selfy."

Martin Grossman had been on death row since 1984. Brewer thought of him often. She even wrote him a letter. "Because I never looked the monster in the eye" was her reason. "Looked him in the eye at the trial, yes sir, did that. But hid the part about how sadness can eat your soul."

She wrote him about the dark nights of her own soul. Months passed; one day she opened her mail and found his Christmas card. That was their last correspondence.

In Florida, condemned prisoners have the option of choosing lethal injection or the chair. Brewer hoped Grossman would choose electricity on his big day. She said she'd volunteer to throw the switch.

"I'll flick it on and off a few times."

Her enthusiastic switching might cause a power outage and put out the lights for miles.

Melissa Sue Brewer hated to hurt even mosquitoes. She never slapped them; that would be killing. She fanned them away. "It's not a good day unless I'm bitten at least once," she said. In the summer, mosquitoes accompanied the dark skies of Myakka City. Even biting things made her philosophical.

"You a creationist?" she asked from her pitch-black driveway. She was science minded, but she also liked provocative talk about how the universe was formed. Did life originate out of thin air? Was there a mysterious Big Bang, an explosion of star stuff that got everything going?

Did God create the universe? If there is a God, is he or she responsible for everything good, from the awesome bowl of stars and the sassy scrub jays to the rambunctious foxes that showed up in the garden at dusk? If God is responsible for good, what about evil, like the evil that happened to Peggy Park so long ago on another dark night?

The heavens answered those questions the only way they could.

The constellation Scorpius showed starkly against the southern sky. The Big Dipper was prominent and bright; Virgo was rising; Hercules blinked down from the zenith.

47 Firefly Doc

"Can you meet me back here at 8 o'clock?" Jim Lloyd asked. Eight
P.M. was three hours away. I told him returning on time should be no
problem.

"You won't be late?" Lloyd asked. "We will only have a nineteen-
minute window, after sunset, to see the fireflies. After nineteen minutes,
that particular species turns off for the night."

Professor Lloyd, a University of Florida animal behaviorist, was known
as the "Firefly Doc." He had studied them four decades and probably knew
more about them than any other person alive. Which hardly meant he
knew everything. To hear him tell it, one of the charming things about
fireflies was their mystery. They resisted understanding.

Some people might have said the same about the Firefly Doc. Visitors
to his unlighted Gainesville office developed eyestrain in the dim light. I
asked if he were trying to preserve his night vision. "Ah. Well," he said
after a moment. "It's as good an excuse as any."

He had pursued fireflies all over the world, in open fields, in jungles, in
swamps, in the mountains, and along the shores of tropical islands. He
edited *Fireflyer Companion,* an eclectic journal with an international read-
ership of several hundred *Homo sapiens.* There were waiting lists of students who hoped to take his honors classes, "Biology and Natural History
with Fireflies" and "Advanced Fireflies." In his crammed campus office,
which smelled of mothballs, he reached for a trunk brimming with data.
"My monograph," he said about the fruits of more than three decades of
night labor. One of these days, he said, he'd get around to writing up
everything he knew, but in the meantime there were so many fireflies, so
many projects, so little time.

Worldwide, 1,900 species of fireflies—some people called them "lightning bugs"—had been formally named, though Lloyd thought the number was understated by half. More than 170 species had been described in
North America. Florida, with fifty-six known species, was the richest of

all firefly states. If you drew a line from Northwest Florida's "Big Bend" to Southeast Georgia's Okefenokee Swamp, you passed through the nation's densest firefly belt.

Lloyd had spent as much time as possible prospecting within the belt, either alone or with students, whom he called his "fireflyers." When I met him he was a sixtyish scientist who believed in getting out of the office and the classroom and doing old-fashioned field work. "Modern science seems to think it can only function in the laboratory," he sniffed.

He functioned best among his beloved beetles, being charmed.

"If you spent your childhood with the flashing species of eastern North America, then fireflies are more than mere insects," he wrote in the *Fireflyer Companion*. "They are glowing stripes smeared on shirts and foreheads, a Mason jar of flashes gathered from the front lawn at dusk and carried quickly off to bed to be watched under the pillow where it was really dark. Flashing fireflies met the colonists in Jamestown, and danced on the prairie with a fiddle and Sweet Betsy from Pike."

Often he wondered if they were disappearing. If they were vanishing, like Florida panthers, family farms, and starry nights, then he wanted to do something about it. He was just not sure what.

Where was Doc? As the sun raced for the pines, the nineteen-minute firefly window was beginning to close. Had he forgotten our date? He emerged from the entomology building, grinning. "You ready to do some fireflying?" he asked, sounding elated. His hair was wild and gray, and his piercing brown eyes were topped by brows that might have inspired an entomologist. Your basic caterpillars, they were black and bristly and undulated with enthusiasm. He said he liked nothing more than showing off the natural world to someone new. If he had his way, he said, everybody would study a single species of insect from childhood to old age. They would learn volumes about life, period.

"I have been teaching for thirty-five years, and I still love it," he said. When I met him, Jim Lloyd was poised to teach another swarm of students in the upcoming semester. As always, they would mostly be non-science majors, which he preferred. Non-science majors, he had found, were likely to come to his classes with open minds. "I want you to do science like the humanities," he would tell them.

English majors ended up writing firefly poetry. A philosophy major wrote about existentialism and fireflies. A religion major wrote about evolution and creationism. Lloyd published their papers in a section of the *Fireflyer Companion* he called "Essays by Little-Known Authors."

On the opening night of class he always handed them Crayolas, and they attacked a sheet of paper called "My Own Fireflyer Coloring & Work Book." Sometimes they sculpted fireflies out of clay. Doc hung photographs of his students on a bulletin board he called "my refrigerator."

Instead of lecturing—"I despise the lecture system"—he preferred handing out "Letters from Doc," informal writings covering the basics of fireflyery. He ended his lectures by wishing his students "Quiet and mysterious trails."

"Science is not voodoo," he told me. "Amateurs should be able to do it. But a lot of students today think science requires lots of expensive technology and a laboratory." The accessibility of science was his favorite theme. He once wrote an essay about the subject, inspired by Ralph Waldo Emerson, the New England transcendentalist who encouraged naturalist and writer Henry David Thoreau:

"Foregoing generations of students beheld nature face to face; ours, through their eyes, poorly," Doc wrote, capturing the flavor of Emerson's nineteenth-century prose. "Why should not our students also enjoy an original relation with their universe? Why should not our learners have a poetry and philosophy of insight and not of tradition, and a science by revelation to them, and not merely through the history of others? Surrounded in nature, whose floods of life stream around and through them, and will invite them by the invigoration they supply to actions that reach to achieve new heights of insight, why should our students grope among the dry bones of the past, or the molecules or electrons of some wanting future, and live themselves as role-playing facades they know from TV?

"The sun shines today too. There are things to be explored and found again, fresh."

Fireflies, of course.

I asked Jim Lloyd how he evolved into the Firefly Doc. He said it was a complete accident. He grew up in New York State and loved watching fireflies, but even more he relished hunting and fishing. "I hated school," he said. "I would leave my books on the bus rather than take them home and study. I actually joined the navy before somebody could ask me to go to college." Back from sea, he had no idea what he wanted to do when he grew up. So he sold shoes. He worked in a cracker factory, stirring batter in 109-degree heat. College suddenly seemed attractive.

A basic science class, taught by an enthusiastic professor, caught his fancy. "The stuff I had wondered about when I was fishing or hunting actually mattered," he told me as we drove away from the campus. He intended to teach high school science, but his gifts led him to graduate school at the University of Michigan, for his master's, and to Cornell for his doctorate, and finally to the University of Florida, for his job.

Fireflies became his field of interest—for reasons romantic and practical. Fireflies, beautiful and mysterious enough to inspire poetry through the ages, had been relatively unstudied. They were virgin territory.

My fancies are fireflies,
Specks of living light
Twinkling in the dark.
—Tagore, Indian poet

The Firefly Doc might have added "Amen." Or he might have explained that the firefly's living light, which is a form of chemiluminescence known as bioluminescence, is neither electrical spark nor brief glimpse into a flaming furnace within. A chemical called luciferin, a light-emitting molecule known as ATP, and an enzyme, luciferase, flip the switch.

"They're just neat," he said.

Doc's transportation to nightly firefly fandangos was no horse-and-buggy but his prized old Ford Festiva, missing the rear seat. "I have converted my car into the most basic kind of pickup truck," he explained.

Full dark was approaching. The compass on his dashboard pointed northeast. We were in the country now, and looming ahead was Newnan's Lake. We stopped, not to look at fireflies, but to admire the water. Doc liked the lake, where he used to sail and fish for bass. Sometimes he and Dorothy, married thirty-eight years, drove to the lake for a picnic of wine and cheese. After dark they watched fireflies.

Many modern Floridians, he said, complain about a firefly deficit. Lloyd had a notion that some species had gotten rare or even disappeared. But it was only a suspicion, unproved. It could even be wrong.

"Maybe people see fewer fireflies because they have stopped looking," he said. People stayed indoors and watched television. They didn't sit on the porch in the evening and read the newspaper. They didn't play catch with their children in the darkening back yard. Neighborhoods were brightly lit by high-intensity crime lamps, making fireflies hard to see.

The other side of the argument also made sense to Doc. Great hunks of firefly habitat had been destroyed, paved over, bulldozed, plowed. Many a suburban neighborhood was doused regularly with mosquito poisons that were lethal to fireflies. "Herbicides and pesticides have been used to encourage sterile monocultures of socially approved vegetation," Doc said. He was describing a perfect lawn.

"But all of this is complicated," he went on. It could take the rest of his life to try to prove that fireflies were disappearing. And if he managed the proof, it would be as difficult to explain why. The ultimate answer, he told me, likely would point to overpopulation of humans. We were intruding on firefly territory.

"When Wall Street sees that China has two billion people, it doesn't see a human population problem. It sees a business opportunity—new customers. And that's how many powerful people think these days.

"We live in a different kind of world now. Things are changing. Ways of life are going. Little family farms are disappearing. Do you think anybody will get worked up about saving fireflies?"

As it grew darker, his mood lightened. We were on a lonely two-lane road that snaked along the shore of the lake. Just as he suspected: The firefly window had opened. They were in fields and along the roadside by the thousands.

Out went his car's headlamps. We rolled along the highway by feel; fortunately traffic was light. "There are a whole lot of fireflies here," Doc whispered as his tires dropped onto the road shoulder with a jolt. "Oh, look. *Photinus collustrans*. It means 'with a light.'"

He said he was interested in the nuts and bolts of the natural history of fireflies but was more fascinated by firefly behavior. He was wild about their blinking. To me, it looked like fireflies were blinking for the heck of it; he explained otherwise. The blinking was about sex and probably murder.

"The fliers are all males," he explained. "They're looking for females that have just come out of their burrows. The females don't have wings. She'll flash, and a male will generally find her within six minutes."

When Doc arrived at the topic of firefly sex during speeches to garden clubs or church groups, he was likely to announce: "Propriety insists that I stop right here," a statement that usually provoked chuckles. Reporters are notoriously difficult to embarrass, so Doc plowed ahead, using a mild slang word often used to describe sex between humans. "Afterward, within about a minute, she'll be back under the ground, where she'll lay her eggs and eventually die. He'll go back into the air and look for more opportunities to have sex."

I asked about firefly mayhem.

In the 1950s, he explained, some bright entomologist wondered whether certain fireflies were imitating the blinks of other species as a way of inviting them to dinner. In the 1960s, Doc proved the theory, thanks to personal observation and photography. An unsuspecting male, hoping for a sexual liaison, lands near a prospective mate's frantic flash. Only it isn't a female of his own kind. She wolfs down the poor fool.

"Oh, what a tangled web we weave, when we first practice to deceive!"

When Sir Walter Scott wrote *Marmion*, he did not have fireflies on his mind. But Doc did, so he quoted it anyway.

He handed me a weird fishing pole. A switch near the handle activated a tiny light hanging from the tip. With the pole I could imitate the flash of a female firefly. I hoped I might entice a male to land too. I would not eat him, though Doc had been known to out of curiosity about how they taste.

I blinked my pole. To my humiliation, the fireflies ignored me. "It's not as easy at it looks," Doc said kindly. To human eyes, all firefly flashes may look alike. But not to fireflies. Their flash is language in an alien vocabulary that Doc had taken the trouble to try to learn. Alas, there are thousands of species, and thousands of combinations of colors, patterns, and duration. Still, he had made progress. He could identify many species by the way they flashed, and he could talk to them, in a manner of speaking, with his light pole. He told me that if you know what you are doing, and you are in the right area of Florida, you could drive from spot to spot and talk to fireflies for much of the night.

"They're lovely," he said, "and we'll never quite figure them out. That's what makes them appealing, that there are things humans probably will never find out."

Standing in the tall grass, my pole pointed at the ground, I was surrounded by thousands of fireflies, flashing frantically. Feeling foolish, I tried to engage them in a sexy dialogue. "You don't quite have it," Doc said, sounding more impatient than annoyed. "What you want to do is try to run in front of a firefly, then get ready. Put your light close to the ground. When he flashes, wait a half-second and flash in return."

Trotting along the roadside with my pole, I hoped to intercept some neon-lit Casanova. I twirled in place, my fish pole winking suggestively. It was too dark for me to see if some Zoot-suited firefly suitor—carrying a flower bouquet, no doubt—was coming a-courting.

Doc sauntered away. In the distance I saw his own light, a flashlight, blinking. Cars slowed to watch but didn't stop. More than once he had been questioned by police who saw him cavorting with his firefly lights and wondered if he needed a lift to the mental hospital at Chattahoochee. Usually the officers ended up learning something interesting.

He was shouting me advice but was too far away to be heard above the roar of Southern bullfrogs and the high-pitched screeches of bush katydids. I remembered what he had told on the drive over, when I asked why he studied fireflies. He said lots of people asked him that question, and he had a stock answer.

"I tell people that if they have to ask, they won't understand the answer."

Quiet and mysterious trails.

Credits

THE FLORIDA HISTORY AND CULTURE SERIES
Edited by Raymond Arsenault and Gary R. Mormino

Al Burt's Florida: Snowbirds, Sand Castles, and Self-Rising Crackers, by Al Burt
(1997)
Black Miami in the Twentieth Century, by Marvin Dunn (1997)
Gladesmen: Gator Hunters, Moonshiners, and Skiffers, by Glen Simmons and
Laura Ogden (1998)
*"Come to My Sunland": Letters of Julia Daniels Moseley from the Florida Frontier,
1882–1886*, by Julia Winifred Moseley and Betty Powers Crislip (1998)
The Enduring Seminoles: From Alligator Wrestling to Ecotourism, by Patsy West
(1998)
Government in the Sunshine State: Florida since Statehood, by David R. Colburn
and Lance deHaven-Smith (1999)
The Everglades: An Environmental History, by David McCally (1999), first paper-
back edition, 2001
Beechers, Stowes, and Yankee Strangers: The Transformation of Florida,
by John T. Foster Jr., and Sarah Whitmer Foster (1999)
The Tropic of Cracker, by Al Burt (1999)
Balancing Evils Judiciously: The Proslavery Writings of Zephaniah Kingsley,
edited and annotated by Daniel W. Stowell (1999)
Hitler's Soldiers in the Sunshine State: German POWs in Florida,
by Robert D. Billinger Jr. (2000)
Cassadaga: The South's Oldest Spiritualist Community, edited by John J. Guthrie,
Phillip Charles Lucas, and Gary Monroe (2000)
Claude Pepper and Ed Ball: Politics, Purpose, and Power, by Tracy E. Danese (2000)
Pensacola during the Civil War: A Thorn in the Side of the Confederacy,
by George F. Pearce (2000)
Castles in the Sand: The Life and Times of Carl Graham Fisher, by Mark S. Foster
(2000)
Miami, U.S.A., by Helen Muir (2000)
Politics and Growth in Twentieth-Century Tampa, by Robert Kerstein (2001)
The Invisible Empire: The Ku Klux Klan in Florida, by Michael Newton (2001)
The Wide Brim: Early Poems and Ponderings of Marjory Stoneman Douglas,
edited by Jack E. Davis (2002)
*The Architecture of Leisure: The Florida Resort Hotels of Henry Flagler and Henry
Plant*, by Susan R. Braden (2002)

Florida's Space Coast: The Impact of NASA on the Sunshine State,
   by William Barnaby Faherty, S.J. (2002)

In the Eye of Hurricane Andrew, by Eugene F. Provenzo Jr. and Asterie Baker
   Provenzo (2002)

Florida's Farmworkers in the Twenty-first Century, text by Nano Riley and photographs by Davida Johns (2003)

Making Waves: Female Activists in Twentieth-Century Florida, edited by Jack E.
   Davis and Kari Frederickson (2003)

Orange Journalism: Voices from Florida Newspapers, by Julian M. Pleasants (2003)

The Stranahans of Ft. Lauderdale: A Pioneer Family of New River,
   by Harry A. Kersey Jr. (2003)

*Death in the Everglades: The Murder of Guy Bradley, America's First Martyr to Envi-
   ronmentalism,* by Stuart B. McIver (2003)

Jacksonville: The Consolidation Story, from Civil Rights to the Jaguars,
   by James B. Crooks (2004)

The Seminole Wars: The Nation's Longest Indian Conflict, by John and Mary Lou
   Missall (2004)

Seasons of Real Florida, by Jeff Klinkenberg (2004)